THE GREEN BREAST OF THE NEW WORLD

The Green Breast

LOUISE H. WESTLING

of the New World

Landscape, Gender, and American Fiction

THE UNIVERSITY OF GEORGIA PRESS
Athens and London

© 1996 by the University of Georgia Press

Athens, Georgia 30602

All rights reserved

Designed by Sandra Strother Hudson

Set in 11 on 14 Bembo with Centaur display

by Books International

Printed and bound by Thomson-Shore

Printed in the United States of America

00 99 98 97 96 C 5 4 3 2 1

Library of Congress Cataloging in Publication Data

Westling, Louise Hutchings.

The green breast of the new world : landscape, gender, and

American fiction / Louise H. Westling.

p.   cm.

Includes bibliographical references and index.

ISBN 0-8203-1814-0 (alk. paper)

1. American fiction—20th century—History and criticism.

2. Landscape in literature.   3. Pastoral literature, American—

History and criticism.   4. American prose literature—History

and criticism.   5. Fiction—Authorship—Sex differences.

6. Body, Human, in literature.   7. Sex role in literature.

8. Women in literature.   I. Title.

PS374.L28W47   1996

813'.50936—dc20   95-39094

British Library Cataloging in Publication Data available

The wood engravings of wild grapevines are by William G.

Haynes, Jr., and are from *The Marshes of Glynn* by Sidney Lanier,

© 1957 and 1984 by William G. Haynes, Jr., The Ashantilly Press,

Darien, Georgia.

To GAW

CONTENTS

PRELUDE

All my reading life I have been fascinated by archaeology and the records of ancient civilizations. In the beginning it was just a child's wonder at what was old and strange, but gradually I came to believe that we cannot truly know ourselves as humans without seeing the continuity of our lives on the planet as fully as possible. Since specific origins are impossible to conceive, we must look to the cultural records to piece together a sense of who we are and how we have explained to ourselves our existence within this living planet.

My previous work with the literature of the American South, and particularly the fictions of Eudora Welty, Carson McCullers, and Flannery O'Connor, led me into a consideration of landscape imagery and its centrality for identity and meaning that has grown into the present broader project. What I found in the writing of *Sacred Groves and Ravaged Gardens: The Fiction of Eudora Welty, Carson McCullers, and Flannery O'Connor* was that these women writers' relations to landscape had to be seen as resonating with ancient mythological patterns especially apparent in modernist writing and that they revealed long habits of gender conflict at the heart of European-American culture. I decided to move on to look at the fiction of male writers as well. My strategy was to choose several pairs of American fiction writers from the same general regions and time periods and to see what relationships might emerge when I questioned the presence of gender in the treatment of landscape and environment.

First, however, I needed to establish a sense of the deep historical context that I believe must be understood as lying behind the symbolic practice of contemporary writers. My method is always to pose large framing questions at the beginning of a research project and select representative texts that I think will repay examination, but then to use an inductive approach that seeks what the texts can teach me about those questions. In the process, the texts open out and out in ways I could never have anticipated. Max Oelschlaeger's ambitious book *The Idea of Wilderness* appeared in 1991 as a kind of godsend to help frame the "deep history" I sought to define, and then the next year Robert Harrison published *Forests: The Shadow of Civilization*, which also attempted this kind of long view. Both

Oelschlaeger and Harrison were interested in many of the Sumerian, Babylonian, and ancient Greek texts, such as *The Epic of Gilgamesh* and Euripides' *Bacchae,* that I had been using for my own explorations, so I felt encouraged to be in the company of others who were beginning to shape ecological perspectives on philosophy and literature.

Once I had sketched out the possibilities for deep history that I felt needed to stand as background for consideration of American literary traditions, I moved to Emerson and Thoreau, who established a specifically American approach to landscape imagery. Their work demonstrates the tensions that I believe still trouble most writing about the land and also are central to important problems in American identity and history. To see how these tensions have played out in our own century, I turned to two pairs of writers, one male and one female, from each of two regions of the United States that seem to produce especially powerful fiction about the relation of humans to the land. I trust that my choice of Willa Cather, Ernest Hemingway, William Faulkner, and Eudora Welty is understandable in light of this purpose. Cather, Hemingway, and Faulkner are especially identified with the landscapes of their fictions, and Welty offers a rich and useful contrast with Faulkner in her treatment of the Mississippi Delta region. Louise Erdrich's novels struck me as deeply engaged with the ecological questions my study explores, and as my work progressed, I began to see how involved Erdrich's fictions are in a dialogic relationship with these fictional predecessors. As a Native American writer, Erdrich can draw on many symbolic traditions outside the European-American context, and she uses these with the history of her Ojibwa community to rewrite the story of the American frontier and revise the landscape imagery that most American pastoral writing supports.

My study ends by suggesting enormous unresolved problems that the close investigation of selected modern American texts raises about the ways people should understand their place in the life of the earth. Much further thought must be expended by others, particularly, I think, in the study of science fiction, which I was only able to glance toward with a few remarks about the provocative work of Octavia Butler. I hope at least to have demonstrated the importance of redirecting our questions about American fiction in the ecocritical directions which I and others have been striving to define.

In the writing of this book, I have benefited from the help of many colleagues and friends. Marija Gimbutas's encouragement in Austin,

Texas, in the summer of 1990 and the astonishing wealth and mystery of Neolithic civilization that she began introducing in the 1970s are especially important. I owe a debt to Mary Kuntz, who taught me Greek and was a stimulating and generous friend, and also to Jeffrey Hurwit, who has helped over the years to chasten some of my mythological excesses. I am grateful also to the archaeological advice of Madonna Moss and to the careful readings Karen Ford has given to various drafts of the project. Glen Love has been an unfailing support in the effort to ground my ecocritical education in the whole range of writings scattered through many disciplines. He is the true founder of this emerging field of literary inquiry and has been tireless and generous in helping scores of young colleagues get established. Among these young scholars, Cheryll Burgess Glotfelty, Mike Branch, and Scott Slovic have also played an important role in organizing the Association for the Study of Literature and Environment, creating bibliographies, and writing books and articles that help to define the field. Bill Rossi has been of great help in pointing me toward relevant Thoreau scholarship. Peter Redfield sat with me looking out over the sea at the Camargo Foundation in 1991 and sketched a list of challenging anthropological readings, many of which became central to my thinking. I would also like to thank my longtime editor Karen Orchard at the University of Georgia Press for believing in this somewhat idiosyncratic project and waiting patiently as I slid past deadlines. Finally, I want to thank my husband, George Wickes, who helps me keep my prose as clean as I can manage and who has been willing to listen for more than ten years to my ideas about this subject, as well as to grope through caves in the Dordogne, to explore Irish and Breton and Spanish passage graves, and to wander through the rubble of Mycenaean Greece and Minoan Crete in search of ancient landscape symbols.

I
Backgrounds

You ask me to plow the ground. Shall I take a knife and tear my mother's breast? Then when I die she will not take me to her bosom to rest.

You ask me to dig for stone. Shall I dig under her skin for her bones? Then when I die I cannot enter her body to be born again.

You ask me to cut grass and make hay and sell it and be rich like white men. But how dare I cut off my mother's hair?
SMOHALLA, Nez Perce, *Touch the Earth*

License my roving hands, and let them go
Before, behind, between, above, below.
O my America, my new-found-land!
My kingdom, safliest when with one man manned,
My mine of precious stones, my empery,
How blest am I in this discovering thee!
JOHN DONNE, "To His Mistress Going to Bed"

And as the moon rose higher the inessential houses began to melt away until gradually I became aware of the old island here that flowered once for Dutch sailors' eyes—a fresh, green breast of the new world. Its vanished trees, the trees that had made way for Gatsby's house, had once pandered in whispers to the last and greatest of all human dreams; for a transitory enchanted moment man must have held his breath in the presence of this continent, compelled into an aesthetic contemplation he neither understood nor desired, face to face for the last time in history with something commensurate to his capacity for wonder.
F. SCOTT FITZGERALD, *The Great Gatsby*

CHAPTER I

Lost Innocence

What accounts for the contrast between John Donne's joyful exploration of his new America and Fitzgerald's elegiac disappointment about that feminized landscape in 1925? Donne employed a trope common to his era, the same historical moment that Nick Carraway imagines at the deflated end of *The Great Gatsby* (182). Even though Donne used geographical imagery to describe a woman's body, he was expressing actual attitudes toward the New World, and perhaps expressing them with unusual explicitness *because* they are projected into an intimate setting that seems merely personal and playful. For seventeenth-century Europe,

3

the Americas represented an immense geographical body ripe for conquest, the erotic dimensions of which Annette Kolodny has detailed in *The Lay of the Land*.[1] All was delicious possibility, licensed for eager exploration and despoiling by roving bands of adventurers and colonists.

But for Fitzgerald's young hero of three hundred years later, the new continent's promise has betrayed its admirers. The famous "valley of ashes" passage early in the novel presents a grotesque parody of the pastoral dream that attracted so many colonists and still remains central to the mythic identity of the United States. Instead of the rural paradise of yeoman farmers described by Hector St. John de Crevecoeur, Nick sees "a fantastic farm where ashes grow like wheat into ridges and hills and grotesque gardens; where ashes take the forms of houses and chimneys and rising smoke and, finally, with a transcendent effort, of men who move dimly and already crumbling through the powdery air" (23). This is one of the sardonically disillusioned pastoral moments Leo Marx has traced through the novel (354–65; Tichi 253), leading to the final elegy of betrayal that I have used as the third epigraph above. What neither Marx nor Kolodny has mentioned, however, is the subtle rhetoric of blame that informs the final projection of the "fresh, green breast of the new world." Fitzgerald suggests that this voluptuous landscape was purposive; it flowered and its rustling leaves "pandered in whispers" to seduce the Dutch sailors. The desire that Fitzgerald actually portrays in *The Great Gatsby* is not for the aesthetic contemplation that Nick claims the Dutch sailors felt. Donne is closer to the truth of their lust. Men like the brutal, careless Tom Buchanan are the real culprits whose drive for power denuded the landscape and produced the valley of ashes. Fitzgerald makes Tom's wife Daisy, whose name suggests the deceptive appearance of natural freshness, the literal cause of the novel's tragedy, displacing the guilt of the rapacious industrialists in a parallel to the way his final description of Long Island displaces the blame for the landscape's ruin upon the victim "her"self.

Fitzgerald's Nick Carraway is only one of many central characters in twentieth-century American literature haunted by the lost dream of Eden in the New World. A half-century before chain saws droned through the last of the continent's ancient forests, fictional observers of the landscape such as Willa Cather's Jim Burden, Ernest Hemingway's Nick Adams, and William Faulkner's Ike McCaslin grieved over the end of the wilderness with its fecundity, its mysterious otherness, and its endless promise. They worship and feel healed in a natural world that is crashing down all around them, and they know that its demise is a guilty part of their heritage as white men. Nick Carraway's grieving vision of the aboriginal continent is a particularly succinct expression of the ambivalent relation these sensitive observers feel toward the dying wilderness, but all of them share the failure to confront their own complicity with the forces of destruction. They all participate in a cultural habit of gendering the landscape as female and then excusing their mistreatment of it by retreating into a nostalgia that erases their real motives, displaces responsibility, and takes refuge in attitudes of self-pitying adoration.

Renato Rosaldo has coined the term "imperialist nostalgia" to define a widespread tactic used by colonial powers to cover up their domination and "transform the responsible colonial agent into an innocent bystander"(70). The North American manifestation of this strategy, as Philip Fisher argued in *Hard Facts*, several years before Rosaldo, was the radical cultural work of erasure. "Cooper 'made up' the wilderness; the Indian and the killing of the Indian; the process of settlement and, along with that process, the single white figure, Leatherstocking, who made morally tolerable the ethical complexities of settlement and the superseding of the Indians that was the basic secondary fact within settlement" (6). Rosaldo generalizes the kind of argument Fisher has made, applying it globally as an imperialist practice but also pointing out its relevance for the environmental wreckage of American colonization: "[the] attitude of reverence toward the natural developed at the same time that North Americans intensified the destruction of their human and natural environment" (71). Neither Fisher nor Rosaldo looks closely at the function of gender in this process, though Fisher might have noticed how both D. H. Lawrence and Leslie Fiedler had delineated its centrality to Cooper's Deerslayer novels previously.[2]

The following discussion will suggest that gender is a field of imperialism central to more obvious political and historical forms of colonization. Attention to gender can do much to explain the puzzle of ambivalence in American literary responses to landscape and nature. My approach proceeds from an interested perspective, of course—that of a woman desiring to unravel the strange combination of eroticism and misogyny that has accompanied men's attitudes toward landscape and nature for thousands of years. These attitudes are not at all empty tropes but instead are part of a complex evolution from the most ancient human past, in which an analogy seems to have been assumed between the body of woman and the fruitful body of the land.[3] Such attitudes survive in many remnants of ancient cultures, such as Australian aborigines and Amerindian tribes in North and South America.[4] Rigoberta Menchú, a contemporary Quiché Maya woman who grew up in the traditional village culture of upland Guatemala, explains, "We think of the earth as the mother of man, and our parents teach us to respect the earth. We must only harm the earth when we are in need. This is why, before we sow our maize, we have to ask the earth's permission" (57).

"We have yet to realize the full implication of the mother as a primary landscape," says Paul Shepard in *Man in the Landscape* (98), and he goes on to assert that neither Freudian nor Jungian psychological theory provides adequate exploration of the evolving metaphor of landscape as maternal (98–105). I would argue that both Freud and Jung represent essentially nineteenth-century views on the subject, however much they may have contributed to our understanding of human psychology. Their scientific training was primitive by present-day standards of cognitive research, and they persisted in unexamined assumptions about the naturalness of masculine control of society and culture. A much more historicized, self-critical effort must be made to understand the continued submerged functioning of the archaic habit of gendering the land, and some attention must be paid to cognitive science of our own time. Thus as a background for examining modern American fiction, I propose to sketch out in this chapter a suggestion of what the study of prehistory might have to teach us about our ancient ancestors' sense of themselves in the landscape, to discuss a model of cognitive functioning analogous to the working of culture, and then to look at a few examples of the earliest literary treatments of the subject in Western civilization—Sumerian hymns to the goddess Inanna and the *Epic of Gilgamesh*.

Although we cannot recover the exact cultures of prehistory, an enormous accumulation of archaeological and ethnographic evidence over the past one hundred years now allows for tentative suggestions. The increasingly common tendency to sentimentalize the primitive must be avoided in this process, so that we recognize that humans have been hunting animals to extinction for thousands of years, that they have been practicing fire management of landscapes from Australia to North America for an equally long period, and that overgrazing by domesticated flocks occurred in places such as the British Isles as early as 1,500 B.C.E. (Darville 108). The Mayan ancestors of Rigoberta Menchú may have shared her people's reverence for the earth, but they seem nevertheless to have exhausted their farmland soils during the classical period and been forced to abandon their monumental cities. Some of the cultural dynamics involved in historical events such as the collapse of ancient Anatolian and Mesopotamian agricultural civilizations and those in Central America are reflected in the Sumerian literature.

Before turning to the American subject of this study, I also want to provide a bridge from the extremely archaic material of prehistory and Sumerian literature to the more directly European traditions that colonists brought with them to North America in the sixteenth and seventeenth centuries. The Judeo-Christian biblical heritage and the closely related Hellenic complex of myth, literature, and philosophy from ancient Greece embody central cultural patterns that continue from prehistory into the self-consciously modern literary milieu of the English Renaissance. Brief commentary on attitudes toward the landscape in Genesis and in Euripides' treatment of the worship of Dionysos in the *Bacchae* will provide a basis for moving my argument into the medieval and then the modern period of American exploration and settlement by Europeans. I trust that a continuum of symbolic practice from the deep past into the modern era will emerge in this long introductory background discussion to serve as an illuminating context for Ralph Waldo Emerson's *Nature* and Henry David Thoreau's *Walden*, arguably the founding manifestos for American writing about landscape.

Since the beginnings of systematic archaeology in the nineteenth century, students of culture have been trying with varying degrees of attention and evasion to account for the thousands of female figurines found in sites from Paleolithic caves in France and digs in Siberia to late Neolithic cities of Mesopotamia and pre-Columbian America. Contact with living tribal peoples such as the Iroquois, West African tribal cultures, and Indonesian tribal societies has also provided examples of matriliny and female political power (Parker 19, 29–30, 74–79; Tanner 129–56). German cultural historian Johann Jacob Bachofen was one of the first to try to explain the importance of this information, with his influential *Mother Right* in 1861. There he argued that they were the symbols of matriarchies that preceded the historical eras. His work was important for Marx and Engels's views of social origins, it influenced Sir James Frazer's enormous compendium *The Golden Bough,* and it informed basic assumptions behind the *Prolegomena to the Study of Greek Religion* by Cambridge classicist Jane Ellen Harrison.[5] Such ideas were unsettling for the paternalistic imperial cultures of late-nineteenth-century Europe, and an ideological battle ensued that is still in progress.[6] Nevertheless, most present-day students of ancient cultures will agree that, whatever the dubious possibility of prehistoric matriarchies, the female body has been associated with the vegetative energies of the earth and the reproductive powers of other animals for as long as humans have been producing symbols.

Decades ago in *The Gate of Horn,* G. R. Levy attempted to demonstrate the continuity of religious history from Paleolithic culture of twenty-five thousand years ago to the present. She linked the beliefs of surviving aboriginal societies with Stone Age peoples in seeing earth as both womb and tomb for living things (54–167). More recently, though we still lack access to the precise coding of patterns in cave art, increased attention has been paid to its complexity and its close relation to symbolic forms and practices of the cultures that developed after it.[7] Max Oelschlaeger suggests that a major paradigm shift is under way among students of human cultural evolution and history, based on the new findings about prehistory. He calls the new thinking "Posthistoric Primitivism" and sees it as gradually developing a deep history that should henceforth be the perspective from which we evaluate particular cultural phenomena.[8] In the several million years of our species' history, our Stone Age ancestors are really quite recent, much like ourselves:

> Local variations aside (tools, geography, game), our prehistoric
> ancestors lived well by hunting and foraging; they buried human
> remains and were religious; they had an understanding of nature's
> ways that reflects an intelligence equal to our own; and their art
> reveals a rich imaginative life. In short, Paleolithic people were not
> the ignorant, fierce brutes that civilized humans imagine, a fact that
> places the onus on us—especially on those who would grapple
> with the idea of wilderness—to reassess our self-concept. We
> come from that green world of the hunter-gatherers. (6)

Although Paleolithic culture goes back at least thirty thousand years (Delporte 46–47), the skill of its art and the sophistication of what Alexander Marshack takes to be its calendrical computations indicate that these people were already laying the foundations of astronomy and were minutely attentive students of the seasonal cycles of plant and animal life. Henri Delporte has defined five major regional types for Paleolithic art in *L'image de la femme dans l'art prehistorique*:

1. The Pyreneo-Aquitainian Group
2. The Italian Group
3. The Rheno-Danubian Group
4. The Russian Group
5. The Siberian Group

In finds through all these regions, the human image is usually female, emphasizing large bellies, full breasts, and otherwise ample dimensions. The form of the vulva or pubic triangle is clearly etched on both wall carvings and drawings and on three-dimensional sculpted mobilary pieces. Often this vulvic form becomes stylized as a design and appears separate from a recognizable body (Leroi-Gourhan 199–201, 513–20; Marshack 281–340; Delporte 14–19, 209–40). Delporte sees these forms as the essential translation of the female body into a widespread Paleolithic symbol of femininity (47). In the contexts where these feminine images are found, much attention is given to reproducing (or imitating, or trying to capture) in visual images the physical signs of fertility in other animals and in plants. For example, Marshack's microscopic photographs of bone carvings reveal careful and anatomically accurate etchings of the female and male salmon in spawning season, wild grasses in seed, the buds of flowers, gravid aurochs, female and male seals, and so forth (169–234). Delporte defines the general pattern of figuration found all over the vast geographic region of Paleolithic remains as one presenting the static forms of woman opposed, in an almost systematic fashion, to the dynamic forms of animals.

All things considered, it seems to us, we emphasize, that it is this woman-animal duality—and not the woman-man, or feminine-masculine, for the masculine element is among the most rare—that best suits as an explicatory hypothesis for the nature and morphology of Paleolithic figurations. . . . it seems to us that this relation, almost dialectic in essence, between Humanity represented in preferential fashion by the woman, and the living World represented by the animal, is not far from bringing us, along with others, the total explanation of the exceptional adventure that was Paleolithic Art. (312, my trans.)

One might quarrel with Delporte's opposition of "static" female humans to "dynamic" animals, suspecting that he is seeing the varied and often active images in both mobilary and parietal cave art from within a reductionist modern pattern that assumes the "feminine" to be passive and in dialectical opposition to active "nonfeminine" principles and forces. This is a long tradition in Western thinking, as Carolyn Merchant, Evelyn Fox Keller, and many others have established,[9] that has clearly served the purposes of the dominant masculine culture wishing to portray itself as controlling inert matter and docile women. An alternative, equally plausible way of interpreting the relation of female images and sculptures to images of animals and plants is to posit a sacramental vision of interrelatedness for Paleolithic humans, according to which women are seen as analogous to pregnant horses, spawning salmon, egg-laying birds, ripe grains, and flowers as fertile sources of new life. We know many examples of such views in ethnography and in ancient literature. Because all hypotheses about the meaning of Paleolithic art can only be speculative, we must seek guidance from what we know of living hunter-gatherer cultures and ancient texts. Even then, we must continue to acknowledge geographical, chronological, contextual, and stylistic variations in the evidence and realize how partial our understanding remains.

Archaeologist Marija Gimbutas has concentrated her voluminous publications on the Neolithic period, but she has assumed, with Bachofen, Frazer, and Levy that the symbolic practice of Neolithic peoples evolved from the Paleolithic, simply adapting the more ancient habits to changing conditions of life. As I have suggested, this evolutionary view is shared by Paul Shepard and is the basis of Max Oelschlaeger's theory of deep history. Gimbutas's work on Indo-European migrations has established the hypothesis that patriarchal warrior-pastoralists descended upon the peaceful Neolithic agriculturalists of Mesopotamia and the Mediterranean area and displaced the goddess-centered cultures with aggressive masculine cosmologies.[10] Shepard sees pastoralism as intrinsically hostile to the land.

The fierce, hierarchic society of nomadic pastoralism is partly a result of grappling with the hazards and problems of a fringe environment: the world between desert and forest, low in productivity, where herds of grass-eating mammals exist by eating their way across a very large surface. . . .

The pastoralist's watch over and breeding of a stock is a continuing lesson in the relationship between authority and lineage, a confirmation of the extension of paternity, of a creative patriarchate. . . . Women have low status. The gods are omniscient, arbitrary, and manlike. This stern sophisticated view is ameliorated when pastoralism is mixed with farming and town life. But its homocentric, patriarchal, dualistic, abstract view of nature is the background of a hierarchical and divided universe. (50–52)

Gerda Lerner sees even plant cultivation as leading to the gradual emergence of masculine control and cultural distancing from feminine nature. The working hypothesis she offers in *The Creation of Patriarchy* is that the Neolithic revolution of plow agriculture and animal husbandry demanded the strength of men and resulted in the accumulation of surpluses that then had to be guarded, while women's physical activity was limited by the bearing and nursing of offspring. Furthermore, "since all agricultural societies have reified women's and not men's reproductive capacity, one must conclude that such systems have an advantage in regard to the expansion and appropriation of surpluses over systems based on complementarity between the sexes"(51–52).[11] As we shall see in literary examples from Mesopotamia and Greece, a constant in this equation is the analogy assumed between the productive, cultivated earth and the fertile bodies of women.

The emotional result of these changes is described by Paul Shepard in *Nature and Madness* as grave psychological debilitation. As Max Oelschlaeger puts it, "The Neolithic mind no longer thought of itself as the child of Magna Mater, and wild nature increasingly loomed as an enemy, a foe opposed to human intentionality that must be conquered"(29–30). It seems reasonable to assume that the domestication of both animals and plants gradually detached humans from their archaic sense of enmeshment in the web of life and led them to assume the ability to stand outside of the rest of Nature and control it. Pastoralism may have induced a greater degree of this detachment, as Shepard argues, and a more active habit of physical coercion of other creatures and of women and children as analogous to the beasts in their herds. But there is ample evidence all over the earth for the ambivalence and frequent hostility of masculine culture toward both women and the natural world with which they have been identified apparently from the deepest past.[12] The dynamics of this tension can be seen in some of the most ancient and most formative literary texts remaining from that period when human self-consciousness emerges from the preliterate Neolithic, through writing in the earliest civilizations.

The study of ancient cultures by archaeologists, linguists, and textual scholars has come to emphasize their evolutionary status. One hundred years of Indo-European studies and Sumerian and Semitic cuneiform studies, as well as textual criticism of the Bible and of the Homeric epics and their development from oral poetry, have all revealed the layered, accretive quality of written texts (Puhvel, Tigay, Nilsson, Lord, Schneidau). As we examine representative texts, therefore, we must keep in mind that none is "original." Instead each is an arrested moment in an evolution we can only trace back linguistically a few thousand years but that actually goes back to the beginning of consciousness among our remotest ancestors. Each literary work is an agglutination of mythic, metaphoric, narrative, and linguistic elements combined in a multivocal dramatic or dialectic texture. Each has purposive structure but is best understood as a series of danced conversations, staged and arrested in a moment of performative balance that temporarily satisfies the needs of a particular author or community.

The complexity and dynamism of cultural texture, and the way it is performed in specific works, parallels the texture and performance of language, which Maxine Sheets-Johnstone bases in physical experience deriving from a biological evolution of meaningful interaction in the preverbal hominid environment. Using the infant's gradual movement from babbling to speech as a model, Sheets-Johnstone infers that sounds were made, experimented with, and related to experiences in a looping back and forth from individuals to environment and among themselves.

What is discovered in perception flows back into burgeoning powers of articulation and vice versa. There is a complex of active awareness rooted in physiognomic perception. . . .

In the passage to verbal language, a further and final stage along a sensory-kinetic continuum and in sensory-kinetic integration is achieved. The tactile/aural tongue becomes witness to a preeminently visual world: the tactile/aural tongue becomes a tactile/aural/visual organ. Its enunciations are of things—or *relationships* seen. The most distant sensory world is thus brought within the realm of touch. This linkage of tactility and visuality might in fact explain why verbal language is sometimes thought of as having magical powers. (161)

Thus the process of speech is linked with visual powers in "the corporeal appropriation of the visual"(162). In one further evolutionary step, that of literacy, speech became encoded in physical objects outside the body, but recent cognitive imaging shows clearly that reading activates the brain in many of the same complex ways that physical speech does, and it involves the deepest mechanisms used for direct physical sense impressions.[13]

On this model literary culture, as a linguistic construct, is the performance of dynamic systems of meaning that have evolved from thousands of years of the actual physical lives of our fellow beings. It has never been arbitrary; it has never ceased to be centered in the body: "it is *thought* in terms of corporeal being," and is therefore naturally anthropomorphic at heart (Sheets-Johnstone 296). Arnold Trehub sees the most natural cognitive processes as metaphoric. "The stream of passive thought is often not constrained by the principles of deduction or the application of rules of inference; the succession of conscious impression seems to proceed rather along analogical and metaphorical links" (169). And this thinking is essentially visual, tuned to the physical environment in a pragmatic and opportunistic way for "the solution of ecologically relevant problems" in the course of its evolution (300). "The cognitive brain has a remarkable capacity to learn the ecologically significant properties of the visual world and to model these properties within its neuronal structures" (290).

By rough analogy of thought processes to the evolution of brain structure, we might assume that language and culture were gradually built up by a process of accretion that is rehearsed or repeated in the ontogeny of each individual. As the brain developed over the millennia (and develops in the growth of each fetus), the simplest sensing mechanisms gave rise to the spinal column, which then enlarged on its anterior end to form primary brain vesicles, each of which later developed into one of the areas of the mature human brain. Present neuroscience sees these parts as forming a kind of living physical history of evolution, with the most primitive, ancient structures of hindbrain (or brainstem) and then midbrain superimposed on the spinal column as regulators of cardiac and respiratory activity, as well as the coordinators of locomotion (Glees 24–27). This part of the brain is the most ancient and is shared by mammals and reptiles, thus informally called the reptilian or R-Complex. It also plays an important part in territoriality, aggressiveness, reproductive drives, and ritual (Sagan 60). The paleomammalian brain, or limbic system, is superimposed upon the R-Complex and governs emotions and perhaps altruistic behavior. It regulates and interacts with impulses from the R-Complex, in turn transmitting them and interacting with the most recent evolutionary part of the brain, the neocortex or cerebrum, which is the site of conscious thought, visual processes, and linguistic behavior (Sagan 69–76; Isaacson 239–57). Robert Isaacson emphasizes the special freedom that recently developed linguistic capacities allow humans:

> With language, humans can override the demands both of their internal environment and of the outer world. . . .
>
> To exercise this freedom, humans must override and suppress the well-learned or genetically determined behaviors that are presumed to be properties of the R-complex. Therefore, the neocortical mechanisms must overcome the habits and memories of the past, either indirectly by activating some portions of the paleomammalian brain, or by a more direct control process. In short, the neocortex, too, is profoundly concerned with suppressing the past. (254)

Here Isaacson defines cognitive functioning as dramatic interplay, indeed conflict among the different areas and functions of the brain that are concrete, living phases of evolutionary history. This is an oversimplification of a much more complex mechanical model of brain function that is itself debated by specialists.[14] And Isaacson does not adequately acknowledge how all parts of the brain work together to integrate our mental activity. Nevertheless, he does at least indicate the historical qualities embedded in physical structures and reveal how regulation of their living processes involves contestation, repression, channeling, and control. My guess would be that Trehub is closer to the evolutionary truth of cognitive evolution in stressing the pragmatic and opportunistic results of these activities over the course of humanity's evolutionary history. After all, too much overriding of biological imperatives means extinction.

The deepest levels of language and culture can be seen to articulate in similar ways with those that are more consciously controlled. The oldest cultural structures work more or less unnoticed in present behaviors, activating and interacting with all other levels. At this level are appeals to the senses, especially taste and smell, and the most elemental emotions such as fear, mother-child bonds, aggression, joy, and sexual desire. Jay Appleton suggests that primitive responses to habitat are basic in aesthetic judgment of paintings and architecture (12–22). Surely landscapes of safety and freedom, such as caves, wooded springs, high vantage points, and wide vistas evoke basic responses in literature as well, both as narrative settings and as metaphors or symbolic places.

Consciously constructed narrative surface would be parallel in function to the most recent evolutionary part of the brain, the cerebrum, where the linguistic function seems concentrated in the left forebrain. I do not mean to make facile comparisons between physical functions and cultural ones, or even fully to accept the mechanistic model of cognition, but the physical function of the brain can serve as a practical analogy. The physical organ described by cognitive scientists has evolved over millennia and preserved its earliest structures and functions, yet at the same time it is a living process of chemical/electronic conversations and interactions among its parts. Culture seems to work similarly, and individual cultural artifacts can be seen as physical embodiments of the process.

To return to the literary evidence—the civilization of ancient Sumer was emerging from the Neolithic period and into the Bronze Age when it created cuneiform writing and made possible the transmission of cultural records. Clay tablets inscribed around 2,000 B.C. describe Inanna, "Sumer's most beloved and revered deity," according to cuneiformist Samuel Noah Kramer (Wolkstein and Kramer xiii). Hundreds of tablets contain hymns, myths, and psalms to this goddess, and their metaphoric and narrative references to the land and growing things upon it reveal that this early culture saw the fruit- and grain-bearing earth as analogous to women's bodies.

In Sumerian hymns celebrating the sacred marriage of Inanna and the shepherd Dumuzi that brings fruitfulness to the landscape each year, however, moments of partially submerged conflict suggest an uneasy coexistence of competing symbolic forces.[15] When marriage is proposed by her brother Utu, the agriculturally identified Inanna at first rejects the idea of the pastoral Dumuzi in terms that may anticipate or at least parallel the conflict between Cain and Abel in the Bible, indicating conflict between pastoralists and farmers. Inanna prefers the farmer to the rough, wool-clad shepherd whom she defines as alien. After urgings from her brother Utu and her powerful mother, Ningal, however, she consents to the match. In the stanzas that follow, an unusual synthesis of agricultural and pastoral imagery creates the ecstatic atmosphere of sexual union. What seems particularly strange is the way Dumuzi is identified at some points with growing plants but at others with the potent bull. It seems as though the hymn is attempting to synthesize two contesting definitions of masculinity, a vegetative one in harmony with and subordinate to the fertile landscape (Anderson and Hicks 34–43), and a more active animal one moving about its surface.

Inanna identifies herself with the land as she asks,

> Who will plow my vulva?
> Who will plow my high field?
> Who will plow my wet ground?
> (Wolkstein and Kramer 37)[16]

Dumuzi answers that he will complete this task, and when Inanna accepts him, he is described in potently vegetative terms.

> At the king's lap stood the rising cedar.
> Plants grew high by their side.
> Grains grew high by their side.
> Gardens flourished luxuriantly.

Inanna sang:

> "He has sprouted; he has burgeoned;
> He is lettuce planted by the water.
> He is the one my womb loves best.
>
> My well-stocked garden of the plain,
> My barley growing high in its furrow,
> My apple tree which bears fruit up to its crown,
> He is lettuce planted by the water."
> (37–38)

In the dialogue that follows, Dumuzi affirms that Inanna's body is her fertile field pouring out plants, grain, and water for him as her servant.

> O Lady, your breast is your field.
> Inanna, your breast is your field.

Your broad field pours out plants.
Your broad field pours out grain.
Water flows from on high for your servant.
Bread flows from on high for your servant.
(37–39)

When she answers by identifying him with the wild bull who provides thick milk for her, she retains the basic relation between herself as
representing the enduring land to her consort as representing the transitory forms of life upon it. But plants are fixed in the earth, where they
will wither and die at the end of the growing season, while the powerful
bull moves about the surface of the land and lives through many seasons.
According to Shepard's and Gimbutas's hypotheses about the greater
mobility of pastoralists and their hostility to the feminine and the natural
world, the cattle-herding aspect of Dumuzi already indicates the presence of cultural and political forces that will gradually come to dominate a previously matristic or egalitarian ideology based on harmony
with the natural world.[17] Lerner's theory would lead to the expectation
that masculine control of culture and detachment from Nature would
be inevitable in any case, because of the habit of manipulating land and
plants for intense agricultural productivity. But continued involvement
in plowing and irrigating required continued psychic interaction with
the feminine earthy source of life inherited from the Paleolithic. At the
cultural moment when the courtship hymns were produced, Inanna remains the giver of life and the legitimizer of Dumuzi's kingly power,
and in another major poem of Sumerian literature, "The Descent of
Inanna," she causes him to be sacrificed into death as a substitute for
herself after her heroic but almost fatal journey into the underworld
(Wolkstein and Kramer 52–89).

Other Sumerian texts, however, present a very different gender dynamic, with a correspondingly different attitude toward the landscape and
natural world. This is the heroic, tragic mode of the epic, which explicitly
breaks away from identification with the cyclical processes of physical life.
Joseph Meeker helps focus its premises in his definition of an ecological
form of literary criticism in *The Comedy of Survival*, which values the
inclusiveness, compromise, and paradox of comedy over the destructive
heroic idealism of tragedy. Meeker blames the ancient Greeks for the creation of tragedy, claiming that the Athenian mind "built tragic drama on

this unprecedented combination of transcendence and annihilation and set a standard which men and writers since have tried to match" (50). Konrad Lorenz agrees, seeing in Platonic idealism a "morality which encourages man to detach himself from his animal origins and to regard all nature as subject to him" (xvi). However, both Meeker and Lorenz neglect the critical importance of gender conflict that can be seen emerging much earlier in the heroic warrior code of the Sumerian *Epic of Gilgamesh* of the second millennium B.C.E. This work may represent a chronologically later moment of cultural ideology than what Meeker would call the "comic" mode of the Inanna poems. Kramer defines the Heroic Ages of Greek, Indian (subcontinental), and Teutonic civilizations, as well as that of Sumer, as belonging to the "rather adolescent and barbaric cultural stage" that follows the penetration of more primitive tribal peoples into a civilized power in the process of disintegration and the carving out of their own kingdoms and wealth within it (237–38). This somewhat crude developmental stage produces a synthesis of the invading group's traditions and those of the more advanced civilization that they have taken over. As we have seen with the hymns to Inanna, the texts recovered by archaeologists and linguists include uneasy combinations of these varying traditions. Kramer explains that they reflect at least a thousand years of oral traditions among contending groups who settled in the fertile river valleys of Mesopotamia (181–98).[18] Our knowledge of the most famous Sumerian heroic poem, the *Epic of Gilgamesh*, comes from a confusing welter of cuneiform texts representing Sumerian and later Akkadian, Babylonian, and Hittite versions of the story, with all the varying adaptations each of these peoples brought to the story they received from their predecessors.[19] According to Jeffrey Tigay, because of the durable quality of clay tablets, as opposed to the perishable materials of biblical and classical literature, the history of certain Mesopotamian compositions can be traced "through several stages over a span of nearly two millennia" (2). Ancient texts are beginning to seem much closer to oral performances of traditional material than we have been accustomed to thinking, and in fact modern literary works are also more like momentary performances in complex, evolving cultural conversations than we had been prepared to acknowledge until the work of Mikhail Bakhtin pointed out the dialogic qualities of most literary productions.

Although the Babylonian versions of *Gilgamesh* are clearly based upon earlier Sumerian texts, the latter are thus far available in only a fragmentary and partial state. Thus my comments about the epic will refer primarily to the composite version prepared by N. K. Sandars, which comes predominantly from Old Babylonian sources but uses Sumerian materials to fill some gaps.

Central to all the versions of *The Epic of Gilgamesh* is a conflict between the hero and the goddess Inanna/Ishtar,[20] with Gilgamesh standing in violent opposition to the forces of natural vitality and the landscape that we saw identified with Inanna in the Sumerian courtship poems. Gilgamesh's heroic identity is predicated upon his desire to transcend death, destroy the flourishing life of the wild cedar forest, and reject the goddess's power. We see the antagonistic sexual force of this heroic mode especially against the value system implied in the hymns to Inanna. In contrast to the social and ritual order of events in the courtship of Inanna and Dumuzi, a rhythmic enactment of proper traditional behavior whose object is the repetition of cyclical patterns of renewal for landscape and community, the narrative movement of Gilgamesh is a series of violent outward thrusts.

In the Sumerian tablets translated by Samuel Noah Kramer, Gilgamesh's heroic journey to the cedar forest is set in motion by an understanding of his own mortality and human limitations:

> I peered over the wall.
> Saw the dead bodies . . . floating in the river;
> As for me, I too will be served thus; verily 'tis so.
> Man, the tallest, cannot reach to heaven,
> Man, the widest, cannot cover the earth.
> (177)

And so the hero begs the god Utu for permission to enter the sacred wilderness, the "Land of the Living," and set up his name as an apparent assertion of transcendent personal value against the power of natural forces in the landscape. As the action unfolds, the setting up of his name seems synonymous with the destruction of the forest and its guardian Huwawa, a monstrous creature who personifies wild nature. The chopping down of the forest is paralleled by Gilgamesh's rejection of Inanna's offers of love in a closely related text, but the evidence is still so fragmentary that Gilgamesh's stated reasons cannot be recovered (Kramer 189).

Interestingly, all through the narrative of these exploits, Gilgamesh and the unmarried young men who are his followers are defined as sons of mothers, rather than of fathers. The father seems to occupy a minimal role in the son's life. Gilgamesh prays for success against Huwawa, "By the life of Ninsun, my mother who gave birth to me, of pure Lulalbanda, my father, / May I become as one who sits to be wondered at on the knee of Ninsun, my mother who gave birth to me." It is the mother who will validate the son's success. Similarly, when Gilgamesh urges Enkidu for mercy to the defeated Huwawa, he says, "Let the caught man return to the bosom of his mother" (178–79).

The later Babylonian version of the epic defines a much more aggressive and potentially disruptive hero, who first appears as a young man of "arrogance beyond bound," whose voracious appetites for violence and sex ravage the city of Uruk. "His lust leaves no virgin to her lover, neither the warrior's daughter nor the wife of the noble; yet this is the shepherd of the city, wise, comely, and resolute" (Sandars 62). Gods must intervene to save the city from the rampage of the one who ought to be its guardian.

In a curious doubling technique, a distraction is created for Gilgamesh in the form of a wild man whose hairy appearance seems to match Gilgamesh's disorderly, uncivilized behavior. When he is first created, however, Enkidu dwells peacefully in the natural world: he "ate grass in the hills with the gazelle and lurked with wild beasts at the water-holes" (63). Innocent of humankind, Enkidu tears up the traps of the hunters and protects his fellow beasts. Enkidu's life among wild creatures also prefigures the monster Humbaba who guards the sacred cedar forest and its inhabitants. In a reversal of the power stimulated by the sacred conjunction of Inanna and Dumuzi, Enkidu is robbed of his strength and his bond with the natural world by sexual experience with a harlot who is sent by the gods to humanize him. Then he is ready to go to Uruk and challenge Gilgamesh.

Enkidu replaces women as the object of Gilgamesh's attention; even before he arrives in Uruk, Gilgamesh dreams of a meteor and a magic axe, both of which attract him "like the love of a woman." Gilgamesh's mother Ninsun explains that both represent a strong companion who is on his way to the city. She says, "You will love him as a woman and he will never forsake you" (66). On his arrival in the city, Enkidu blocks Gilgamesh from performing the ritual marriage to Ishtar (Inanna), Queen of Love (68). Annually Sumerian and Babylonian kings joined with a priestess representing Inanna or Ishtar in the performance of the ritual marriage found in most archaic cultures of the Mesopotamian/ Mediterranean world. This is the ceremony invoked in the Sumerian courtship hymns to Inanna and Dumuzi, and ordinary human procreation was understood to be similarly sacred (Wolkstein and Kramer 124–25; Harrison 534–51; Burkert 108–9; Lerner 126–27; DuBois 40–42; and Oelschlaeger 40). Yet the epic sets the fertility ritual in a negative context and locks the king in violent combat with the *doppelganger* Enkidu instead. Grappling together like bulls, the two smash the doors of the House of Marriage. When Gilgamesh finally throws the challenger, the two embrace and become inseparable companions. The male bond replaces Gilgamesh's connection with female fertility, and it is the basis for the series of heroic adventures that define his stature. Clearly Enkidu is a consort who replaces the wife in the narrative; when he dies Gilgamesh covers his body with a veil, "as one veils the bride" (95).

This replacement of male-female conjunction with male bonding is important as a corollary to the replacement of reverence for the natural landscape by violent conquest and destruction in the *Epic of Gilgamesh*. The epic begins with the breaking of Enkidu's bond with the wilderness and climaxes with his and Gilgamesh's combined attack on Humbaba and their chopping down of the magical cedar forest. At the heart of this forest wilderness was the throne of Ishtar (Inanna), suggesting the ancient worship of the Mistress of Animals recorded in many places in the ancient world and surviving in shadowy form in the worship of Greek Artemis and Roman Diana.[21] When Humbaba falls, the forest shudders, and Enkidu's essential connection with the natural world is implied by the sickness that causes his death soon after.

Ecological tragedy is thus the very ground of Gilgamesh's heroism. His triumph also rests upon the rejection of the feminine power of life that the Sumerians and later Semitic traditions located at the heart of the wilderness. On his return to Uruk, Gilgamesh rejects Ishtar's proffered love, and thus symbolically refuses to participate in the fertility mysteries of traditional Mesopotamian religion. His contemptuous speech to the goddess blames her for infidelity to previous lovers. Clearly the power of independent sexuality that was earlier in the hands of Inanna has been transferred to male control in the economy of the masculine epic.[22] It is ironic that the Gilgamesh who rejects Ishtar for her promiscuity is the same young king whose unbridled lust at the beginning of the epic drove the city fathers to enlist the gods to restrain him. The gender dynamics of the epic are somewhat confused, for as we have seen, the narrative retains elements of matriliny and worship of the goddess associated with the landscape and natural world. But the primary emphasis lies upon the imposition of aggressive male will upon the world, however tragic might be the results of the wreck of the forest or however futile Gilgamesh's journey to the land of the dead. Violence and death have replaced sexual union, harmony, and regeneration.

Because thou hast hearkened unto the voice of thy wife, and hast eaten of the tree of which I commanded thee, saying Thou shalt not eat of it: cursed is the ground for thy sake; in sorrow shalt thou eat of it all the days of thy life.
GENESIS 3:17, King James Version

CHAPTER 2

European Tradition and Figuration of a New World

The Judaic creation stories in Genesis descend from the same Mesopotamian culture that worshipped Inanna and Ishtar but gradually moved toward a male-dominated pantheon and heroic values. Judaic concepts of the supernatural and of the human relation to the land and its creatures represent a radical divergence from the sensuously celebratory vision of the Inanna poems, and even from the assertive vision of the Gilgamesh epic. As Max Oelschlaeger points out, the epic retains a respect for nature's powers in spite of Gilgamesh's attack on the forest. It describes his initial awe in the wild cedar forest, and the death of Humbaba engenders a sense of guilt (Oelschlaeger 39). The epic's treatment of the doomed monster vacillates from fear to contempt to sympathy, and a terrible punishment results from his murder and the parallel destruction of the holy forest surrounding the sacred mountain and throne of Ishtar.

In contrast, as many commentators have established, the cultural subjectivity of the Hebraic pastoralists developed in separation from the landscape, defining itself in a master narrative of guilt, punishment, and antagonism toward the vegetative capacity of the earth (Shepard, *N&M*, 47–73; Schneidau 21–49; Teubal 20–48; Oelschlaeger 41–53; White 346–48; Puhvel 23). While the creation stories of both cultures emphasize a primeval sea from which the universe was engendered, a separation of heaven and earth, the fashioning of man from clay, a catastrophic flood, and the creative power of divine word (Wolkstein and Kramer 122–23), no feminine presence has been retained in the Judaic concept of the supernatural, and the relation of humans to the physical world is one of separation and domination.[1]

Herbert Schneidau emphasizes the Hebrew antagonism to the sacramental tradition of sacred landscapes in the ancient cultures of the region. "Yahweh, who was never localized, claimed the whole of the promised land as his (Lev. 25:23) and thus dispossessed all the chthonic spirits" (74). This biblical deity is a disembodied voice distinct from the physical universe he calls into being. In Genesis 1:28, God blesses the males and females he created in his own image and tells them to *subdue* the earth and have *dominion* over all other life. The older, more detailed version of this event,[2] and the more familiar one told in Genesis 2, makes male creation primary and defines Adam's female companion as a mere "rib and crooked piece" of the original whole human, as Sir Thomas Browne gleefully worded it in *Religio Medici* (110). It is the male who is placed in the Garden of Eden and told "to dress and keep it," the male Adam who is invited to define the newly created animals by naming them. Thus even before the alliance between the female and the subtlest beast causes the Fall, man is separate from the rest of nature and identified with the nonmaterial God not only by the similarity asserted in Genesis 1, when God is said to make man in his likeness, but also in Genesis 2 by the creative power of the word in the act of naming the other animals and by his formative dominance over the garden and its creatures. This separation is of course intensified by explicit antagonism between man and land in God's punishment for Adam and Eve's disobedience. Schneidau thinks the author's overdetermined efforts to curse the ground were probably part of the wider cultural effort "to repudiate autochthonic ideology" (161).[3]

> And unto Adam he said, Because thou has hearkened unto the voice of thy wife, and hast eaten of the tree of which I commanded thee, saying Thou shalt not eat of it: *cursed is the ground for thy sake:* in sorrow shalt thou eat of it all the days of thy life; Thorns also and thistles shall it bring forth to thee; and thou shalt eat the herb of the field; In the sweat of thy face shalt thou eat bread, till thou return unto the ground; for out of it wast thou taken; for dust thou art, and unto dust shalt thou return. (verses 17–19, my emphasis)

In a curious shift here, the very earth receives the divine curse for human disobedience, and man's primary identification is no longer with the disembodied and controlling divine but with the embodied, cursed, and decaying essence of the ground that he will battle all his life. Lost forever is the celebratory vision of the Sumerian Inanna poems, with its sympathy between human sexuality and the fruit-bearing trees, the grain ripening in furrows and the flowing waters where the lettuce springs. Theologians and textual scholars have debated the meaning of the Genesis passages for many centuries, but for our purposes, the juxtaposition of this biblical material to the Inanna texts makes a clear enough contrast between the harmonious connection of the sacred couple Inanna and Dumuzi to the earth and the doomed, embattled version of that relation in the story of Adam and Eve.[4]

In *Sowing the Body*, Page DuBois has examined similar changes in the evolving culture of classical Athens. The close interrelation of Greek and Minoan civilizations with the entire Eastern Mediterranean/Mesopotamian world has long been understood, and recent work on Anatolian languages has made it clear that much of Greek religious thought is directly descended from Hittite and other Near Eastern sources (Puhvel 21–32, 126–43). Rather full evidence of the historical evolution of Greek literature and its relation to substratal and adstratal material is available in Greek literature and philosophy, for we have texts from the Homeric epics reflecting the Mycenaean world and other early materials such as

Hesiod and the Homeric Hymns, and then a relatively unbroken body of materials from Attic culture ranging from the eighth century B.C. down through to the fall of Rome (Chadwick 6–11). This was in most respects an urban, settled culture in contrast to the often nomadic world of the early Hebrews. Rich archaeological remains from the Mycenaean world and Minoan Crete allow the tracing of some aspects of Greek culture back to the second millennium B.C. Linear B goes back to the fourteenth century B.C. and is Greek; names such as Demeter and Dionysos can be found on the Linear B tablets and establish links between Mycenaean Greek and Minoan culture.

The point is that change is perhaps more visible here than in the area of transition from Sumerian to Hebrew. Instead of the fiercely patriarchal Judaic priesthood that erased most evidence of its development from an ancient dual-gendered pantheon, the Greeks retained a polytheistic religious base that includes various kinds of female and male powers identified with forces and processes in the natural world. In some of the earliest Greek literary documents, such as Hesiod's *Theogony*, we find a body of metaphor in seeming flux, where, as DuBois remarks, contradictory elements exist "in a synthesis that provides contesting political groups with the mythic vocabularies they can use to argue for dominance or for sharing" (63). These contesting political groups seem to have been centrally interested in gender. In particular the creation story in the *Theogony* moves from primal *Chaos* (a neuter noun meaning an undifferentiated nether world) to *Gaia* ("wide-breasted Earth," a feminine noun and adjective) who is *hedos* ("the eternal, immovable seat of all things") and the parthenogenic mother of her consort Ouranos and then in conjunction with him, of all life. DuBois sees this passage as demonstrating "the primacy of the màternal body for the Greeks. It is the male consort who is a supplement in Derrida's sense, that is, an addition and/or substitution" (43). But this ancient account is enclosed in a strangely uneven patchwork of narrative focused on the patriarchal pantheon that began with the squabbles of father/son pairs from Ouranos down to Zeus. Jaan Puhvel calls the attempted synthesis of indigenous chthonic pre-Greek, diffusionary Anatolian, and Indo-European materials "a somewhat rickety hodgepodge" that still shows its seams (130, also 27–30).

Long catalogs of the daughters of Nereus and the daughters of Electra and of Ceto sit next to descriptions of the battles among the terrible male children of Chronos and Rhea. More than fifty lines are given over to the monstrous Medusa and her even more horrible serpentine children who live in the mysterious and frightening hidden places of mother earth. The term for these places, *keuthesi gaiēs*, is symbolically the womb, later figured as *lochos*, simultaneously bed, site of childbirth, and place of ambush for Uranos. Chronos jumps out from it with his jagged sickle and castrates his father, in a horrifying masculine vision of birth as castration (*Theogony*, lines 158, 174, 178). Yet Zeus forces goddess after goddess to submit to his lovemaking, he appropriates the powers of the all-knowing Metis by putting her inside his own body and thus claiming to be the parthenogenic parent of Athena, and so on.

As DuBois explains, the material contains both "evidence of reverence and awe for earth and woman and evidence of a desire to bypass the female, to appropriate her powers and to represent the male as self-sufficient" (58). Lerner sees these attitudes as part of a gradual transformation occurring generally in archaic cultures as they moved away from preagricultural focus on independent fertility of the female earth and into systems of male dominance based on intensive crop cultivation and animal husbandry (141–60). Because humans have never moved beyond dependence on the land for food and on women for human reproduction, the transformation has never been completed, and masculine attitudes toward land, nature, and materiality have continued to reflect the kind of ambivalence DuBois finds in the ancient Greek materials.

As Greek culture matured, the desire for appropriation overcame that reverence and awe, or at least buried it deep beneath a master narrative of male primacy whose construction DuBois closely analyzes.

> The ideology of the woman's body as fruitful, spontaneously generating earth gives way in time to a cultural appropriation of the body that responds to and rewrites that primary image. Men claim that they must *plough* the earth, create fields, furrow them, and plant seeds if the earth is to bear fruit. They see female bodies as empty ovens that must be filled with grains and made to concoct offspring. They see the female body as analogous to a writing tablet on which they write: the stylus (plough) carving the lines (furrows) of letters (sown seeds) in the body of the mother. (28)

All of these metaphors are rewritings of the earlier metaphoric analogy made between agricultural production and human reproduction that we saw in the Inanna poems, an analogy that probably derives itself from a much older habit of connecting the fertile body of woman with the uncultivated landscapes of the Paleolithic era.

Euripides' *Bacchae*, a text that DuBois does not discuss, offers a disturbing battle between repressive masculine forces and archaic traditions linking fertile landscape and food, to the female body that we saw earlier in Mesopotamian and Anatolian sources. The treatment of these materials is extremely ambivalent, portraying the conjunction of natural fertility and female assertion as powerful and essential but threatening to masculine civic order (Segal, "Menace," 195–200). The *Bacchae* is a revealing transitional text in which liquid foods flow from the land in conjunction with the flow of milk from women's bodies, but in a precarious context threatened by male coercion. E. R. Dodds remarks on the archaic substance and form of this play, which preserves rituals that feature women in positive roles (xxv–xxxviii). Nevertheless, Euripides wrote it for a male audience in an insistently masculinist society, and it reflects deep uneasiness about the wild spirit and fruitful magic of women and landscape.[5] Young King Pentheus goes too far in his efforts to control the women of Thebes and punish them for their rebellious worship of Dionysos, but when the tragedy has run its course, the women who worked the god's will in destroying Pentheus are themselves condemned.

The association of women's bodies with food and the land remains a sacred mystery in spite of these ambiguities. Two passages in the *Bacchae* make this clear, the first occurring early in the play when the seer Tiresias reprimands Pentheus's refusal to take Dionysos seriously.

> Young fellow,
> mankind is blessed with two supreme natural powers:
> Earth power and Liquid power. Demeter,
> or Goddess Earth—call her whichever you like—
> gave us our dry life-nourishing bread.
> Another god then came to complete her good work:
> Semele's child Bakkhos,
> who found a vital juice in the grape cluster—
> (Bagg 28)

Demeter is the grain-giving earth, closely related to Asiatic Cybele (Dodds 76), and Dionysos is the grape. In worshiping him the Maenad releases magical nourishment from the land: "Beneath her the meadow is running with milk / running with wine / running slowly with the nektar of bees" (Bagg 24). A herdsman reports just such a scene to Pentheus, which he and fellow shepherds witnessed in the hills outside of Thebes.

> . . . mothers whose new babies were back home
> eased their aching breasts by picking up
> gazelles and wild wolf cubs to suckle
> with white human milk.
>
> . . . .
>
> Then one struck her wand
> to a rock—out jumps icy springwater!
> Another pushed hers gently into the pasture
> feeling for Bakkhos—she found the god
> who made wine flood up right there!
> Women eager for milk raked the meadow
> with their fingers until it oozed out,
> fresh and white.
>
> Raw honey was dripping
> in sweet threads from their wands.
> (Bagg 42–43)

Dodds explains that the Maenads' playing with the young of wild creatures has a ritual meaning: "the fawn or wolf-cub is an incarnation of the young god, and in suckling it the human mother becomes a foster-mother of Dion" (163). The isomorphism between the spontaneously nourishing power of landscape and woman is quite obvious in this scene, in spite of references to the use of the thyrsus or the power of the god.[6]

Such traditions of independent fertility are entirely suppressed in the writings of Plato. In a reading of Plato that takes the complex traditions of Greek landscape imagery into account, DuBois shows how the male philosopher appropriates traditional agricultural metaphors for woman, "assuming the role of the earth, the field to be filled with the lover's seeds" (28). In the *Phaedrus*, "The field, furrow—the dominant metaphors used for reproductive intercourse from the time of Homer—are here assimilated to a situation of pederasty and philosophy. . . . This field yields not human children, a new generation to populate the *polis*, but *sperma*, seed. The philosopher who erotically implants his seed, his words, in the soul of the beloved will begin an endless process of purely masculine reproduction, where the produce is more words, more seeds" (178). According to DuBois, Aristotle completes the process Plato had begun and thus defines woman's inferior place for centuries. "The male philosopher becomes the site of metaphorical reproduction, the subject of philosophical generation; the female, stripped of her metaphorical otherness, becomes a defective male, defined by lack" (183).

Thus by the fifth century B.C. in Athens, a philosophical and literary tradition is established that will mesh comfortably with the gender definitions of Judaic culture and that will echo the same notion of male subjectivity that transcends the decaying and debased materiality of the body and the earth. According to DuBois:

> What is perhaps most interesting about all these data is the way in which the description of the female by the male who sees her, who is the "theorist," varies according to the demands and needs of culture. The rewriting of the particular metaphor earth/woman's body is transformed over the centuries, and . . . is contested by other metaphors that dominate at other moments. My emphasis is on the contestation, the challenging and putting into question of cultural "sets." There is always a vocabulary of possible signs to be used, transformed, and generated, and the choices made by individuals—poets, dramatists, vase painters, urban planners—must be seen as choices within situations of conflict. (63)

The Virgin Mary serves as a similar focus for such energies and symbolic associations in Christian culture, which of course is heavily encrusted with Hellenic and Roman religious traditions and iconography. Marina Warner explains how the ecstatic traditions of eroticism and food from the *Song of Songs* and related pagan iconography (for instance, Isis-Horus), were always under the control of the male clergy, manipulated to encode but also control and enclose female bodily mysteries within a transcendent, disembodied, and ascetic ideology (132–33).

Caroline Walker Bynum has more recently emphasized the gender reversal in Christian tradition, that places Christ in the feminine role of food preparer and nourisher and exhorts the male priesthood to see itself as feminine in relation to the male God. Since this symbolic move takes place within an overall code in which "male is to female as spirit is to flesh, food receiver to food generator, . . . divine to human," it represents a masculine appropriation of physical life and its sources, in the service of a disembodied power. "The fundamental contrast seems to be between (a) constructs of laws, patterns, forms, erected at some distance from, if not in opposition to, nature, and (b) a more instinctual, internal, biological 'human' nature" (282–83). Nevertheless, Bynum argues that the presence of rich imagery of food in medieval Christianity, deriving both from the Old Testament *Song of Songs* and the New Testament ritual of communion, continued to acknowledge the centrality of flesh, suffering, and the feminine principles of fertility. Christ's wounds continued to be associated with wine and with women's bodies in menstruation and birth giving, and women continued to be linked with the milk of heavenly grace and the food of the Eucharist (270–71). With the advent of modern industrial Europe under the control of a Protestant, masculinist deism, these remaining habits of thought linking the fertile earth and its life with the meaning of human experience were pushed farther and farther into the background.[7]

To speak of the increasing desacralization of the natural world during the passage from medieval Christianity to the modern industrial age is more or less commonplace by now (Collingwood, Shepard, Merchant, Oelschlaeger). Lynn White, Jr., sees these tendencies developing much earlier than is usually granted, for northern European peasants had already invented a deep-slicing plow by the seventh century, while the intelligentsia was busily absorbing Greek, Roman, and Islamic science during the next three hundred years.

> The leadership of the West, both in technology and in science, is far older than the so-called Scientific Revolution of the 17th century or the so-called Industrial Revolution of the 18th century. These terms are in fact outmoded and obscure the true nature of what they try to describe—significant stages in two long and separate developments. By A.D. 1000 at the latest—and perhaps, feebly, as much as 200 years earlier—the West began to apply water power to industrial processes other than milling grain. This was followed in the late 12th century by the harnessing of wind power. From simple beginnings, but with remarkable consistency of style, the West rapidly expanded its skills in the development of power machinery, labor-saving devices, and automation. (344)

Intellectual historian R. G. Collingwood and historian of science Carolyn Merchant give particular emphasis to the mechanical metaphor that came to dominate Western thought and allow the manipulation of objects in a physical world defined as inert.[8]

Carolyn Merchant and Evelyn Fox Keller have insisted that we recognize the implicit gendering of the scientific project. In *The Death of Nature*, Merchant surveys medieval and renaissance ambivalence about a feminized nature that was at once nurturing source of abundance and disordered source of diseases, tempests, and pests. The figure of the witch symbolized natural violence and became the emblem of disturbances in social and economic terms as well. Scientific discoveries of men like Galileo and Copernicus shook Christian cosmology, voyages of discovery in Asia and the Americas destabilized European economies with a gradually increasing flow of raw materials and exotic goods, and knowledge of other lands and whole populations of exotic peoples disrupted traditional cultural assumptions. Merchant sees the seventeenth-century obsession with witches as a projection of anxiety born of these changes, giving birth to a mechanized view of nature that was violently misogynist at its heart (148). Francis Bacon's self-conscious construction of a mechanistic new science was deliberately framed in hostility to female nature, as revealed by the title of one work, *The Masculine Birth of Time*, in which he announced, "I am come in very truth leading to you nature with all her children to bind her to your service and make her your slave." He saw the new learning as a vigorous exploration in a theoretical landscape, operating by "digging further and further into the mine of natural knowledge" or "entering and penetrating into these holes and corners," and asserted that nature can be "forced out of her natural state and squeezed and molded" by the hand of man (qtd. in Merchant 168–71). The underlying violence of these metaphors is set in the coercive context of seventeenth-century gender politics in Merchant's assertion that "the interrogation of witches as symbol for the interrogation of nature, the courtroom as model for its inquisition, and torture through mechanical devices as a tool for the subjugation of disorder were fundamental to the scientific method as power" (172).[9]

Max Oelschlaeger sees the Enlightenment as consolidating "a number of diverse intellectual elements and historical moments into a powerful, virtually overwhelming cultural paradigm" of nature as a machine. This movement he terms modernism and sees still ruling the world long after the Industrial Revolution that gave it rise (91). The romantic movement was a counterforce to this paradigm, but it remained limited to philosophy and the "decorative" arts of literature, painting, and music, failing seriously to divert or slow the powerful advances of the scientific/industrial machine. The romantic embrace of wild nature as source of power, inspiration, and solace was thus a movement of resistance to the soulless mechanism of industrialism and a reassertion of religious habits that had come unmoored from orthodox Judeo-Christian dogma as a result of the cosmology presented by modern physics and astronomy.[10]

In terms of the long cultural tradition I have defined and the gender ideology that Merchant and Keller have revealed at the heart of the scientific revolution, the romantic retreat from science and turn toward nature was an implicit move into the archaic, the primitive, and above all, the feminine. The idea of Nature as feminine clashes with the mechanical metaphor and takes us back to the fact that new ways of figuring land and nature did not wholly displace older patterns of thinking about the physical world. As in the development of the brain, older layers of symbolic behavior continued to operate simultaneously with newer ones in a dynamic interplay among different submerged metaphors that stand for conflicting philosophical and moral positions. Man's reverence for a personified female Nature is quite different from Bacon's treatment of nature "as a female to be tortured through mechanical inventions" (Merchant 168) or man's power over a post-Enlightenment nature defined as a lifeless machine. Deep emotional responses are involved when nature and landscape are personified, while the idea of manipulating a machine is a merely formal, utilitarian matter.

When the European explorers first encountered the immense new continents of North and South America, they naturally projected familiar expectations upon what they saw before them: mythical conceptions of the Golden World from Hesiod, Edenic visions from Judeo-Christian culture, pastoral expectations from the classics, exotic stories of Asian riches from folklore and popular travel lore, and various ancient traditions of fear and hostility toward unfamiliar, dangerous wild places (Marx 34–88; Nash 8–22; Slotkin 14–24; Todorov 14–17). Annette Kolodny has detailed the ways in which many of their imaginings were highly gendered, though the meaning given sexual metaphors varied with the needs and experiences of the Europeans who invoked them. In Kolodny's view, for the first waves of European colonists "at the deepest psychological level, the move to America was experienced as the daily reality of what has become its single dominating metaphor: regression from the cares of adult life and a return to the primal warmth of womb or breast in a feminine landscape" (6). Such a characterization must refer to a romanticized picture of a much more complicated physical reality, for at least half the original colonists at both Jamestown and Plymouth died of starvation and disease before their first year in the new land was over. Physical hardships and challenges required adjustment of the colonists' expectations, as William Cronon explains in *Changes in the Land: Indians, Colonists, and the Ecology of New England*. On the other hand, what the colonists found was hardly a wilderness. We now know that the landscapes of the Americas were carefully managed for thousands of years by indigenous peoples. Much of New England was parklike woodland, with open grassy spaces under the trees—all controlled by seasonal burning. Similar practices were used across the continent.

Thus the encounter with the new landscapes and their indigenous inhabitants began complex processes of definition, ideological manipulation, and acculturation that continue today. Richard Slotkin's *Regeneration through Violence* summarizes many of the ways these processes are recorded in the development of our national literature during its formative stages, and he explains the double nature of the exchange. European colonists had to adapt their ideas about the landscape to the desperate project of surviving its rigors, and the perspectives and practices of the tribal peoples already on the land were crucial to their success (Cronon 34–127). Slotkin describes the deeply disorienting effect of life among the Indians for Spanish explorer Núñez Cabeza de Vaca, who was no longer able to see the land as an object for conquest but instead became a divided person suffering guilt for his countrymen's despoiling of the environment and slaughter of native populations (33–37). Similar cultural dislocation occurred for later Dutch and English captives. Indeed, many refused to return to "civilization" when they were given the chance, preferring life among the Indians in a more harmonious balance with the landscape (325–31; Axtell 131–206). "In ways so subtle that they were often ignored," says Bruce Johansen of the Iroquois influence on the northern colonies, "the Indians left their imprint on the colonists' eating habits, the paths they followed, the way they clothed themselves, and the way they thought" (34).

Similarly, the Indians had to adapt to the presence of the intruders and to the radical changes they soon made in the landscape. Native American oral traditions began to reflect this changed reality (McLuhan 45–123), and as Oglala Sioux Chief Luther Standing Bear later reflected, the native peoples' harmony with the land was radically changed as the white man moved steadily westward.

> We did not think of the great open plains, the beautiful rolling hills, and winding streams with tangled growth, as "wild." Only to the white man was nature a "wilderness" and only to him was the land "infested" with "wild" animals and "savage" people. To us it was tame. Earth was bountiful and we were surrounded with the blessings of the Great Mystery. Not until the hairy man from the east came and with brutal frenzy heaped injustices upon us and the families we loved was it "wild" for us. When the very animals of the forest began fleeing from his approach, then it was that for us the "Wild West" began. (McLuhan 45)

Slotkin provides a useful summary of the complex relations of attraction and revulsion between the two cultures (25–56, 190–99; McWilliams 123–57), but his assignment of the Indians to a "primary, Moira stage" of mythopoeic vision in contrast to the sophisticated conventions of the Europeans is rather condescending and too heavily reliant on Jungian and psychoanalytic models. Indians and Europeans began to appropriate each other's tools, practices, clothing, and political arrangements.[11] In gradually winning control of the land and dispossessing its earlier inhabitants, the Europeans became aware of the profoundly sacramental understanding of Nature found everywhere among the natives, and they had to come to some terms with it. The southern colonists tended to see the wilderness in erotic terms of feminine allurement and fertility, as Kolodny has shown (10–16; Tichi 86). Thus they adapted pastoral conventions of contemporary European literature to their experiences in a positive scheme that could be reconciled with the Indians' concepts of harmony and kinship with the land and its creatures. Indeed, descriptions of native peoples were fed back into European thought, where they influenced the political philosophy of Hobbes and Locke, and fed the older concept of the Noble Savage in a romantic primitivism that eventually found a powerful propagandist in Rousseau (Slotkin 200–205 and 370).[12]

From the first, with William Bradford's description of the Plymouth landing in a "hideous and desolate wilderness, full of wild beasts and wild men," the New England Puritans consigned the inhospitable wilderness to the realm of Satan. As Slotkin puts the matter, "it was quite appropriate to destroy the natural wilderness in the name of a higher good—and quite inappropriate for anyone to worship, as the Indians did, the world or the things of the world, such things being evil by nature"(51). Cotton Mather used a vivid agricultural metaphor to express this idea in *The Wonders of the Invisible World*, describing the Puritan colonists as "the vine which God has here planted, casting out the heathen, and preparing a room before it, and causing it to take deep root, and fill the land, so that it sent its boughs unto the Atlantic Sea eastward, and its branches unto the Connecticut River westward, and the hills were covered with the shadow thereof."[13] This image of plantation in a hostile landscape echoes the kind of language King James I had earlier used in directing colonizing companies to extirpate the "barbarian" Scottish clans of the Hebrides Islands and "plant those isles with civil people" (MacLeod 32). As we have seen, such imagery expressed a gendered ideology supporting the domination of feminized landscapes and "alien" peoples, and it is the same ideology so vigorously advanced by the king's counselor Francis Bacon for the violent coercion of female Nature by masculine science.

The consolidation of the United States as a nation at the end of the eighteenth century and the romantic movement that swept in from Europe during the early decades of the nineteenth merely softened and secularized these metaphoric habits of defining the wilderness. Thus, as Lawrence and Fiedler observe, works like Cooper's Deerslayer novels consign Native Americans to an already existing European category of unconstrained and dangerous passionate feminine power in contrast to the domesticating, controlling power wielded by men, a category I have traced back to Greece, Palestine, and Sumer (Lawrence 86–90; Fiedler 184–200). At the same time, two conflicting landscape metaphors are being employed, essentially paralleling these categories—howling, disordered wilderness as opposed to benign and abundant pastoral paradise. It is no accident that this opposition also corresponds with two radically opposing views of the feminine in European culture, that of the pure virginal or maternal source of life and comfort, and that of the demonic witch. These qualities play out an unresolved tension in Hawthorne's "Maypole of Merrymount" and *The Scarlet Letter*. The latter work in particular sets up the forest as home of sinister Indians who teach Chillingworth the lore of poisonous herbs and site where witches gather, but also the one place where a benign Nature allows a moment of happiness and love for Hester Prynne and Arthur Dimmesdale.

The negative construction of the landscape justified its violent domination, but the simultaneous operation of the pastoral vision, usually employed to describe landscapes already under human control, led to confusion and guilt in the emerging national consciousness. Leo Marx has explained the guilt as deriving from an uneasy sense of mechanical violation, while Kolodny sees the problem almost solely in terms of gender. There is justice to both views, but the complex, evolving historical dimension of the matter is more fully explored by Slotkin and Fisher. Slotkin takes his hint from D. H. Lawrence's claim that the true American hero is a killer "who lets his consciousness penetrate in loneliness into the new continent. His contacts are not human. He wrestles with the spirits of the forest and the American wild, as a hermit wrestles with God and Satan" (86, 90). Thus fictional efforts at constructing a national hero began with biographies of Daniel Boone and led to Cooper's creation of an archetype in Natty Bumppo. Fiedler, also following Lawrence, has called our attention to the male bonding between the hunter and his native, dark-skinned companion, which substitutes for the more conventional male-female bond of civilized community in Cooper's fiction, a pattern that settled into an American archetype but that we have seen already fully articulated in the ancient Mesopotamian *Epic of Gilgamesh.* This "is a relationship which symbolically joins the white man to nature and his own unconscious, without a sacrifice of his 'gifts'; and binds him in life-long loyalty to a help-meet, without the sacrifice of his freedom. This is the pure marriage of males—sexless and holy, a kind of counter-matrimony, in which the white refugee from society and the dark-skinned primitive are joined till death do them part" (200–205).

The arrangement serves several crucial psychological purposes for the dominant class of white males in the new country. Fiedler labels them sentimental but clearly indicates their relation to a collective sense of guilt.

> Though the Leatherstocking romances are, first of all, entertainments, they are also propitiatory offerings. There is in all of them, at one point or another, a reflection of Cooper's quarrel with himself (with the "Indian" deep within him): the sound of an inner voice explaining, justifying, endlessly hashing over the appropriation of the land, on which Cooper's own wealth and status so directly depended. His first means of coming to terms with his guilt-feelings is by identifying himself with the injured party, dissociating himself

from the exploiters. In reading his romances, the American boy becomes for a little while the Indian, the trapper ... [and] finds it easy to think of himself as somehow really expropriated and dispossessed, driven from the Great Good Place of the wilderness by pressures of maturity and conformism. (186)

At this point Fiedler does not confront the gendered associations of that place that we have already seen, associations he himself mentions frequently elsewhere in *Love and Death in the American Novel*. The Great Good Place is seen as an erotically seductive virgin landscape or the maternally comforting lap or bosom of Mother Nature that both Emerson and Thoreau will invoke only a few decades after Cooper.

In more directly theoretical and less sympathetic terms than Fiedler's, Philip Fisher defines the mechanism of historical erasure in a cultural imperialism that softens the killer by making him a mediating force sympathetic to Indians, while villains of both races effect the work of genocide, and greedy white bullies tear down the forest and slaughter its wildlife. By an even more sinister sleight of hand, Fisher tells us, Cooper's brand of historical fiction assumes as already complete an extermination of native peoples that has never in fact occurred (29–39, 83–86). Such an erasure is constantly wished and encouraged in popular media even today. What is important for my argument is the alliance of Indians, land, and the feminine in these ideological formulations by white men, and the resulting problems of affect and moral responsibility to which they unrelentingly led. Among Indian people, to this day, the association has continued to evoke reverence in the traditional way, but also deep grief for the sacrilege that has occurred across the continent.

Every rational creature has all nature for his dowry and estate.
RALPH WALDO EMERSON, *Nature*

Nature is hard to be overcome, but she must be overcome.
HENRY DAVID THOREAU, *Walden*

CHAPTER 3

Pastoral Ambivalence in Emerson and Thoreau

What James Fenimore Cooper defined through fiction as white Americans' innocent inheritance of the landscape, Ralph Waldo Emerson and Henry David Thoreau addressed explicitly in *Nature* and *Walden*, through deliberate acts of self-evaluation and national mythmaking (Lewis, *American Adam*, 13–27; Nash 2–10, 67–95). Oelschlaeger claims that as Thoreau's reputation has grown, Emerson has come to be seen more as a popularizer of European ideas than as an original thinker (133). But among scholars of American literature Emerson has experienced renewed popularity as a deconstructive thinker in the past fifteen years. In any case *Walden* grows so directly out of *Nature,* and echoes it so richly, that the two works must be considered together. *Walden* is as interlaced with European learning as *Nature* is, in spite of both writers' protestations of independence from the past. We have already seen how masculine opposition to the feminine metaphoric identification of land and nature is implicated in that past, and David Leverenz's *Manhood and the American Renaissance* reveals the intense ambivalence of Emerson's reliance on the self-conscious virility of his day (42–71). Because Emerson and Thoreau approached the question of American identity and the landscape so directly and were so influential, they define the basic ground of our modern assumptions and illustrate the dynamic play of gender at their core.

Emerson chose to make his first claim to literary prominence with *Nature,* an ambitious attempt at philosophy focused on what he must have considered central to the identity of the new nation. As scion of a long line of Puritan clerics, Emerson's intellectual inheritance was the best classical and theological education Boston Latin School and Harvard College could provide. He added to it an enthusiastic absorption of German philosophic idealism gleaned from Coleridge and Carlyle. But when he set out to formulate an independent American vision of human destiny, the basically untamed physical landscape of North America was all the new culture could claim as its own. Thus, in Roderick Nash's paradoxical formulation, "Wilderness was the defining symbol of the national civilization" (xv). As we have seen, the idea of wilderness was intimately entangled in troubled relations with indigenous peoples just beyond the range of Emerson's vision.

There were also personal reasons leading Emerson to turn his attention to the natural world for his first major literary effort. Evelyn Barish describes the salutary effect of the warm natural paradise of Florida on his health at the age of twenty-three, when the family malady of tuberculosis had nearly blinded him, crippled his hip, and literally threatened his life (177–97). In fleeing the harsh New England climate, Emerson was also escaping the oppressive weight of a paternal theological heritage that he resisted in an agony of doubt. He turned away from this bookish realm to the languorous physical world of virtually unsettled Florida tropics around the little village of St. Augustine where he spent several months. A visit to the Jardin des Plantes in Paris five years later, on a voyage taken to relieve his grief after the death of his first wife, also seems to have turned him toward Nature as an alternative to the burden of history and the European cultural heritage (Barish 239, Ellison 85).

Many have remarked upon the fierce rejection of cultural fathers that begins *Nature*, and Eric Cheyfitz urges us to read the work as an oedipal drama of deeply conflicted sexual identity in which the narrative sings "the siren song of a savage, hermaphroditic figure that, aligning itself with a growing feminine power, is luring us into drowning in a dream of the FATHER" (113, 167). Cheyfitz's study ingeniously explores the sexual ambivalence of the work, but I would argue that the essential identification of the narrator is always firmly masculine, however complex his oedipal hostilities may be. This is a son eager to escape from the dry bones and sepulchres of the cultural fathers, but one seeking access to the supreme Father who legitimizes his oracular voice: the God behind Nature. The most profound anxiety revealed in *Nature* is fear of the feminine, with a corresponding need to ensure the subjective distance from it that defines male control. That Nature is feminine is a cultural given, as we have seen. It is everywhere apparent in the essay, from the consistent use of feminine pronouns to explicit personification of Nature and feminine clothing metaphors. The problem for Emerson's persona is an infantile yearning for passive bliss in a maternal embrace. This "effeminacy" must be fought and overcome by manly assertions of will.

Emerson lived in an era deeply troubled by the emergence of women into the cultural mainstream of the West. Ann Douglas has described a general nineteenth-century feminization of the American clergy and popular culture, placing Emerson in its midst and alluding to his fear of effeminacy (19–20). And Cheyfitz cites Tocqueville's reactions to the confident and assertive "virile" women of the new country as background for the sexual ambivalence of Emerson's narrative voice (132–41). The problem must have been intensified for Emerson by his deep personal reliance on his aunt Mary Moody Emerson, the only positive parental figure in his childhood and the major intellectual influence in his upbringing.[1] She introduced him to Mary Wollstonecraft's *Vindication of the Rights of Woman* and prepared him to be responsive later in life to strong women like Margaret Fuller, the aggressive Muse he invited to lay siege to him (Douglas 275). In a defensively "virile" intellectual culture (Leverenz 60–61), Emerson must have felt especially uneasy about his lifelong identification with strong women.

Given this background, it is neither surprising that *Nature* should reject the patriarchal past and yearn to be "embosomed" in the life-giving floods of nature, nor that the essay should ultimately reassert the language of the FATHER and retreat from an identification with the feminine world of the "not me." Toward the end of *Nature* Emerson self-consciously protests, "I have no hostility to nature, but a child's love to it. I expand and live in the warm day like corn and melons. Let us speak her fair. I do not wish to fling stones at my beautiful mother, nor soil my gentle nest" (28). He is guiltily aware of the central paradox in this manifesto that ends with a call for the realization of "the kingdom of man over nature" (36). Reverence for nature's power and the contrasting will to conquer oscillate through the essay in a tension that is reiterated in the more complex texture of Thoreau's *Walden.*[2]

In the famous transparent eyeball passage of Emerson's essay, the human subject ecstatically communicates his union with the sublime, healing natural environment that is his direct access to Truth and God. "Standing on the bare ground—my head bathed by the blithe air, and uplifted into infinite space,—all mean egotism vanishes. I become a transparent eyeball. I am nothing. I see all. The currents of the Universal Being circulate through me; I am part and particle of God" (6).

From this early point on, however, Emerson's essay quivers with ambivalence toward physical Nature, and in its course the passive ecstasy of the transparent eyeball passage is quickly relegated to a lower, effeminate level of apprehension so that the male will can properly assert itself over the material world and a Platonic movement up the hierarchy toward the disembodied ideal can be effected. As Myra Jehlen puts it, "The stillness and the pull of oceanic surrender are there in *Nature*, but so is a thrusting energy that can at any moment turn Emerson's movement out of himself, all the way around, and make God part or parcel of *him*" (97). Just before the passage, Emerson had asserted that "Nature never wears a mean appearance," but just after it he claims that "nature is not always tricked in holiday attire" but is changeable, and in fact ultimately depends on the male observer's moods for her aspect (5–6). "Tricked" is a demeaning pun that suggests feminine ornamentation designed to mislead a male admirer. It harmonizes more effectively than Emerson may have realized with the Greek word *kosmos,* meaning both order and women's clothing and decoration (Liddell and Scott 447), which he uses to characterize Nature's beauty in chapter 3. Emerson betrays an uneasiness about the physical beauty of Nature, arguing that it is mere appearance and requires a "higher, spiritual element," the controlling human will, which preserves the onlooker from "effeminacy." Exemplars such as Spartan warrior king Leonidas and Swiss military hero Arnold Winkelried show how "every rational creature has all nature for his dowry and estate" (10–11). The goddess Nature who clothes her darling child Columbus with the beautiful landscapes of the New World and "stretcheth out her arms to embrace man" in chapter 3 becomes by chapter 5 "thoroughly mediate," receiving the dominion of man "as meekly as the ass on which the Saviour rode" (19). Emerson bestows only a guilty backward glance upon the mother with her gentle nest, as his prose marches on to the heroic call to conquest in the essay's final passage.

Emerson's cavalier refusal to be bound by the kind of consistency he called "the hobgoblin of little minds" delighted iconoclastic readers like Nietzsche and has led recent commentators to celebrate the dialectical play of the essays. But many others have been troubled by profound contradictions such as those in *Nature* and have tried to reconcile them.[3] Because Thoreau followed Emerson in this rhetorical habit, obviously in part to discomfit his readers and wake them out of complacency just as Emerson wished to do, the problem of how the pronouncements of both are to be taken is central to my discussion. It should be clear by now that I think both writers accountable for participation in a long tradition of gender politics that is not part of any complex philosophical exploration or mimetic representation of a difficult and confusing world. While Emerson may have conflicting impulses regarding the feminized Nature that is the subject of his essay, I think he comes to a decision about them by the end. His narrative movement is hierarchical, recalling the movement of Plato's *Symposium*, and in its light there is no doubt about the gender or position of the speaker of the final paragraphs. Emerson cannot both adore Mother Nature and urge his readers to conquer her. As David Leverenz remarks, "Emerson's ideal of manly self-empowerment reduces womanhood to spiritual nurturance while erasing female subjectivity" (44).

Nature was published when Thoreau was a senior at Harvard and became so central to the younger man's thinking that his own writing began immediately to echo Emersonian terms like "not me" in assertions of the opposition of nature and mind (Sattelmeyer, *TR*, 22–23). Critical readers of *Walden* have often noticed the conflict between Thoreau's desire to become part of the natural environment at the pond on the one hand and his need to maintain distance and control on the other.[4] But dismissals of this conflict as source of productive intensity or useful irony fail to acknowledge what seems an implicit betrayal of the original pastoral purpose. Although Thoreau experiments more playfully with subjective positions and distances from nature than Emerson does, "she" is always other than himself; the witty narrator is always a male in control of the relationship. I think we must recognize that in spite of lifelong efforts to immerse himself in the natural world, Thoreau is trapped by his literary heritage and masculine loyalties into a position very similar to Emerson's.

While Emerson retreats almost dizzily from imaginative fusion with Nature in his essay and appears to have had little interest in physical experience of the natural world, Thoreau physically sought "the occult relation between man and vegetable," mineral, and other animals that Emerson only rhapsodized about. Yet Thoreau also finally shrinks away from the feminization inherent in too close an identification with the nonhuman world. As he shaped his journal entries into the increasingly literary form of the published *Walden*, he exalted the "father tongue" of the written word and his intellectual heritage over the "mother tongue" of embodied speech, which he called "almost brutish" (101). He too withdrew from immersion in the physical world, most obviously in the much-discussed ascetic chapter "Higher Laws" and in his departure from Walden Pond at the end of his experiment, but also in many more subtle ways while he still lived there. *Walden*, like *Nature*, enacts a dramatic dance back and forth between attraction and repulsion, love and disgust, in an imagined female presence from which the author's masculine identity compels him to distinguish himself.

At the time Thoreau was writing *Walden*, advances in natural science and movement toward technological human control of the American landscape placed his ruminations at the pond in a complex, ironic matrix. Robert Sattelmeyer and William Rossi have discussed Thoreau's debt to geologist Charles Lyell in his emphasis on minuscule presence of humans in earth's evolution.[5] Yet at the same time, humans seemed to be gaining ever greater control of the vast landscape that had seemed an inexhaustible wilderness only a generation earlier. By the beginning of the nineteenth century, the deforestation of New England was almost complete, and the region's Indians were equally devastated, reduced to small bands of ragged paupers by European disease, colonial appropriation of

land and natural resources, and ecological transformation that made traditional subsistence impossible (Cronon 102–56). Philip Fisher explains
that it was clear by the 1840s to thoughtful observers like Francis Park-
man that the continent was tamed and its native peoples soon to be
swept "from the face of the earth" by streams of white settlers (38). With
the Indians, of course, wildlife and an older ecological reality would also
be swept away. Something parallel was happening in medicine, regarding
that other landscape that loomed so large in the deep cultural imagination. In the 1840s American gynecologist Marion Sims was describing
himself as a Columbus discovering the vagina as his "New World" landscape, so that traditional gendered definitions of landscape and geography
were projected back onto the female body in gynecological research of
the time (Gilbert and Gubar 2: 33). In sum, though natural history de-
centered humans in the physical world, modern industrial civilization's
enormous project of controlling the landscape of North America seemed
to have success in view. A colonization of the female body as a kind of
landscape was simultaneously under way among medical pioneers.

Thoreau's Walden Pond was a microcosm of the already corrupted
American landscape. As many have observed, it was no wilderness but
instead a colonized space from which Indians and most wildlife had already been removed. During his sojourn there, it was used as a quarry
for raw materials like ice and lumber.[6] Thoreau himself calls attention to
the instability of the physical place he idealizes in his book. He is only a
mile and a half from Concord and can see the village through a vista
opened up by the deforestation of a nearby hill (86–87). He makes his famous bean field in an area cleared fifteen years previously (156), and he
indicates that Walden has been destroyed in his lifetime. The pond of his
boyhood, "completely surrounded by thick and lofty pine and oak
woods," is by the final writing of *Walden*—some years after he lived
there—circled by denuded shores laid waste by woodchoppers like the
Canadian used in the narrative as a model of the natural, heroic man
(191–92). In the end, Thoreau was not as interested in a particular place
as he was in seeking to use his experiences as rhetoric, "for the sake of
tropes and expression" (162). Most of the experiences he describes in
Walden are defined by literary and philosophical allusion in a sort of
free-floating Platonic realm of traditional ideas. Thus we must question
Oelschlaeger's claim that Thoreau "becomes a man of Indian wisdom, a
person-in-contact with wild nature, with the Great Mother" (170). The

gender dynamics of *Walden* reveal that sustained contact with wild nature and the Great Mother are exactly what he cannot afford.

Thoreau's *Journal* unselfconsciously uses gendered definitions of the landscape and natural world, as when he refers to the Indian's cleanly use of his "untrimmed mistress" the earth, in contrast to "something vulgar and foul" in the white farmer's greater closeness as a tiller of the soil (*J* 2: 100). Similarly, botanical imagery used to describe the mind relies on a female earth and erotic processes of masculine penetration:

> So the mind develops from the first in two opposite directions: upwards to expand in the light and air; and downwards avoiding the light to form the root. One half is aerial, the other subterranean. The mind is not well balanced and firmly planted, like the oak, which has not as much root as branch, whose roots like those of the white pine are slight and near the surface. One half of the mind's development must still be root,—in the embryonic state, in the womb of nature, more unborn than at first. For each successive new idea or bud, a new rootlet in the earth. The growing man penetrates yet deeper by his roots into the womb of things. The infant is comparatively near the surface, just covered from the light; but the man sends down a tap-root to the centre of things. (*J* 2: 203)

For Thoreau such depth of involvement in "the womb of things" is obviously unfortunate, moving the mind away from the superior sunlit realm of transcendence identified with the masculine.

During the period when he was living at Walden, the journal also constantly defines the place in terms of classical models. His cabin is a place for the gods like the halls of Olympus, the light and air are like the atmosphere that inspired Grecian art, he hears Aeolian music all about him, and his reflections are saturated with references to Homer, Alexander, Achilles, Patroclus, Cicero, and so forth. On July 7, 1845, he writes, "I am glad to remember tonight as I sit by my door that I too am at least a remote descendant of that heroic race of men of whom there is tradition. I too sit here on the shore of my Ithaca, a fellow wanderer and survivor of Ulysses" (*J* 2: 156).

When Thoreau recast his materials for publication, he continued to emphasize the Homeric ideal that had been central to his education, "naturalizing" his citizenship in a culture that defined itself by aggressive action, in opposition to the feminine. Thoreau may cast this tradition in an ironic light, as in the famous mock-heroic descriptions of the ant battle or the bean field, but he never seriously abandons it as the ground of his manly identity. Time and again he contrasts passive "effeminacy" to virile action, as Emerson had done before him in the standard formulation of their era.[7] In "Reading" he champions the reading of Homer and Aeschylus in Greek as a way of avoiding "dissipation or luxuriousness" (100) and opposes this activity to the degeneracy of the majority of his fellows, "a race of tit-men" who content themselves by "sucking the pap" of provincial newspapers and other cheap popular writing (107, 109). High culture is male, low culture unmistakably feminized.

In shaping a statement of purpose for *Walden,* Thoreau applied Homeric military imagery to earlier journal material. On July 6, 1845, he had written: "I wish to meet the facts of life—the vital facts, which where [*sic*] the phenomena or actuality the Gods meant to show us,—face to face, And so I came down here. Life! who knows what it is—what it does? If I am not quite right here I am less wrong than before" (*J* 2: 156). The revised version states his purpose in terms that are much more specific and forceful: "I went to the woods because I wished to live deliberately, to front only the essential facts of life. . . . I wanted to live deep and suck out all the marrow of life, to live so sturdily and Spartan-like as to put to rout all that was not life, to cut a broad swath and shave close, to drive life into a corner" (90–91).

Echoing Francis Bacon's language of violent attack upon Nature to open her secrets, Thoreau presents "life" as an animal he must kill and eat, a field he must harvest, or some hunted beast he must drive into a trap. The Emersonian sense of "life" as wild nature or the "not me" is clearly implied here (Rossi, "Limits," 94). Man the predator and domesticator of the landscape is only half hidden in these metaphors, as Slotkin noticed some years ago (519).

The chapter ends with a paragraph that decribes his enterprise, not in terms of physical involvement with the material environment of Walden Pond, but rather as a primarily intellectual effort: "The intellect is a cleaver; it discerns and rifts its way into the secret of things. I do not wish to be any more busy with my hands than is necessary. My head is hands and feet. I feel all my best faculties concentrated in it. My instinct tells me that my head is an organ for burrowing, as some creatures use their snout and fore-paws, and with it I would mine and burrow my way through these hills" (98). Thoreau is definite about not wanting to waste time with physical tasks here. Yet once again he uses the imagery of physical attack. The reference to a cleaver brings to mind the butcher shop and hacking of flesh. His imagining his head as "an organ for bur- rowing" at first might suggest the relatively benign work of some animal like a mole or badger that seeks only a nest and safety in the earth. (And of course there is the possibility of a phallic pun.) But the word "min- ing" differentiates his work from that of such creatures, linking it to large-scale industrial processes that ravage and poison the landscape. Even though Thoreau refers to intellectual activity in this passage, his violent metaphors are related to the physical work that he says allows him to know the Nature around him at Walden Pond. For instance, when he fells a number of pine trees to frame his little house, the pitch (their lifeblood, in effect) imparts a fragrance to the bread of his lunch and creates a sense of intimacy. "Before I had done I was more the friend than the foe of the pine tree, though I had cut down some of them, having become better acquainted with it" (42). The action of knowing in this friendship is the action of killing.

At the heart of *Walden* is Thoreau's extended meditation on "The Ponds" describing Walden's shape, exact physical measurements, aspect in various weathers, colors under various skies, and most important for Thoreau, its meaning in the landscape: "A Lake is the landscape's most beautiful and expressive feature. It is earth's eye; looking into which the beholder measures the depth of his own nature. The fluviatile trees next the shore are the slender eyelashes which fringe it, and the wooded hills and cliffs around are its overhanging brows" (186). Here Thoreau has elaborated the transparent eyeball image of Emerson, but he has com- pletely changed its reference. Emerson defined himself as speaking sub- ject, transformed into an organ of vision or into the function of vision. Thoreau has transposed the metaphor onto the landscape, thus personify- ing earth, which we have already seen is consistently feminized and set apart from the poet.

This feminine "other," which is the land and all living things outside the male subject, is beautiful and magnetic but somehow horrifying in its material being, subject to decay like the body. His ambivalence to- ward his body and sensuality in general is most fully displayed in "Higher Laws," a section whose rhetorical structure seems designed to follow the Platonic progression from physical to higher spiritual realms that Emerson mirrors in the structure of *Nature*. "Higher Laws" begins with a wild, Dionysiac urge toward *sparagmos* and *omophagia*, expressing Thoreau's desire to snatch up a woodchuck, tear it to pieces, and eat it raw. One wonders whether Euripides' *Bacchae* might not be hovering behind Thoreau's conscious construction here. But very soon he backs away from these impulses almost in horror; these are the antithesis of man's higher, moral being. "We are conscious of an animal in us, which awakens in proportion as our higher nature slumbers. It is reptile and sensual, and perhaps cannot be wholly expelled; like the worms which, even in life and health, occupy our bodies" (219).

Eating, drinking—even the Puritan's brown crust and water—are potential experiences of degradation and brutishness. By the end of the section, Thoreau has decided, "Nature is hard to be overcome, but *she* must be overcome" (221, my emphasis). As Michael West remarks, "Thoreau remains haunted by a profound ambivalence toward the body and toward those excremental processes that he explicitly undertakes to defend in 'Higher Laws'" (1046). This material reality is feminine, and the consumption that was ravaging Thoreau's own body and would cause his early death was blamed by popular medical theory on "effeminacy," which could be counteracted by an ascetic regimen (West 1054).

It is no wonder that when Thoreau describes his most peaceful and intimate moments of communion with Walden Pond, he is really abstracted from it, as in the emblematic description of fishing in the pond at night.

> These experiences were very memorable and valuable to me,— anchored in forty feet of water, and twenty or thirty rods from the shore, surrounded sometimes by thousands of small perch and shiners, dimpling the surface with their tails in the moonlight, and communicating by a long flaxen line with mysterious nocturnal fishes which had their dwelling forty feet below, or sometimes dragging sixty feet of line about the pond as I drifted in the gentle night breeze, now and then feeling a slight vibration along it, indicative of some life prowling about its extremity, of dull uncertain blundering purpose there, and slow to make up its mind. At length you slowly raise, pulling hand over hand, some horned pout squeaking and squirming to the upper air. It was very queer, expecially in dark nights, when your thoughts had wandered to vast and cosmogonal themes in other spheres, to feel this faint jerk, which came to interrupt your dreams and link you to Nature

again. It seemed as if I might next cast my line upward into the air, as well as downward into this element which was scarcely more dense. Thus I caught two fishes as it were with one hook. (174–75)

From the outset his purpose is predatory. Yet he defines the scene as a cozily domesticated space in which animals serenade the fisherman and in which charming fish pattern the moonlit water for his benefit. Separated from the pond by his boat, he only communicates with its life by a deadly fishing line. Though it may appear that he gives himself over to the forces of Nature by allowing his boat to drift to and fro in the darkness, this movement is circumscribed because the boat is *anchored*. He condescendingly describes his prey as being of "dull, uncertain blundering purpose."

Not only is Thoreau physically separated from the body of the pond, but also he is abstracted from the life of his own body. He describes his thoughts transcending his physical being and wandering "to vast cosmogonal themes in other spheres" so that he needs the jerk of the captured fish, struggling vainly to escape death, to link him up to Nature again. (One of my students suggested that the fishing line could be seen as a kind of umbilical cord connecting Thoreau to the body of Mother Nature. If so, it is temporary, carefully controlled, and dangerous.)

Water, of course, is traditionally connected with the feminine. Such associations permeate Celtic mythology, European literature is full of them, Freud made much of them, and Klaus Theweleit adduces scores of examples from nineteenth- and twentieth-century literature that express a combination of ecstatic sexual abandon and horror at the dissolution of ego boundaries accompanying male immersion in water (276–88). Perhaps such associations led Thoreau to concentrate his attention upon his manageable experiences with the water of the pond rather than to provide close descriptions of his daily morning swim or other experiences of immersion, in spite of all his emphasis on bathing.

Even the famous celebratory description of the thawing spring earth late in *Walden* is darkened by an undercurrent of physical revulsion accompanying the emphasis on liquid metamorphosis that, as we might expect, is identified with the feminine. Thoreau likens patterns of flowing liquid and sand to foliage and "such a foliaceous mass as the vitals of the animal body." The divine male Artist who made the world sports erotically in the spring muck of the crumbling bank, making the very atoms pregnant with these designs. Man is "but a mass of thawing clay," part of this exhilarating riot of physical life (306–7). Along with his excitement, Thoreau mildly admits an uneasiness that flowers into an image of the ruptured bodily boundaries of Mother Earth, an excremental and chaotic mass of internal organs flowing across the surface: "True, it is somewhat excrementitious in its character, and there is no end to the heaps of liver lights and bowels, as if the globe were turned wrong side outward: but this suggests at least that Nature has some bowels, and there again is mother of humanity" (308). Attempting to pull out of this morass, Thoreau retreats into the more distanced terms "frost coming out of the ground," "Spring," the analogy of mythology preceding true poetry for the mucky liquid earth "that precedes the green and flowery spring." Yet as the passage concludes, he returns again and again to suggestions of excrement and decay as the essential facts of the living maternal earth.

Nevertheless, Thoreau genuinely sought to reconcile his philosophical heritage with his physical experiences at Walden Pond and with the natural science of his day. He attempted to define an Eden in the middle ground between the frenzy of industrial civilization and the inhuman wastes of wilderness. Robert Sattelmeyer says that Thoreau saw Native Americans as potential guides "toward some wisdom gained through the appreciation of nature that had been lost by civilized people" but was never able to adapt his voluminous notes on Indians for his own literary pursuits (100). I would argue that he could not do so because of his entrapment within the insistently gendered consciousness central to both the literary heritage he shared with Emerson and the emerging scientific paradigms of his time. He represents what Donna Haraway would call "one half of the system of desire mediated by modern science and technology, the half dreaming of reclosing the broken cosmos" (136). His understanding of himself was defined by the ethic of heroic assertion and exploitation at the heart of this system that can be traced all the way back to Gilgamesh, destroyer of the wild cedar forest sacred to Inanna/Ishtar. Like Cooper and Emerson before him, Thoreau was genuinely drawn to the idea of Nature and the landscape as alternatives to the sepulchres of the European cultural fathers. But their authority as writers remained grounded in a semiotic network that defined itself in opposition to the feminine. The emergence of women into nineteenth-century intellectual and political life threatened the position of men like

Emerson and Thoreau in "nonvirile" professions at the historical moment when science was emerging as the new field for heroism. Science had manipulated the traditional female codes for earth, in Donna Haraway's words, "in order to legitimate deeper penetration by a virile lover/actor/knower" who could hardly afford to identify with "the natural-technical objects of knowledge which his fertile mind and hands generated from her raw materials" (136).

Thus Emerson and Thoreau move insistently to abstract themselves, no matter how reverently they may speak of the beauties of the physical world. What has been associated in the popular mind with the most benign appreciation of Nature has actually been an ultimate rejection of the physical because of its "feminine" identification. Both writers consolidate the imperialist nostalgia that has always been at the heart of American pastoral—a sentimental masculine gaze at a feminized landscape and its creatures that masked the conquest and destruction of the "wild" continent. As Lawrence Buell has recently advised, there is much to be gained from seeing American pastoral in this kind of postcolonial context (477).

At least Thoreau dramatized the problem in the record of his ingenious, multifaceted, and passionate efforts to live a different reality than the one his culture imposed upon him. He understood and tried to accept the necessary violence involved in human survival—the sacrificial logic of sparagmos and omophagia by which we must destroy and eat other living creatures. If he was also horrified by the fact of our decaying materiality, he was honest enough to articulate the paradox. As we move to our primary focus on twentieth-century fiction, we will see that Thoreau's version of American pastoral has been reiterated by male writers down to our own time. Hemingway's Nick Adams and Faulkner's Ike McCaslin perform similar escapist nest-building rituals in eroticized landscapes, and gendered responses to Nature even motivate environmentally conscious essayists like Edward Abbey and Barry Lopez. In contrast, women writers usually identify with and draw strength from symbolic landscapes. But all this behavior locks them into patterns of meaning appropriate to our ancestors of fifteen thousand years ago—patterns that are inappropriate and dangerous for the threatened Earth at the end of the twentieth century. The radical experiments of twentieth-century art and philosophy may have exploded, estranged, and scrambled much of our cultural heritage, but they have not apparently shaken these deep and ancient habits of thought. In fact the mythological and anthropological interests of twentieth-century writers may actually have restored the vigor of the mythic heritage. The question we must ask as we examine the highly charged landscapes of twentieth-century fiction writers is whether they succeed in breaking out of the destructive gender oppositions and imperialist nostalgia endemic to American pastoral traditions and find a way to project a more realistic and responsible sense of Americans in their land.

II

Landscape in Twentieth-Century Fiction

Come my tan-faced children,
Follow well in order, get your weapons ready,
Have you your pistols? have you your sharp-edged axes?
Pioneers! O Pioneers!

. . . .

We detachments steady throwing,
Down the edges, through the passes, up the mountains steep,
Conquering, holding, daring, venturing as we go the unknown ways,
Pioneers! O Pioneers!

We primeval forests felling,
We the rivers stemming, vexing we and piercing deep the mines within,
We the surface broad surveying, we the virgin soil upheaving,
Pioneers! O Pioneers!
WALT WHITMAN, "Pioneers! O Pioneers!"

CHAPTER 4

Willa Cather's Prairie Epics

Ralph Waldo Emerson's 1871 trip to California on the new transcontinental railroad signaled the end of the "wild" North American continent and celebrated the dominion of man over nature that he had exhorted his readers to achieve almost half a century before. This journey westward culminated rather symbolically in a meeting with a young disciple, John Muir, in one of the great redwood forests that Muir would later define as the cathedrals of his new conservation movement. Ironies abound. The railroad had been completed only two years earlier (Creigh 66), and George Pullman himself had stocked the private railway car that Emerson's wealthy friends had leased from Pullman for the trip. The finest foods would therefore accompany the little party of northeastern sophisticates across a landscape just barely wrested from the tribes of Cheyenne, Sioux, and Arapaho who had fought desperately to prevent the slaughter of the buffalo herds and the invasion of their ancestral home. The success of the railroads' campaign against those guardians of the land can be measured by the fact that the only buffalo Emerson saw on the trip was one in captivity. Emerson wrote his wife, "There is an awe & terror lying over *this new garden—all empty as yet of any adequate people*, yet with this assured future in American hands,—unequalled in climate & production. . . . I should think no young man would come back from it" (Allen 248–50, my emphasis). The railway car was named the *Huron*, memorializing a tribe vanquished earlier in the settlement process. When they reached California, John Muir, then working in a sawmill, introduced Emerson to the great trees named for Sequoia, the Cherokee who had tried to help his people accommodate to the white man's ways (an effort rendered somewhat vain by the forced removal to Oklahoma along the Trail of Tears). Emerson was asked to choose a tree to be saved and labeled in memory of his visit. He named it Samoset, for the Plymouth sachem who had aided the Pilgrims two centuries earlier (Allen 647–51). Thus white men counted coup, labeling their new possessions with the names of Indians they displaced.

Though the Indian wars would continue for a while longer, their outcome was never in doubt. The indigenous peoples were the indicator species whose demise spelled the collapse of the "wild" plains ecosystem through the kind of martial aggression celebrated in Whitman's "Pioneers! O Pioneers!," first published in *Drum Taps* in 1865, when the end of the Civil War allowed the nation's attention to turn westward again. Whitman's martial rhythms, his references to weapons and detachments, and the "resistless restless race" of conquering settlers felling the primeval forests, stemming the rivers, and upheaving the virgin soil were logical extensions of Emerson's rhetoric in *Nature*.

A daughter of those pioneers translated Emerson's and Whitman's sentiments into prose epics celebrating both the heartland of the Plains and the people who conquered it. Willa Cather had been borne westward by this wave of settlement, migrating at the age of nine with her family from Virginia to the Republican River Valley of southern Nebraska in 1883 (Woodress 31–36; Lee 30). This land paralleling the Kansas border to the south and the old Oregon Trail to the north was offered for sale by the railroads and the state at low prices, to promote immigration, which "was integral to the accelerated pace at which Nebraskan lands were wrested from the Indians and consolidated as white property" (Fischer 31–35, 41). When Cather came into maturity as a writer, she turned her energies toward this landscape, transposing her childhood memories of Nebraska into her finest novels and creating a public myth that grants literary validation to the process of exploitation that the railroads set in motion.

In some respects, Cather was a legitimate heir of Emerson, Thoreau, and Whitman. The title of her first Nebraska novel, *O Pioneers!*, claims this kinship in its explicit echo of Whitman, and the novel echoes Emerson at its climactic turning point. In describing heroes like Columbus, Emerson had claimed that "the New World clothes his form with her palm-groves and savannahs as fit drapery" and said that "an act of truth or heroism seems at once to draw to itself the sky as its temple, the sun as its candle.... Willingly does she follow his steps with the rose and the violet and bend her lines of grandeur and grace to the decoration of her darling child" (*Nature*, ch. 3). As Cather's Alexandra gazes in love and yearning over the land she will soon buy up and plow under, "the Genius of the Divide, the great free spirit which breathes across it, must have bent lower than it ever bent to a human will before" (*OP* 170).[1]

Yet that passage also signals the central problem of Cather's writing life—her illegitimacy as a woman in the heroic masculine literary tradition. Cather feminized Alexander the Great, made the emblematic Pioneer a woman, and thus symbolically placed the nation's destiny in her hands. Sharon O'Brien claims that Cather successfully challenged the masculine tradition of American pastoral by these means, "collapsing the traditional nineteenth-century distinction between 'public' and 'private,' male and female space" and thus "suggesting that a female hero and a female author could write stories that both sprang from and transcended female experience" (433–34). I do not think the case is quite so simple. In fact, it seems to me that Cather's whole writing life is complicated by the problems of gender identification that O'Brien so sensitively anatomizes in her study of Cather's literary apprenticeship. Contrary to O'Brien's depiction of the epic hero as a communal projection that counters the solitary masculine subjectivity of the American pastoral, I think we need to remember the disastrous separatist egotism of Homer's Achilles and the colorful but foolhardy risks taken by Odysseus as he wandered and returned alone to Ithaca after a twenty-year absence. Alexandra Bergson does indeed represent a new kind of epic hero, a woman who stays home and works the land, representing her community's triumph and bridging spaces and activities usually ascribed to separate female and male spheres, but she is a loner at the same time. As a young woman she frightens men with her Amazon fierceness and remains independent of the erotic and domestic spheres that define the other women of her community. Her dying father anoints her his heir despite her sex. Once she assumes this "male" role, she stands alone as leader in her family and the surrounding countryside, initiating a new relation to the land. In turning her adolescent hero Alexander into an Amazon and appropriating Virgilian pastoral tropes for her epic struggle with the land and later for that of the Bohemian peasant heroine of *My Ántonia*, Willa Cather "is intervening in a masculine language of epic pastoral" (Lee 5). She is, however, more seriously at odds with the ideological terms of these tropes and types than were Emerson and Thoreau before her.

Willa Cather was a trespasser in masculine psychic disguise, having formed her imagination, as most intellectual girls have always done, by immersing herself in the writings of her cultural fathers (Fetterley, *RR*). But Cather's version of the trespass was more extreme and long-lived, for she adopted a defiantly masculine personal style in childhood, continued it through adolescence, and went on to establish her career as a professional writer through a male persona.

Much recent discussion of Cather's fiction has focused on her personal gender ambivalence and the androgynous character of her narrative persona (Woodress, Rosowski, O'Brien, Lee, Fetterley). While I agree with Sharon O'Brien that problems associated with lesbianism and conflicted sexual identification were central to Cather's imagination (215), I would urge a less psychoanalytic and more practical approach, along the lines of Hermione Lee's discussion of the tension among several related contrarieties in Cather's life and work.[2] In practical terms, it is not surprising that lively, ambitious girls might tend to identify themselves with activities that are traditionally coded as masculine. "I will venture to affirm," wrote Mary Wollstonecraft in 1789, "that a girl, whose spirits have not been damped by inactivity, or innocence tainted by false shame, will always be a romp, and the doll will never excite attention unless confinement allows her no alternative" (43). American feminist critics in the

1970s such as Ellen Moers and Carolyn Heilbrun showed how strategies of masculine disguise and identification were used to gain access to previously forbidden realms of action throughout the nineteenth century and into our own era by literary and professional women.

Cather's was a form of male mimicry that was at least tolerated in bourgeois American life of the mid-nineteenth century, according to Caroll Smith-Rosenberg, though it received increasing opprobrium as the century drew to a close (264–65). For a brief time there seems to have been a fluidity of gendering for women that allowed the emergence of the New Woman, the founding of women's colleges and social improvement organizations, and of course the steadily increasing movement for suffrage (Gilbert and Gubar 1: 3–62; Smith-Rosenberg 245–96). Women writers began to earn serious prominence during this era, though they often hid behind male pseudonyms, the most celebrated examples being the Brontës, George Eliot, and George Sand. The young journalist Willa Cather applauded all of them (Lee 12), and she found another popular examplar of male impersonation in Sarah Bernhardt's Hamlet. Other "tomboys" of Cather's generation who would go on to notoriety included Natalie Barney and Gertrude Stein.[3] But all such transgressors paid a price, as Virginia Woolf was the first to point out in *A Room of One's Own*. Gilbert and Gubar's *The Madwoman in the Attic* explores the contortions of literary imagination that resulted, such as the failure of George Eliot to allow real agency for her women characters. In a later study, *No Man's Land*, they argue that "the male mimicry practiced by these Victorian women artists functioned to signify their acquiescence in their own (female) inferiority: by mimicking male precursors, they sought an influx of patriarchal power" (1: 185) and denied their feminine legitimacy in the process. Smith-Rosenberg sees the adoption of male symbolic constructs by their descendants, the New Women of the turn of the century, as "a fundamental act of alienation" (266) that ultimately placed them on the cultural margins when the male establishment refused to share power. Willa Cather was caught in this dilemma as an androgynous New Woman when the male backlash of the 1920s began to enforce more conventional behavior and rebuild symbolic gender boundaries that women writers had been working to erode (Smith-Rosenberg 296), but she could never have predicted these changes when she was groping her way toward a literary and professional life in the 1890s as a confused young woman in the raw frontier world of Nebraska.

Red Cloud, Nebraska, may have been surprised or even outraged by Cather's adolescent cross-dressing, her boy's haircuts and insistence on signing herself "William Cather, Jr." or "William Cather, M.D.," but she was tolerated and was even the favorite of some of the town's leaders. One friend who was particularly important for her intellectual development was a transplanted Englishman, William Ducker, who tutored adolescent Willie Cather in classical literature and language for some seven years. With this passionate amateur classicist and scientist, she studied Latin and Greek and read Virgil, Ovid, the *Iliad*, and the Odes of Anacreon, as well as carrying out scientific experiments with him in his home laboratory (Woodress 43–53). She carried her male attire and assertiveness to the state university in Lincoln, quickly establishing herself as a campus literary figure and a professional journalist. There she continued her study of Latin and Greek, added French and German, and immersed herself in English literature of the grand male tradition. Though she was persuaded by a friend's mother to let her hair grow and wear dresses during her second year, she continued the male persona in her journalistic life (Woodress 55–111; O'Brien 82–165). Thus the theatre and book reviews she wrote for the *Nebraska State Journal* during college and for several years following her graduation are full of disparaging remarks about women writers and feminine weakness in general (Lee 12–13). *Tom Brown's School Days* and *Tom Brown at Oxford* were her idea of good children's fiction: "stirring, honest and manly" books. Her review of these books is completely male in identification, opposing "namby-pamby sentimentality" and advocating a return to the old days when a boy read serious English prose and "was pounded through a dozen books of the *Aeneid*" to gain "the foundation of a pure and classical literary taste" (337–38). She championed Rudyard Kipling's stories of love, war, and "boundless freedom," in exotic countries where "there are temples and jungles and . . . mountains whose summits have never been scaled, rivers whose sources have never been reached, deserts whose sands have never been crossed" (Slote 317). Here was fiction that depicted with gusto the late-nineteenth-century imperial version of the classical heroic spirit Cather had absorbed from her studies of Homer and Virgil. She wrote this review in 1896, only four years before Theodore Roosevelt was elected president, bringing the Kiplingesque spirit to the forefront of American politics.

Hermione Lee believes that this masculine identification was Cather's way of appropriating a male literary tradition, "an appropriation which had everything to do with her sexual alienation from conventional femininity" (10). It seems clear that the male persona preceded Cather's literary ambitions and remained a central, deeply troubling ambivalence in her psyche all her life. She was, in effect, a lifelong "tomboy," who only partially acceded to the fact that she was biologically female (Kaye 28). Her close relationship with Isabelle McClung and her crucial encounter with Sarah Orne Jewett somehow freed her enough to admit her femininity and at least partially ally herself with women for a time, and that frame of mind produced the great novels of heroic femininity: *O Pioneers!*, *The Song of the Lark*, and *My Ántonia* (O'Brien 236–38, 334–63; Lee 69). These novels achieve the goal Jewett had set before Cather, of writing about her own country and in her own direct, realistic way (O'Brien 345–46). Even when she followed this advice, however, she was not able to take the further step that Jewett recommended, and write as a woman of the love of women (O'Brien 336–37). Instead she continued to maintain the male narrative voice and gaze, which Frances Kaye argues was a lifelong identification linked to a distaste for everything conventionally female. Cather's heroic women characters are always exceptional, set apart from the community of women defined by domestic life and heterosexual love (Kaye 1–28). Even Ántonia Shimerda shrinks away into drabness when she marries and enters the domestic round. After the burst of creative accomplishment that produced the novels of heroic womanhood, Cather began to retreat back into her male persona. *A Lost Lady* is distanced from its female object much more than *My Ántonia*. After that, with the exception of her last two novels, she seems to feel more comfortable with male characters in a male world, as in *The Professor's House* and *Death Comes to the Archbishop*.

In spite of Cather's eventual retreat from identification with women's lives, her Amazon heroines are centrally connected to the celebration of the American heartland that remains her distinctive contribution to American literature. Ellen Moers was the first to call attention to "the brilliant landscape writing that women have devoted to open country," a deeply gendered attraction to "open lands, harsh and upswelling, high-lying and undulating, vegetated with crimped heather or wind-swept grasses, cut with ravines and declivities and twisting lanes" (262). Willa Cather is one of the most important inscribers of these women's landscapes, enacting her femininity in a profound creative connection to the long cultural identification of women and land that we examined in archaic literatures. But what allowed this implicit declaration of allegiance to the despised gender she had spent much of her life denying, and how can it coexist with the male classical models that shape Cather's pastoral imagination?

O'Brien and Lee have sought to answer these questions by describing the richly supportive foundation of female society and cultural precedent that remained somehow almost invisible until the recent wave of feminist Cather scholarship. We now know that strong women dominated Cather's extended family in childhood. She turned to these matriarchs, as well as to impressive older women and school acquaintances in Red Cloud, when she wrote the novels set in Nebraska. As she described their world, she used domestic activities like quilting, sewing, and gardening as images of literary and artistic creativity (Fryer 248, 257–58; Lee 18–19). As Ann Romines shows in her close reading of "A Wagnerian Matinee," Cather was already trying to direct the gaze of a male protagonist toward positive acceptance of the domestic as early as 1904 (128–33). In addition, she drew upon feminine artistic and literary precedents such as the goddesses of her classical studies, the theatrical and operatic stars she reviewed for the Lincoln newspaper, the Valkyries of Wagnerian opera, and nineteenth-century women novelists, like the Brontës, George Sand, and George Eliot, who had successfully invaded the literary mainstream (O'Brien 11–58, 166–92; Lee 27, 129–30). By grafting such women's traditions and experiences onto classical literary forms, she created liminal Amazon figures who invade and subvert male literary space through androgyny.

The literary and cultural materials that Cather blended together do not naturally cohere, though she managed most of the time to create the surface impression of harmony. The classical pastorals that have been established as her primary literary models (Randall; Rosowski 45–61; Lee 90–99) are stubbornly male, yet she places strong women at their center. Lee shows that the practical rural rituals of Virgil's *Georgics* were especially formative in her pictures of Nebraska farm life, yet Virgil's long-domesticated rural setting is very different from Cather's wild, harsh prairie landscapes. Arguably the dominant narrative tradition in American culture is the violent one described by Lawrence, Fiedler, and Slotkin. This is the realm of renegades from civilization, those Deerslayers and Ishmaels associated with wild adventure and bloody predation.[4] This whole tradition is at odds with the calm, philosophic Virgilian mood

Cather created around her Nebraska materials. While the violent adventures of the frontier hero might reasonably have been linked with the classical epic that hovers in the shadows of Cather's practice, her purpose was to erase this element of the American story, for reasons we will explore later.

A personal ingredient in this confused mixture is Cather's own ambivalence about the landscape. She loved the wide skies and long vistas of the Plains, but she also knew their bleakness. Sometimes she felt she would strangle, suffocate, or be blotted out in the huge, blank spaces of the West. Her first encounter with Nebraska at the age of nine she later remembered as "the end of everything—it was a kind of erasure of personality," and even as an adult she feared that in the vastness of the West she would fall asleep, die, never get out (Woodress 35–37; O'Brien 62–67; Lee 29–31, 87).

Cather had female local colorists like Sarah Orne Jewett, Mary E. Wilkins Freeman, and Kate Chopin immediately ahead of her as examples of what could be done by using a woman's gaze and women's experiences when she began to try to put all her materials together for the first time in O Pioneers! She said to a friend at the time (Elizabeth Shepley Sergeant, Lee 107–8) that her book was like the land, without a skeleton or hard lines but instead all soft form. Teresa De Lauretis has shown, however, that our culture's narrative traditions code plot geographically, with the landscape as female space. As "an element of plot-space, a topos, a resistance, matrix and matter," the feminine is the very ground of the male hero's linear progress to his goal (119). Cather tried to take narrative space away from male control, maintaining the feminine identification of the land but moving male characters to the side and granting a new kind of agency to female protagonists. She sought to weave all these conflicting discourses together—the classical pastoral, the American frontier adventure, the Kiplingesque imperial epic, the immigrant tale (Lee 5–6), and the domestic stories of female nest-building and gardening rituals. The cohesive force was her own desire, creating an exclusively female dynamic of erotic attraction and identification in which the Nebraska landscape and Alexandra Bergson are dual protagonists in a passionate interplay that moves from strife to yearning, to ecstatic conjunction.

First the land is "wild," with "ugly moods," its genius harsh, "unfriendly to man," and seen in the huge frame of geologic time that renders humans insignificant.

Of all the bewildering things about a new country, the absence of human landmarks is one of the most depressing and disheartening. The houses on the Divide were small and were usually tucked away in low places; you did not see them until you came directly upon them. Most of them were built of the sod itself, and were only the unescapable ground in another form. The roads were but faint tracks in the grass, and the fields were scarcely noticeable. The record of the plow was insignificant, like the feeble scratches on stone left by prehistoric races, so indeterminate that they may, after all, be only the markings of glaciers, and not a record of human strivings. (*O Pioneers!* 147)

This "bewildering" and "disheartening" picture implies that comfort and pleasure come only when the land's forms are dominated by the shapes of human artifice. The earth must be inscribed by the plow, with a determinacy that obliterates the records of Nature's rhythms and patterns of change.[5] The passage begins in the voice of the novel's anonymous narrator but slides into the mind of the dying John Bergson where it defines the standard masculine habit of distinguishing the wild from the tame. "It was like a horse that no one knows how to break to harness, that runs wild and kicks things to pieces" (22).

Once Alexandra inherits the farm, however, the language changes. Her father pronounces a kind of Georgics in his dying speech bequeathing control to her. He tells his sons to "be guided by your sister," and he gives instructions on breaking and efficiently using the land (26–27). This signals the end of the patriarchy and the beginning of a heroic female dominion in which Alexandra's foresight and common sense are worth more than physical strength.

John Bergson's death is followed by his daughter's symbolic visit to a strange figure who combines European folk traditions of magical dwarf and Natural Fool and connects her with the powers of the land that must be courted if she is to have success as a farmer. Crazy Ivar is a Norwegian hermit who lives on "unproductive" land in an almost invisible dugout "without defiling the face of nature any more than the coyote that had lived there before him had done"(36). He dislikes the clutter of human dwellings, finds the wild sod cleaner and tidier, and feels that his Bible is truer to him there. Through him, Cather erases the original inhabitants of the Plains whom the white man had evicted not long before the time of the novel. She replaces the Pawnee, Crow, Cheyenne, and Arapaho with a European immigrant literally dug into the American earth to establish his legitimacy and supplant Indian ways of living on the land. Ivar has special kinship with all animals, and his "spells" of raving and hallucination mark him as touched by the God of his comforting Norwegian Bible who now owns the land. Alexandra absorbs Ivar's secret connection to the divine force of nature by consulting with him about her livestock and making him an ally. Thereafter, Ivar is gradually domesticated. He moves indoors (though he always sleeps in her barn) to a life as her dependent, a magician-in-residence who can cure cows and horses and dispense his folk wisdom to his queenly protector. Cather has thus absorbed his mediating function into her protagonist. Ivar represents the midpoint of European domestication of the land through a sleight of hand that sanitizes and naturalizes the process.

After this episode, we are told briefly and in an almost biblical fashion about three years of plenty followed by three years of drought, "the last struggle of a wild soil against the encroaching ploughshare" (47). But this is not a struggle we witness. Instead, the coda to this first major section of the novel is Alexandra's rapturous vision of the land as she begins to imagine its successful exploitation. "For the first time, perhaps, since that land emerged from the waters of geologic ages, a human face was set toward it with love and yearning. It seemed beautiful to her, rich and strong and glorious. Her eyes drank in the breadth of it, until her tears blinded her. Then the Genius of the Divide, the great, free spirit which breathes across it, must have bent lower than it ever bent to a human will before. The history of every country begins in the heart of a man or a woman" (65). Cather creates an epic vastness for this passage by placing it against the immense backdrop of geologic time. Then incredibly, as she sweeps the reader into the romantic ecstasy of Alexandra's emotion, she denies any previous human appreciation of the land, ignoring the Indian people who lived there so long and with such deep feeling for the place that they sickened and died when removed to Oklahoma by the edicts of the white man's government. It is important to note also that the source of Alexandra's joy is her plan to buy up more and more of the high land of the Divide from her bankrupt neighbors and make it productive by planting alfalfa. Cather has inscribed a kind of Manifest Destiny for her entrepreneurial Amazon, masking Alexandra's aggrandizement as joyous eroticism. Before the force of this emotion, the "great, free spirit" of the Divide that had so grimly resisted her father bows to her will.

The situation is complicated a few pages later, at the very end of section 1, for Alexandra herself is identified with the Genius of the Divide. Her bold plan to buy up the land is supported by her sense of connection to "the great operations of nature, and when she thought of the law that lay behind them, she felt a sense of personal security" (70–71). More particularly, she feels akin to the wild creatures of the land, as if her heart has been hiding down in the long grass with them. Thus when "The Wild Land" closes with the statement, "Under the long shaggy ridges, she felt the future stirring," we realize that Alexandra's own being is almost the same thing as this awakening spirit of the landscape. It is feminine.

The middle section of the novel, "Neighboring Fields," begins by completing the erotic conjunction of Alexandra Bergson and her landscape, although Cather's language displaces and distances her desire from the union of plow and earth (Rosowski 50–51). Ten years have elapsed since Alexandra's transfiguring vision, and the prairie's old shaggy coat has been replaced by symmetrical fields making a vast checkerboard of cultivation. The process that has brought fruition to the land is clearly, sensuously sexual; "the brown earth, with such a strong, clean smell, and such a power of growth and fertility in it, yields itself eagerly to the plow; rolls away from the shear, not even dimming the brightness of the metal, with a soft, deep sigh of happiness" (76). This rich brown earth, the place where Alexandra's heart had hidden, in which she had felt the future stirring, and which she later says woke itself up "out of its sleep and stretched itself" (116) actively cooperates in the lovemaking process, rolling and sighing in fulfillment. Some of the language of this passage gestures toward the traditional mating of male sun and female earth, with the land rising to meet the sun and the air and earth "curiously mated and intermingled" (76–77), but the central eroticism of the novel is an expression of the same feminine desire for a feminized object that Judith Fetterley finds in *My Ántonia* and defines as "the key to Cather's genius and achievement" (161).

Cather makes explicit the gender of the land and its connection to Alexandra, saying that on days of particular happiness she feels "in her own body the joyous germination in the soil" (204). This passage might seem to work within the traditional gender coding that Page DuBois analyzed for classical Greek rhetorical practice, in which the plow is the male instrument of penetration fructifying the female earth (39–85). Yet Alexandra has been made the agent of the land's transformation even though she works through male intermediaries. The land is herself, and the land is her lover in a lesbian eroticism only thinly disguised by heterosexual gestures.[6] If Alexandra is lesbian lover of a female landscape, what are we to make of the Demon Lover of her frequent dream, a man yellow like the sunlight, who comes to carry her away over the fields like a sheaf of wheat (206)? I think Blanche Gelfant is right to connect this "Corn God" with death and the romantic "Pyramus and Thisbe" subplot concerning Alexandra's brother Emil and Marie Shabata (xxviii–xxix). This reading links the epic conquest of the Amazon protagonist with the tragic romance that provides a genuinely heterosexual dimension to the novel and identifies human cycles with those of the harvest landscape in a kind of eclogue (Lee 112–13). But we must not fail to notice that whatever impulses Alexandra may have toward easeful Death, she always wakes from her dreamy ravishment "angry with herself" and hastens down to the bathhouse to scrub herself clean and pour buckets of cold water "over her gleaming white body which no man on the Divide could have carried very far" (206).[7]

O Pioneers! ends in an elegiac distancing of narrative presence, describing the aging friends Alexandra and Carl standing on a ridge and gazing down over her land in the sunset: "On every side the brown waves of the earth rolled away to meet the sky" (307). They speak of the deaths of Emil and Marie and the future generations that will know nothing of the passionate conquests and tragedies that make up the old story represented by the tombstones in the graveyard. Alexandra echoes Carl's understanding that it has been written into the land by the best efforts of the pioneers and by the deaths of their most beautiful and promising offspring. All are sacrificial offerings to a vast impersonal Nature that endures in spite of the little comings and goings of humans. "Fortunate country," writes Cather in her final sentence, "that is one day to receive hearts like Alexandra's into its bosom, to give them out again in the yellow wheat, in the rustling corn, in the shining eyes of youth!" (309).

This ripe harvest imagery is meant to spread a comforting glow of golden sentiment over all the discords we have seen shifting under the surface of the novel. O'Brien contends that by planting the epic heroine in the landscape, Cather removes the misogyny from the American pastoral tradition (433), but there is much evidence to the contrary. Alexandra says approvingly that her father left the old country in order to have fine sons and give them a chance for success (117). Her brothers turn on her in her later years, claiming that the property of the family belongs to the men and that they have done all the real work. Cather allows their sullen reproaches to fill most of the scene. "This is what comes of letting a woman meddle in business," says Lou. "You can't do business with women," complains Oscar. Alexandra is reduced to plaintively reminding them of her courage and foresight during hard times (167–73). Cather codes the brothers by making the more benign Oscar the father of sons, while the shrewd and bitter Lou has only daughters. Beautiful, sensuous Marie Shabata is associated with flowers, champagne, sunflower honey, and dancing firelight and, like Alexandra, is identified with the landscape itself (135–36, 202–3). But Alexandra blames Marie for the tragic love affair with Emil and sympathizes with the surly, jealous husband who murdered them (296).

It seems obvious that Cather has not escaped the masculine bias of her culture. This is the conundrum that prevents a consistent voice or tone in O Pioneers! The Nebraska landscape, like the text of the novel, is a contested space in which Cather's impulses toward a positive female agency fail to break out of a masculinist network of codes. She may displace the violent qualities of the epic hero onto negative and marginal male characters like Alexandra's brothers or Frank Shabata and make Alexandra androgynous (Lee 106), but the lesbian eroticism that connects Alexandra to her land finally serves the same purpose of masking and justifying exploitation that heterosexual eroticism serves for male writers. When we move to consider My Ántonia, we find the problem even more clearly marked.

My Ántonia, widely considered her masterpiece, is a more personal book than O Pioneers!; it includes autobiographical materials from Cather's early life in Red Cloud (Rosowski 78) and was written in part as consolation for the recent loss of her intimate relationship with Isabelle McClung. The impulse to return to her roots and reclaim the past may also have been motivated, as Lee suggests, by her horror at the war's devastation of the European world she loved (136). This cultural heritage had been the artistic focus of The Song of the Lark, the novel that followed O Pioneers! Thea Kronberg's early life had also been based on autobiographical details, but Cather had shifted the landscape to Colorado and made even the famous Panther Canyon episode only a spring-board for launching Thea's operatic career in Europe and New York.[8]

With *My Ántonia*, Cather returned to the actual landscape of Ne-braska and reexamined the pastoral materials she had treated in *O Pio-neers!* This time she decided not to write from a third-person stance closely identified with her heroine but instead to use a first-person framing structure borrowed from French and Russian fiction (Lee 135–36). She likened her new heroine to an antique Sicilian jar placed in the lamplight and said she wanted to treat her "like a rare object in the middle of a table, which one may examine from all sides" (qtd. in Lee 137). Her companion Edith Lewis remembers Cather's voice quavering and her eyes filling with tears when she made this pronouncement. Thus powerful emotions were associated with the aesthetic gaze that turned the Czech girl Annie Pavelka into a kind of Nebraska version of Keats's Grecian Urn. The framing devices create the aesthetic objectification that distances and controls Cather's dangerous tenderness toward the warm, sensual, and attractive figure she created in Ántonia.

There are two buffers between herself and her subject: the anonymous narrator of the Introduction, and Jim Burden, the old friend who will tell Ántonia's story. In the 1918 version of the novel, the narrator of the Introduction is a professional woman, presumably a writer like Willa Cather, who "as a little girl" had watched Ántonia "come and go" (713). But Cather removed the reference to the narrator's sex when she revised the Introduction in 1926, perhaps in response to the general backlash of masculine culture against the gains of feminism. What remains in the In-troduction is a cozy masculine reminiscence between two friends cross-ing Iowa on a train. They agree that their prairie background makes them members of "a kind of freemasonry" and they concentrate their nostalgia upon a Bohemian girl who "seemed to mean to us the country, the conditions, the whole adventure of our childhood" (Intro., 1926 ed.). Freemasonry is not an association open to women, and their focus on Ántonia as a distant female embodiment of the land is a male trope. The Introduction functions as a masculine container for the ostensibly male autobiography that follows.[9]

Jim Burden is set up as the man who passionately loves the land and who will define "his" Ántonia as a way of capturing the country and its past. Yet Jim's effort to reach this goal moves away from Ántonia and Nebraska as his narrative traces his escape from the rural landscape he professes to love. He describes his early years on his grandparents' farm with great nostalgia, but his adolescence in the town of Black Hawk is marked by restlessness and gradual withdrawal from local life. Departure to college in Lincoln begins a geographical movement eastward, paralleled by submersion in classical pastorals and European culture that come to define his understanding of place. Virgil's *Georgics* is finally the emblematic text through which he views the Nebraska landscape (Lee 137), and he never again lives in it. Instead, this Virgilian elegist carves out a successful career in New York, working for the railroads that had first opened the West for domestication. The 1916 version of the Introduction identifies him with mining, oil drilling, and other extractive western ventures; his nostalgia is exactly the sort of sentimentalizing of colonized space that Rosaldo describes in *Culture and Truth*. What Cather defines here is a creation myth for the Nebraska plains, more elaborate, sophisticated, and layered in its cultural work than the epic story of Alexandra Bergson because more distanced from its object and artfully embedded in the Virgilian codes of Jim Burden's retrospective imagination. But as Lee points out, there remains a tension between the literal materials of prairie life and the embalming fluids in which Cather seeks to fix them (138).

The dark chaos Jim Burden first encounters on the prairie is "nothing but land: not a country at all, but the material out of which countries are made" (718).[10] This passage is much more negative than the opening landscape descriptions of *O Pioneers!*: there is "nothing to see; no fences, no creeks or trees, no hills or fields . . . No, there was nothing but land" (7). Jim feels he has fallen over the edge of the world and has been erased, blotted out. As Rosowski suggests, we are being prepared for rebirth in a new world (77), but it is a rebirth that remakes the history of place. At the same time, faint markings from the past remain. Most of the novel is set in Black Hawk, named for a vanquished Indian leader, just as Cather's own childhood town of Red Cloud was named for another (Hyde 239, 264; Creigh 77; Lee 31; Fischer 34). The Indians are not quite as completely erased from the landscape in this novel, however, as they were from *O Pioneers!*, and the violent history of the frontier is also faintly recalled in the novel's opening scenes.

The mediating figure of farmhand Otto Fuchs meets Jim's train and conveys him through the formless darkness to his grandmother's farm. With twirled mustachios, a sombrero, a half-missing left ear, and a scar running across one cheek and turning one corner of his mouth into a

sneer, Otto seems to personify the frontier desperados Jim has been reading about in "The Life of Jesse James." His skin is "as brown as an Indian's," but Otto's wilder life is over. Like Crazy Ivar of *O Pioneers!*, Otto
replaces the Indian presence on the land and lives its domestication. Unlike Ivar, Otto bears on his body the signs of the violence involved in the
historical process of conquest. Cather allows one other muted sign of
previous history, the faint pattern of a great circle on the prairie made by
Indians; she aestheticizes it and so disarms it, saying that after a snowfall
it looks "like strokes of Chinese white on canvas" (62).

Thus safely transmuted into the charming tracery of Oriental art, the
Indian way of life can be replaced by constructive domesticity, which
Cather marks by digging her immigrant Bohemians firmly into the
ground and documenting their dogged efforts to establish homes and
rituals of community imported from another continent. Such feminized
activity substitutes for the male violence of buffalo slaughter, Indian
wars, and the lawless antics of desperados that actually preceded settlement and was required to "clear" the land of its traditional inhabitants.[11]

These peasants from traditional central European lands are inserted
into a space of pulsing energy that is alive with the "wildness" of former
inhabitants who seem still present just beneath its surface. The prairie is
covered with a sea of wine-red grass, "and there was so much motion in
it; the whole country seemed, somehow, to be running." Jim feels this
wild energy in his very body, "as if the shaggy grass were a sort of loose
hide, and underneath it herds of wild buffalo were galloping, galloping"
(15–16). In fact, the buffalo herds had been deliberately slaughtered by
settlers, hide-hunters, and agents of the railroads, partly in order to de-
prive the Indians of their central resource for food, clothing, and shelter
(Creigh 130–32). Cather moves Jim's response to the land from the running surface of the grasses, up into the focal image of a hawk, thus dis-
embodying and abstracting the power these vast herds represented. She
projects their force into a kind of transcendental freedom that allows Jim
to imagine floating off into sky and sun "like the tawny hawks which
sailed over our heads making slow shadows on the grass" (16). The narrative follows a similar progress as it moves the center of emotional interest
out of the vibrant, dynamic body of the land and into characters who
move off and leave it flat, patterned, and fenced by the end of the novel.

As Rosowski and Lee have shown, Cather makes much use of enclo-
sures and womblike spaces early in the novel, to emphasize the birth of

major characters into a new life on the Plains (Rosowski 77–78, Lee 142–43). My point is that their rebirth is part of the creation myth of the landscape that the narrative constructs. First coded as formless chaos and then as a galloping shaggy animal, the landscape undergoes an evolution into "civilization" as it is "broken" to the plow and domesticated for food production. The complementary child heroes—Jim Burden in his grandmother's cozy underground kitchen and Ántonia in her family's dank dugout—experience a chrysalis phase that must be left behind in metamorphosis toward higher forms of life. For Jim the kitchen is associated with immaturity and dependency on the women's world of his grandmother. His proper destiny is represented by the active outdoor lives of the men who work the farm. Ántonia's family, and indeed all the immigrants living in dugouts, are seen as degraded and bestial. Cather makes a point of connecting them with the cheerful but lowly prairie dogs preyed upon in their burrows by owls and snakes (30, 32). Advancement up the hierarchical ladder of refinement and success requires moving up into the sun and finally off the land and into the town of Black Hawk.

Involvement with the earth is paradoxically a source of strength, and a brutalizing, coarsening, dehumanizing experience. It ties people to matter, wildness, and backbreaking work; it allies them with dumb beasts. The material world is a resource to be mined for the spiritual energy that goes into the making of wealth, technology, and high culture, and it is only this abstraction and transposition that have ultimate value in Cather's economy. A progressive movement out of the earth into freedom can be observed in the growth of Jim and Ántonia from childhood out on the wild prairie to adolescence in Black Hawk, and then on to their adult destinies.

The traditional pastoral bliss or *otium* that young Jim finds in his grandmother's garden is associated by Cather's language with the passive ecstasy of Emerson's transparent eyeball and his reference to expanding and living happily "in the warm day like corn and melons" (*Nature* ch 1., end of ch. 6). Jim remembers lying in the garden on an autumn day: "I was something that lay under the sun and felt it, like the pumpkins, and I did not want to be anything more. I was entirely happy. Perhaps we feel like that when we die and become a part of something entire, whether it is sun and air, or goodness and knowledge. At any rate, that is happiness: to be dissolved into something complete and great" (18). To lose oneself in this sort of happiness is to become a vegetable, perhaps to die, and thus of course it is not a real option for our hero any more than it was for Emerson.

Jim proves his right to heroism in the next garden scene, when he and Ántonia are surprised by a mythically enormous rattlesnake. The violent action by which he kills the snake and saves the maiden seems to follow the traditional male dragon-slaying pattern, but as many have observed, it leaves Jim feeling somewhat fraudulent. The event marks Jim's expulsion from the garden; it is followed closely in the narrative by a loss of innocence with Mr. Shimerda's suicide and the move of Jim's grandparents into town.

As Jim begins a new life in Black Hawk, Ántonia—or Tony, as she then becomes—enters an androgynous period of harsh physical labor after the death of her father. In a broader sense, her work in the fields reflects the freedom and agency of women on the frontier, a liminal space that both allowed and required the blurring of gender roles and a very active outdoor life for women. By the time she is fifteen, she is wearing her father's boots, "her arms and throat were burned as brown as a sailor's," and her neck comes up "strongly out of her shoulders, like the bole of a tree out of the turf" (122). Rather than applaud Ántonia's new form, however, both Cather's narrative tone and Jim's specific reaction to the strong young girl are grudging. "One sees that draught-horse neck among the peasant women in all old countries," says the condescending narrator (122). And Jim is "vexed" by Ántonia's rough pride and strength. Even though Jim's grandfather makes the accurate prediction that her strength will "help some fellow get ahead in the world" (126), the main flow of the narrative supports Jim's disapproval in its positive treatment of Tony's behavior once she moves to town and becomes refined and feminized by life as a domestic servant in the Harling household. The entrapment and vulnerability of this more conventionally "feminine" role is made clear by Wick Cutter's attempted rape. Jim's utter revulsion at having been Ántonia's unwitting stand-in is understandable as the intense feminine response to rape that many have seen Cather projecting into the scene. But Jim's anger at Ántonia for having been the object of a lecherous attack seems terribly unfair, another instance of Cather's complicity with male codes of behavior. Male-identified Frances Harling has no such difficulties with men, for as her father's accountant and factor, she is free to move about town, in and out of the bank and business offices. Eventually Tiny Soderball and Lena Lingard will also achieve that kind of autonomy, but only because they have rejected traditional feminine domestic roles and biological destinies.

Gender and class differences push Jim and Tony farther and farther apart during their Black Hawk adolescence. Tony remains identified with natural energies, the body, and the land, for she is seen in the Harlings' garden and kitchen, baking rich foods, laughing and warmly playing with the children, and later expressing her sensuous physical nature at town dances during the summer. Jim becomes more and more abstracted, lost in his books as he prepares for college, and prevented by his disapproving grandparents from associating with the hearty hired girls at the dances. But one final reunion occurs before he leaves for college, a summer idyll of pastoral *otium* by the river outside of town.

This farewell picnic of Jim and the immigrant girls is the most memorable scene of the entire novel, glowing with an erotic, earthy aura that sets it apart from anything else in the novel and yet seems emblematic of Cather's whole point in some complex way. It is a sort of apotheosis of the land and its reproductive energies, pulsing with feminine lusciousness:

> It was the high season for summer flowers. The pink bee-bush
> stood tall along the sandy roadsides, and the cone-flowers and rose
> mallow grew everywhere. Across the wire fence, in the long grass,
> I saw a clump of flaming orange-coloured milkweed, rare in that
> part of the state. I left the road and went around through a stretch
> of pasture that was always cropped short in summer, where the
> gaillardia came up year after year and matted over the ground with
> the deep, velvety red that is in Bokhara carpets. The country was
> empty and solitary except for the larks that Sunday morning, and
> it seemed to lift itself up to me and to come very close. (232–33)

Jim undresses among wild grapevines and dogwood bushes, swims and lolls in the river, and then is joined by the immigrant girls who have come to pick elderberries. In the lush sandy bottoms along the stream, clouds of blossoming elderbushes grow thickly in terraces down to the water. Jim is "overcome by content and drowsiness and by the warm silence about me. There was no sound but the high, sing-song buzz of wild bees and the sunny gurgle of the water underneath." Jim and Ántonia sit hidden together, down under "the pagoda-like elders," and talk companionably of old times, of her parents, of their homeland far away in Europe. Jim lies back in the hot sand looking up at the sky through the blossoms and feels one last time the passive bliss of earthy, innocent childhood. When he and Ántonia are interrupted by the other girls, the conversation continues to be chummy and relaxed, completely lacking any of the sexual tension one might expect when an adolescent boy is surrounded by lively girls his age in such a setting. It makes more sense to see the scene as an entirely female congregation in harmony with the rich abundance of summer's bounty, much like the classic scenes of happy maidenhood described in the Homeric Hymn to Demeter when the kore plays with her companions among the flowery meadows just before Hades attacks, or in book 6 of Homer's *Odyssey*, when Nausicaa and her companions play beside the stream just before the appearance of naked Odysseus. There is no sense of masculine otherness in Jim's account of the scene.

The vision of the plough magnified against the setting sun that ends their picnic idyll in this quintessentially female space is said by Cather to be "a picture writing on the sun," but its meaning is not at all obvious. Some have read it simply as the heroic symbol of pioneer agricultural conquest, but if so, what is its relevance for the conversation that precedes it, in which the "hired girls" discuss their mothers' hard lot and determine to escape from farm life? If the image of the plough echoes Virgil but replaces Aeneas's sword as emblem of power and thus celebrates the end of the male myth of military conquest, as Paul Olson explains it (284), or stands for a more peaceable form of achievement than the Spanish sword, recalling Coronado's failed explorations, discussed earlier in the scene by the young people, it is nevertheless a traditionally masculine symbol inappropriate for the celebration of domestic abundance feminists have seen as central to the novel. Nor does it harmonize with any of bookish Jim Burden's interests. Mike Fischer reminds us that a farmer's plow unearthed the Spanish sword. He sees sword and plow working together: "In a paradigmatic example of the return of the repressed, the sword and everything it stands for 'turn up' in Cather's narrative at the very place where she most powerfully calls forth the symbolic plow; meant to replace the sword, the plow rediscovers it instead" (37).[12]

Cather herself explicitly undercuts the heroic significance of the image, for she writes that as Jim and the girls whisper together about this vision, the sun sinks below the horizon. "The fields below us were dark, the sky was growing pale, and that forgotten plough had sunk back to its own littleness somewhere on the prairie" (866). And so, as she had done in deflating Jim's triumph over the giant rattlesnake, here she both conjures up and then denies traditional male heroism. Thus Cather signals the end of an era, an end that coincides with Jim's farewell to the Plains. The glory of conquest is past, the land has been tamed, and the cost of victory has been *almost* erased. The rest of *My Ántonia* depicts the process of turning the historical reality into nostalgic art through the prism of Virgilian pastoral. Jim consciously prepares for this task as he completes his education at the university in Lincoln and at Harvard.

When Jim returns to the land as a middle-aged railroad lawyer, he finds a different world than the wild prairie he had left as a youth. Human discipline has replaced the running grasses with static rectangles of fields and roads over the whole land. Jim finds a deflated Ántonia—a flat-chested woman with grizzled hair and few remaining teeth who has poured herself into her family and their farm. The sensuous fullness of her youthful body has been transferred to the fruitful landscape, as Cather is careful to emphasize through the womblike image of her earthen storage cellar or fruit cave bursting with the tumble of her children "running up the steps together, big and little, tow heads and gold heads and brown, and flashing little naked legs; a veritable explosion of life out of the dark cave into the sunlight" (918). Ántonia's apple orchard is another such transposition of her own fecundity to the landscape. She introduces each of the trees to Jim, caressing them and speaking of her pains in raising them much as she did of her children. This orchard in its triple enclosure of protective fence and tall hedges is another magical female space of pastoral *otium*, "full of sun, like a cup, and we could smell the ripe apples on the trees" (920). But like the other such moments of passive bliss in the novel, this one is only a temporary pause. The chapter closes with Jim bedded down for the night in the hayloft with two of Ántonia's lively boys. As he waits for sleep, he transforms the "battered" Ántonia of the present into a series of "images in the mind that did not fade—that grew stronger with time." He abstracts and stylizes his memories of her into static pictures like "the old woodcuts of one's first primer." No longer a distinct person for whom he feels affection or companionship, she becomes a mythic series of "immemorial human attitudes which we recognize by instinct as universal and true." Jim claims that "all the strong things in her heart came out in her body," but what Cather has actually demonstrated is their expression in the landscape.

The final lines of the chapter describe her only as the mother of tall, straight sons, "a rich mine of life, like the founders of early races" (926). Thus Cather has again performed a narrative distancing and epic generalizing similar to that we observed at the end of *O Pioneers!*, in which central individuals become impersonal types seen against a vast historical canvas—or the golden, hazy, romantic backdrop of the French Realist painters like Millet, Bonvin, Breton, and Bonheur, whom Judith Fryer has shown to have been so important for Cather's imagination (232–44).

Once he has conjured these grand images, Jim's interest in "his" Ántonia seems to end, though the novel does not. Two more chapters fulfill the promise of this final section's title, "Cusak's Boys," by focusing on Jim's introduction to Ántonia's husband and plans for future adventures with the Cusak boys in still-wild areas of Nebraska like the Badlands. "There were enough Cusaks to play with for a long while yet. Even after the boys grew up, there would always be Cusak himself! I meant to tramp along a few miles of lighted streets with Cusak" (936).

That *My Ántonia* should not end in Ántonia's kitchen or her apple orchard, but rather with an emphasis on her sons and their father, tells us that she has served only as a catalyst. She has been used up in the process of creating a male world of hunting and fishing and companionable tramping about, where Jim will find his pleasures in the future. This is a very odd ending for the novel, seeming to signal a return to the male adventures of the "classic" American narrative. Jim's final glance in Ántonia's direction carries no conviction, and all his supposed love for the land is reduced to enjoyment of a vacation playground. Once tamed, it is no longer interesting, just as Ántonia, once productive, loses her fascination.

Judith Fetterley sympathizes with what she sees in *My Ántonia* as Cather's response to "the pressure exerted by the definition of the American 'I' as male and the paradigm of American experience as masculine" (159). But it seems to me that the novel's final chapter enacts a major retreat in Cather's imaginative life from identification with women's lives, and thus from some of the deepest sources of her creative vitality. Similarly, it moves away from any effort toward serious contemplation of the human relation to the land. In *A Lost Lady*, many of the same general identifications of landscape with a strong and sensuous woman reappear, but the central woman character is a much more distant object of evaluation by a possessive male narrator whose relation to her is extremely ambivalent. Hermione Lee details Cather's way of making the pastoral landscape and Marian Forrester mirror each other, so that the "seductive words used for scenery are also the words associated with her—twinkling, glittering, crystalline, limpid, fragrant, tender" (198). Simple enjoyment of these beauties is associated with Niel Herbert's innocent childhood: as he reaches manhood he comes to understand and disapprove of Marian's sexuality, the very energy that has charged her husband's social life. The irony that her vitality is natural like that of the seasons and the earth is not very forcefully emphasized, for the narrative unfolds through the perspective of Marian's queasy male admirer. When old Captain Forrester declines and dies, all the magic of the land drains away. Not long afterward, both Marian and Niel leave forever.

These changes should make us see that Marian Forrester was potent only as a possession of the old railroad baron, like his hillside estate. She represents the freshness of the landscape at the charmed moment when the West was won from the Indians by heroes of enterprise like Captain Forrester but before it was ruined by what Cather saw as the degrading forces of modern life represented by grasping low-class opportunist Ivy Peters, who supplants the old captain as Marian's consort for a time. Cather implies Captain Forrester's "organic" fusion with the land in the story of how the willow stick he planted to mark his claim took root and grew into a tree. But he displaced the Indians who used to make their camp on the spot, and his name implies that he is destructive of its natural life. Furthermore, his wife's vitality is implicated in that destruction. When we last hear of her, she is in South America, on another frontier in the process of exploitation, and she has attached herself to another industrialist who is mining its riches. Her allure may be identified with the land, but apparently only at the moment of its domestication. Cather seems to have feminized and eroticized the landscape of colonization at the moment of its conquest, but that charm only exists in a temporary space of lost childhood innocence; it putrifies when seen with adult eyes or observed over time. This is imperialist nostalgia with a rather sinister twist.

The Professor's House and Death Comes to the Archbishop move completely away from this kind of gendered landscape. Both novels are exclusively masculine in identification, and their western settings are like the Territory of Huck Finn's escape at the end of Twain's novel—wide open spaces for male adventure. The Tom Outland story in The Professor's House is a retrospective tale of cozy male partnership out in pueblo country that encapsulates an unobtainable ideal for the sedentary urban protagonist. Glen Love has shown how the overstuffed domestic world of Professor St. Peter's family life is negatively contrasted with the spare, clean Southwest landscape of Tom Outland's adventures at Blue Mesa ("Chastening" 302–5). Cather has obviously turned against the feminine realm of family life here.

Death Comes to the Archbishop repeats Cather's notion of wild landscape as inert material to be shaped into usefulness by European man (109). Indian people are present in this novel, and there is some appreciation of their traditions of living in quiet harmony with their environment. Father Latour feels that traveling with his Indian guide is "like traveling with the landscape made human. . . . It was the Indian manner to vanish into the landscape, not to stand out against it" (270–71). But the whole force of the narrative is allied with the Spanish conquerers who will turn the land and its peoples to their purposes. Mike Fischer excavates the brutal history of that process, insisting that we recognize the violence that Cather has elided.

Cather succeeded in many respects as the epic celebrant of western settlement, but in spite of the androgyny that feminists have seen in her work, her novels of the land remain part of a male semiotic economy of heroic action that inscribes the individual will upon the face of the earth. Her pastoralism is adapted from the example of the first great imperialist poet, Virgil, and, as we have seen, it encodes a benign version of the conquest of the Plains, erasing its violence. But in the early Nebraska novels *O Pioneers!* and *My Ántonia*, Cather's imperialist nostalgia is strongly contested by the disrupting subtext of women's rituals and domestic values and their identification with the land. Perhaps this constitutes the kind of narrative subversion Lee claims, but only a careful reader will catch the ironies. If most have taken the fiction straight as Whitmanesque celebration, still it is the first time an alternate story—the vision of feminine agency and alliance with the earth—enters the mainstream of American fiction. Setting it beside her younger contemporaries Hemingway and Faulkner will demonstrate how deeply Cather's vision challenges the dominant male myth and prepares the way for later women writers like Eudora Welty.

Now, looking out the tunnel of trees over the ravine at the sky with white clouds moving across in the wind, I loved the country so that I was happy as you are after you have been with a woman that you really love, when, empty, you feel it welling up again and there it is and you can never have it all and yet what there is, now, you can have, and you want more and more, to have, and be, and live in, to possess now again for always, for that long, sudden-ended always; making time stand still, sometimes so very still that afterwards you wait to hear it move, and it is slow in starting. But you are not alone, because if you have ever really loved her happy and untragic, she loves you always; no matter whom she loves nor where she goes she loves you more. So if you have loved some woman and some country you are very fortunate, and if you die afterwards it makes no difference.
ERNEST HEMINGWAY, *Green Hills of Africa*

. . . summer, and fall, and snow, and wet and saprife spring in their ordered immortal sequence, the deathless and immemorial phases of the mother who had shaped him if any had . . . but still the woods would be his mistress and his wife.
WILLIAM FAULKNER, "The Bear"

CHAPTER 5

Pastoral Regression in Hemingway and Faulkner

Willa Cather was perhaps the first American fiction writer to make the celebration of her childhood landscape an explicit goal, or as she explains it through Jim Burden's dedication to Virgil's purpose in the *Georgics*, "*Primus ego in patriam mecum . . . deducam Musas,*" to be the first to lead the Muses into her country. But Sarah Orne Jewett, Kate Chopin, and Ellen Glasgow also brought regional settings to life around the turn of the century, as the last two decades of revisionist scholarship have reminded us. While all were well known in their time, Cather gained the broadest audience with her ambitious construction of a national epic to encapsulate the settling of the West. During the formative years of the World War I or "Lost Generation" writers, she was widely regarded as the most important American novelist. Yet when Raymond Benoit writes on "Holy Places in American Literature" in 1980, he traces an exclusively masculine line of descent from Thoreau's Walden Pond to the Mississippi River of Twain's *Huckleberry Finn* and thence directly to Hemingway's "Big Two-Hearted River" and Faulkner's "The Bear." Why have women regionalists, and particularly Willa Cather, been dropped out of the literary genealogy?

The answer to this question is implied in Nina Baym's "Melodramas of Beset Manhood: How Theories of American Fiction Exclude Women Authors." Even though women writers have numerically dominated American literature since the middle of the nineteenth century, they have been defined by the scholarly establishment as the enemy, a damned mob of sentimental scribblers against whom heroic male writers have had to struggle to maintain aesthetic integrity (Baym 124, 130; also Douglas and Tompkins). With the broad European and American backlash against women's gains during the suffrage movement producing a wave of cultural misogyny, "the androgynous language through which [women like Cather] sought to affirm their legitimacy and centrality only confirmed their increasing marginality—to the world of women as well as that of men" (Smith-Rosenberg 295). Gilbert and Gubar have amply documented the strategies of denigration used against women by male writers from Tennyson down to Yeats, Eliot, and D. H. Lawrence during this period (1: 34–46). They make an assertion similar to Baym's, that in the United States a major tactic was "the construction of a literary history that denies the reality of women writers" (153).

This effort continued for decades with such success that beginning in 1950 with Henry Nash Smith's *Virgin Land* and including other influential literary histories such as R. W. B. Lewis's *The American Adam* and Leslie Fiedler's *Love and Death in the American Novel*, critical opinion consolidated around a selective American myth that "narrates a confrontation of the American individual, the pure American self divorced from specific social circumstances, with the promise offered by the idea of America" (Baym 131). Needless to say, this pure American self is male. Even a writer like Cather, whom we have seen to be deeply invested in masculine traditions, is excluded from membership in the elect group of "classic American" writers because she is a woman who also treats "feminine" themes of community, family, and domestic ritual. Baym shows very clearly that the myth is defined in terms that automatically exclude women protagonists and values associated with social life, because its solitary hero is always shaped by two conflicting feminine forces—the trammeling society that seeks to suffocate him and the promising wilderness landscape where he can find freedom and peace. Women characters who take on such roles are criticized by scholars as unnatural (133, 135). Given such a context, Raymond Benoit *must* exclude Willa Cather's Nebraska from his study of holy places in American literature; her fiction is "wrong."

F. Scott Fitzgerald, Ernest Hemingway, and William Faulkner came of age during the fierce early years of the gender wars and grew up to become masculine combatants who shaped the version of American literary history outlined above. They all read Willa Cather, if not also Sarah Orne Jewett, Kate Chopin, and Ellen Glasgow, but they would hardly have wished to follow her androgynous example. Fitzgerald was an open admirer of Cather's fiction (Bruccoli 221), yet as we saw at the beginning of this discussion, he makes the New World landscape a duplicitous accomplice of women who seduce brave men. Glen Love makes a good case for Hemingway's having read much more of Cather's work than her World War I novel *One of Ours*, which he criticized (Love, "Chastening" 307). But Hemingway limited himself to manly predecessors when he discussed his reading. He grew up on the same Tom Brown books and Kipling adventures that Cather extolled as proper for sturdy boys, and though he read omnivorously throughout his life, he spoke contemptuously of women writers and continued to emphasize only male authors as important to him.[1] In *Green Hills of Africa* he complains of a debilitating gender reversal among American writers. "At a certain age the men writers change into Old Mother Hubbard. The women writers become Joan of Arc without the fighting. They become leaders. It doesn't matter who they lead. If they do not have followers they invent them. It is useless for those selected as followers to protest. They are accused of disloyalty" (24). No women writers are named.

As a son of the South, Faulkner undoubtedly read Chopin and Glasgow, and his short story "Golden Land" indicates a debt to Cather in its brief portrait of the Nebraska prairie he apparently never visited (*CS*,

702–3). Critical discussions of Faulkner's literary apprenticeship rarely mention Cather, but Judith Wittenberg has established how many women writers were represented in his library and whom he named late in life as important to his own development. Among them, Cather was perhaps foremost. He said in a 1950 letter that she was one of "the real ones before us who have not yet got the recog. they deserve," and he also mentioned her importance while teaching at the University of Virginia and lecturing in Japan in the 1950s (Wittenberg 288).

In spite of such admissions, Faulkner also traced a masculine literary descent for himself, regarding women as an inferior species. His boyhood idol was his great-grandfather, "the Old Colonel," William Clark Falkner, a Civil War hero who had written *The White Rose of Memphis*, a romance in purple prose celebrating the glories of the Old South. Shakespeare, Cervantes, and the Bible were the kind of ancestors he claimed.[2] When he wrote to Anita Loos to congratulate her for writing *Gentlemen Prefer Blondes*, he suggested that she might have succeeded by mistake, excusing himself for this suspicion by admitting, "I am still rather Victorian in my prejudices regarding the intelligence of women, despite Elinor Wylie and Willa Cather and all the balance of them" (Blotner 496).

Circumstances in the upbringing of Hemingway and Faulkner might have made them especially uneasy about the assertiveness of women and thus susceptible to their generation's tendencies toward misogyny. Both were the eldest and favorite sons of strong artistic mothers who actively promoted their developing talents. Their fathers seemed weak by comparison: a mild-mannered doctor who liked to cook as well as hunt and fish in Hemingway's case, and a somewhat feckless businessman whose parents regularly had to bail him out of failed ventures and find new jobs for him in Faulkner's. Hemingway regarded his mother as domineering his passive father and dramatized his disgust with this arrangement in the Nick Adams story "The Doctor and the Doctor's Wife." As he grew up, he came to hate his mother, though she had been his childhood literary mentor. This is the main thesis of Kenneth Lynn's biography, *Hemingway*. Faulkner's mother seems to have been contemptuous of her husband Murray's weaknesses from early in their marriage. Maude Falkner was the tough authority in the family who fixed the slogan "Don't complain, don't explain" to the kitchen wall and held her sons to that stoical standard. She was William's champion, she fed him books in childhood, and she was a lifelong confidante whom he visited every day as an adult. Faulkner's mentor and friend Phil Stone thought all the Falkner boys were tied to their mother and resented it; he felt that in William's case it led to an animosity toward women in general.[3]

If Faulkner and Hemingway were uneasy about their closeness to their strong mothers and their "effeminate" taste for books and art, believing themselves to have been betrayed or let down by weak fathers, the onset of World War I offered them a chance to prove their manhood. Both eagerly sought the opportunity, Hemingway by joining the Italian Red Cross before the United States had even entered the war, and Faulkner by enlisting in the Canadian Air Force. Neither actually fought. But both came home apparently wounded, though in Faulkner's case the wounds were only fictional, part of a heroic tale that also included stunt flying much like Snoopy's fantasies in *Peanuts*. Both had uniforms custom-made to give them panache when they returned to their home neighborhoods after the war.[4]

In *Male Fantasies* Klaus Theweleit examines the symbolic habits of a group of returning German veterans of the same war, and while elite *Freikorps* officers of Prussian military background might seem to have little in common with their American contemporaries, Theweleit's analysis turns out to be relevant to the whole modernist generation of European and American men. The German situation was admittedly extreme in many ways: *Freikorps* officers returned to a defeated country that seemed indifferent to the proud military and aristocratic traditions in which they had been schooled and for which they had fought under horrible conditions. Threatening social and political changes in Germany were more radical than comparable transitions in the United States. And the United States had been quite distant from the war, relatively unaffected by its aftermath. Nevertheless, that war was a cultural, social, and political watershed for all Western culture that ended many forms of perceived stability identified with the previous century of imperial expansion.

The German *Freikorps* felt that the glorious heritage of their fatherland was in imminent danger from a vile flood of political and social corruption embodied in the Weimar Republic and the rising working classes under the banner of communism. They organized into secret groups that became in effect an underground right-wing military force during the 1920s, committing political assassinations and creating a "White terror" to combat the "red" forces of communism. Later they surfaced politically with the rise of Nazism and formed part of the Third Reich's central structure (18–26).

What is interesting for my purposes is the violent gendering Theweleit's study uncovers at the heart of fascist resistance to social change in Germany. The forces of change are projected symbolically as feminized natural images of dissolution and chaos: floods, slime, and muck in the landscape that correspond with oozes of blood and mucus in the human—and particularly the female—body (37–45, 408–14). In novels written by *Freikorps* men, bestial proletarian women lewdly threaten and laugh at soldier males and in many cases physically assault and castrate them (66–67, 72–74). As Theweleit shows, these German fictional horrors are only part of a much wider masculinist reaction to postwar transition expressed in Irish, English, French, Italian, and American as well as German modernist literature. This is the same phenomenon explored from a feminist perspective by Gilbert and Gubar in *No Man's Land: The War of the Words*. Theweleit's approach is informed particularly by psychoanalysis, Marxism, and the theories of Norbert Elias and Rudolf zur Lippe about modern European cultural development from the fourteenth to the sixteenth century. He sees twentieth-century masculine language as a hysterical development of patriarchal domination of women (229–435). His conclusions accord with the deep history of symbolic practice identifying women's bodies with the body of the earth (294–300), and the psychological states he defines for *Freikorps* officers and modernist writers show remarkable parallels to the tragic Pentheus of Euripides' *Bacchae*, as I shall explain in more detail later.

We have seen how the Sumerian poems to Innana associate feminine fertility with the waters of flooding rivers and how Euripides' *Bacchae* identifies women's bodies with an earth oozing honey, milk, wine, and water. Such ancient traditions linking women's bodies with liquids seem almost universal, and certainly notable in European culture. Sacred springs with guardian nymphs or goddesses are everywhere in Greek and Roman mythology, and Celtic tradition is full of them as well. Many of Europe's famous churches, such as Notre Dame de Paris and Bath Abbey, are set on former sites of Celtic river goddess shrines or sacred springs where the Virgin Mary or other female saints replaced Celtic deities.[5] Theweleit argues that by the modern era, deployment of such associations is ultimately a tactic of control, an "oppression through exaltation" that denies the carnal reality and subjectivity of individual women:

A river without end, enormous and wide, flows through the world's literatures. Over and over again: the women-in-the-water; woman as water, as a stormy, cavorting, cooling ocean, a raging stream, a waterfall; as a limitless body of water that ships pass through, with tributaries, pools, surfs, and deltas; woman as the enticing (or perilous) deep, as a cup of bubbling body fluids; the vagina as wave, as foam, as a dark place ringed with Pacific ridges; love as the foam from the collision of two waves, as a sea voyage, a slow ebbing. (283–84)

Theweleit's soldier male reacted to this tradition with revulsion, imagining liquid contaminations that threatened to dissolve his identity. "His erupted unconscious 'inundated' his thinking in more than just a metaphorical sense. He actually found himself in a process of disintegration, dissolution, molecularization—a process that threatened to completely cancel him out as an entity" (427). These men had to "'halt' and 'stand firm,' a phallus against the dissolution, remaining hard against the onslaughts of surging womanhood" (50) and the floods and slime of political danger. To fight back, they created a counterflood with the bloody bodies of their enemies, distinguishing themselves from the carnage by still remaining firm and hard, guarding against the dangerous fluids within their own bodies as well as the alien ones without (205, 410–11, 434). Male modernist writers in America as well as Europe all too often fell into similar semiotic practices, though as a rule they were not so extreme as the *Freikorps* propagandists. Theweleit's commentary provides a very revealing context for the landscape imagery and the treatment of women in the fiction of Ernest Hemingway and William Faulkner.

Born less than two years apart at the end of the nineteenth century, Faulkner and Hemingway were members of the first American generation for whom the frontier was only the stuff of legend. During their boyhoods, they were initiated into manly frontier arts of hunting and fishing in forests that were literally being felled around them. As timber companies sawed down the last of those aboriginal forests all over the South, Faulkner's father often took him and his brothers to a hunting camp called the "Club House" in the Tallahatchie bottom outside his hometown of Oxford (Blotner 17; Minter 9). Hemingway learned to fish and hunt and cook while camping with his father up near the Canadian border of the Michigan peninsula, where big timber companies were cutting their way through the old forests that once covered the whole region.

Most writers come from the social class that enriches itself one way or another from the gathering and finishing of raw materials; what sets Hemingway and Faulkner apart from someone like Willa Cather is the fact that these men were trained in the male rituals that signal their privilege as conquerers of the land. The survival skills of the Indians and frontiersmen were only a sport for them, nostalgically mimicking the way of life their society was destroying. Yet these sports carry a sacred aura that both writers powerfully convey in their fiction, and to which men at the end of the century still respond as if to a religion of masculine courage, honor, and prowess. We should ask what is at stake in this atavistic code, this appeal to the power of the woods and the first blooding of a young male initiate in the company of the adult brotherhood of weekend predators. After all, most men in the United States as well as Europe and developed nations in Asia spend their lives as virtual cyborgs in cities where machines move them from place to place, food is bought in packages or served up at restaurants, and tracking skills are no more necessary for success than physical strength.

I shall look closely at landscape imagery in the fiction of both Hemingway and Faulkner, particularly at their famous initiation stories of hunting and fishing in the woods of Upper Michigan and Mississippi, to explore the question of their power and the values they encode. Both writers have sometimes been criticized for failing to make their outdoor heroes more active in defense of the wilderness they profess to love,[6] but the bulk of scholarly commentary has been strongly sympathetic to Isaac McCaslin and Nick Adams. And the remarkable success of Robert Bly's *Iron Man* and proliferation of men's groups that go out into Nature to perform primitive Wild Man rituals reflect an almost automatic allegiance to primitive notions of male valor.

Hemingway was surprisingly conscious of the erotic charge and gendered coding of his own and his fictional hero's passion for fishing and for the wilderness. In an early autobiographical passage spoken through the persona of Nick Adams, he frankly admits his ambition "to be a great writer" and sets his aesthetic credo in the context of fishing and male camaraderie that is disrupted by women. The piece was originally written as a coda to "Big Two-Hearted River" but only published post-humously in *The Nick Adams Stories* and entitled "On Writing" by editor Philip Young.[7] Thus it is the literal context for Hemingway's most famous story, constructing his quintessential hero.

Unlike the published story of a man alone with Nature, "On Writing" assumes a community of fishing companions and friends, "the old gang" Nick had lost when he married. Hemingway claims here that the Nick Adams stories are not about himself, but that pretense is belied by references to Paris, Ezra [Pound], [Gertrude] Stein, art galleries Stein had introduced him to, and a wife Helen who was certainly his own first wife Hadley. Marriage to this wife is the cause of his exclusion from the life he had loved "more than anything" (215), of summers with his gang of friends camping and fishing and working outdoors, especially with his friend Bill Smith. The first several pages refer again and again to this loss in a pastoral elegy for the cozy fishing comradeship described as similar to a relationship with a girl. Bill forgave him for the fishing he had done prior to their friendship, "like a girl about other girls." Fishing is the object of passionate male alliances existing in opposition to relations with women. "He lost them because he admitted by marrying that something was more important than fishing. . . . They were all married to fishing. . . . He'd been married to it before he married Helen. Really married to it. It wasn't any joke."

Nick remembers that Ezra Pound thought fishing was a joke, just as "lots of people" think poetry is a joke and Englishmen are a joke (214). In a complex defensive action against what he assumes to be the ridicule of an unfeeling world, Hemingway links his outdoor ethos to literature and to the stoical code of the English upper class that he had absorbed from the Tom Brown books and admired in British officers he met during the war in Italy. This combination is important because it counters the common American male disdain for effeminate qualities assigned to poetry and an "effete" British masculinity in the image of Oscar Wilde. Thus he defines the code that becomes the value system of his fiction.

"On Writing" sets the depiction of landscape as Hemingway's central goal: "He wanted to write like Cézanne painted . . . wanted to write about country so it would be there like Cézanne had done it in painting" (218). This is an idea he adopted from Gertrude Stein, and he has Nick Adams say, "She'd know if he ever got things right" (218). Stein always regarded the painting of Cézanne as a major influence on everything she wrote. Specifically she credited the portrait of Madame Cézanne on her wall for having inspired her own influential early work in *Three Lives*; as she wrote of herself in *The Autobiography of Alice B. Toklas*, "she had this Cézanne and she looked at it and under its stimulus she wrote Three Lives" (41). Hemingway must have heard her tell this story, probably more than once, and must have been introduced to Cézanne in Stein's studio, where he could see more of the painter's work than in the one museum in Paris with Cézanne holdings.[8] Similarly Hemingway writes, "He knew just how Cézanne would paint this stretch of river." In fact he then has Nick standing up and stepping down into the cold and actual water. "He waded across the stream, moving in the picture" (218). This is the "Big Two-Hearted River" itself, but rather than being a uniquely American place, it turns out to have originally been imagined as a French painting. Of course no traces of these associations remain in the published form of the story that did so much to define the modern American hero in an emblematic Great Good Place.

The landscape of the "Big Two-Hearted River" is as familiar to readers of American fiction as Thoreau's Walden Pond, and in spite of Hemingway's later claim that he could not read Thoreau, he must have been aware of the Thoreauvian tradition in which he wrote.[9] The site beside the river where Nick pitches his tent is similar to Walden in being a place already tamed by foresters, a midpoint between "savagery" and "civilization" that is the magic pastoral space of Euramerican tradition. But there is a violence and ruin encoded in Nick's Upper Michigan landscape that is completely absent from most pastoral writing and certainly from Thoreau's Walden Pond. Instead of the town surrounded by forests where Nick expects to begin his hike into fishing country, he finds a place so devastated by fire that even the surface has been burned off the ground. Because Hemingway has kept the description of the fire free of explicit ties to anything else in Nick's life, it can suggest natural disasters or merely psychological wreckage when the story is read by itself. Most readings, however, have linked this fire to World War I, which weaves in and out of the Michigan sections of *In Our Time* like a thoroughbass defining the ground of meaning for the whole. "The story was about coming back from the war but there was no mention of the war in it," as Hemingway explained in *A Moveable Feast* (76; cf. Lynn, "Troubled").

In a deep way, war lay behind everything Hemingway wrote, as a proving ground for the writer and an essential reality against which every other kind of experience must be measured.[10]

Nick is a battered American Adam who seeks healing in the green world of his boyhood. The terrible European war whose supposed glories *In Our Time* does so much to deflate is at the same time the crucible of Hemingway's famous tough-but-tender narrative voice. Nick has gained his manhood by witnessing and surviving the exploding shells, the landscape littered with bloated bodies and fragments of human and animal flesh, the smouldering remains of villages and farms. He embodies the clenched stoicism of men who have withstood the terror of battle and done what they had to do, or broken down under prolonged stress, seen their friends' heads blown off and known the bitterness of lost limbs. Hemingway exploits this kind of grim heroism for all it is worth. It is an exclusively masculine virtue tied to the heroic warrior code of epic and tragedy despite its implied claims of disillusionment. Participating in this heroic tradition is almost too much to bear, however; Nick's psyche is paralyzed by his experience of war, symbolically devastated like the burnt landscape where the train stops and lets him off. The story is almost allegorical, with the modern American pilgrim shouldering his belongings and trudging off, up hill and down, to rebuild his life. He seeks to be restored by the wholesome American landscape in a series of carefully controlled rituals that stop his mind from working on the past. The language of the story is almost desperately tamped down to restore a childlike simplicity to experience.

From "On Writing," the fragmentary rejected coda of the story, we know that in the story's original material, Nick had once felt married to camping and fishing in an implied erotic relationship to flowing water and the landscape around it. In some sense Hemingway means his hero to experience the land and its rivers as feminine. We have encountered similar associations in Emerson and Thoreau, and even in Cather. For male writers, however, as Fiedler, Kolodny, and Baym have explained, escape into the bosom of Mother Nature is imagined as flight from entrapment by society and particularly from women. As Baym puts it,

> Landscape is deeply imbued with female qualities, as society is; but where society is menacing and destructive, landscape is compliant and supportive. It has the attributes simultaneously of a virginal

bride and a non-threatening mother; its female qualities are articulated with respect to a male angle of vision: what can nature do for me, asks the hero, what can it give me? . . . heroes of American myth turn to nature as sweetheart and nurture, anticipating the satisfaction of all desires through her and including among these the desires for mastery and power. (135–36)

But we have seen that Nick's psychic damage in "Big Two-Hearted River" has been caused by war, which the blackened landscape around Seney represents, not by anything feminine. War is the ultimate effort for mastery and power over land masses as well, of course, as over other human males who claim it. In shaping his story for publication, Hemingway seems to have cleared out all the material concerning Nick's enmeshment with society, his marriage, his loss of the companionship of his friends, in order to focus on the heroic individual and his struggle to recover from war. This is an action that occurs frequently *within* other stories in *In Our Time* as part of the larger dynamic that Baym describes—negotiation of a male mythic space between the entrapping social context of active (and threatening) human females and the benign, passive natural feminine in the landscape.

In the stories about the landscape of Michigan, the stage is cleared of (white) women so that males can enjoy companionship in the woods. The whole action of "The End of Something," for instance, involves Nick's ending a relationship with a girl named Marjorie, with whom he had shared fishing. As she leaves the campfire at the end of the story, a male fishing companion walks into the firelight and takes her place. Many other stories involve escape from feminine entrapments or the dangers inherent in them. Harold Krebs of "Soldier's Home" evades his mother's efforts to draw him back into hometown life and responsibility, and though he finds the town girls attractive to look at, he wants no entanglements with them. He thus refuses the kind of social integration identified with women, domesticity, and town life that could help restore him, serving as an antidote to the violent disintegration of the masculine battlefield. He is nauseated by his mother's assertion of her love. Hemingway reinforces this revulsion by objectifying it in the image of grease hardening in the plate of food she has prepared for him (*IOT*, 99). Here is an early example of what Gilbert and Gubar call "the campaign against mothers" (1: 55), with the most basic kind of feminine nurturing used to evoke disgust.

When men are settled in relationships with women, as in "The Doctor and the Doctor's Wife" or "Mr. and Mrs. Elliot," they are portrayed as weak, passive, emasculated. Real manhood is found in the woods or at war.[11]

In opposition to the human females who invade male spaces or relations in the stories is the landscape that Hemingway loved and set out to capture in his fiction. We have seen that it is feminized and eroticized in the unpublished coda to "Big Two-Hearted River." Fishing is the erotic action of this "marriage" that is replaced by the wife. In a later book, Hemingway states the parallels between woman and land even more explicitly: "I loved the country so that I was happy as you are after you have been with a woman that you really love" (*GH* 72–73).

Indians provide a link in the Nick Adams Michigan stories between the two feminine realms—the entrapping social world of families and responsibilities, and the feminized landscape. They are the remnants of indigenous people who still know the woods and practice traditional skills in hunting and fishing. Nick has learned from them, as Hemingway himself must have done. Hemingway proudly claimed that his father had Indian blood, praised the "Cheyenne" qualities of his athletic son Gregory, and held a romantic notion of Indian virtues all his life (Cowley xviii; Love, "Indian Virtues," 201; Lewis, "Long Time," 200–201). But the Indians who populate Hemingway's Nick Adams stories, like Thoreau's Indians, are a degraded group marked by alcoholism, laziness, and petty theft. They are associated with sex and with hunting in Nick's adolescent experience. The first girl he imagines he loves is an Indian girl in "Ten Indians" who turns out to be promiscuous. At the center of "Fathers and Sons" is a flashback to summer idylls in the forest with an Indian hunting companion named Billy, who offers his sister's sexual favors to Nick. The three lounge about on the soft forest floor under giant hemlocks, Nick lending Billy his shotgun in exchange for sex with his sister Trudy. Most powerful of all the stories involving Indians, however, is "Indian Camp," in which Hemingway dramatizes the consequences of sexuality in the horrifying experience of childbirth that Nick must watch as a stunned little boy. At the heart of Nature, in the mists of darkness and the lakes, and at the heart of natural cycles and regenerative energies is the spectacle of this screaming female body opening in pain and blood to bring forth a new life, and so unbearable to witness that her husband slits his throat. Thus integral to the Indian presence is a female sexuality associated with the woods, tied to the debauched remnants of a formerly proud primitive masculinity, and leading to the violent and repulsive and deadly process of regeneration.[12]

But the explicitly aggressive violence in *In Our Time* and the other Nick Adams stories remains masculine, as in "The Battler" and "The Killers" and the vignettes of war. That is what Nick flees in "Big Two-Hearted River" as he sets off alone across the gently undulating pine plain with the line of the river in the distance, glinting in the sun. Once he has passed beyond the fire line, the country is alive again with a covering of sweet fern, clumps of scrubby jack pines, and occasional dark islands of the original pine forest. As he hikes over this uneven, shadeless plain, Nick reintegrates himself by attending entirely to his body and the pleasures it can take from the physical world. As in the basic model Baym describes, the hero's relation to this feminine space is focused on what it can do for *him*. Nick carefully monitors the feel of the sand under his feet, the excessive weight of the pack, the chafing of the pack straps against his shoulders, his heat and fatigue. He comes to one of the big islands of old growth pines and describes it sensuously as a sort of outdoor pavilion with smooth straight trunks, a soft pine needle floor, and a high canopy of interlocking branches moving in the wind. Nick slips out of his pack and lies down in the shade: "He lay on his back and looked up into the pine trees. His neck and back and the small of his back rested as he stretched. The earth felt good against his back. He looked up at the sky, through the branches, and then shut his eyes. He opened them and looked up again. There was a wind high up in the branches. He shut his eyes again and went to sleep" (183–84).

When he wakes, Nick realizes that he has relaxed too completely in this comforting oasis. The sun is almost down, and he must make camp before dark. He feels stiff and cramped, but shoulders his pack, feeling the painful straps, and moves quickly across the fern swale to reach the river. Then follows what I should like to define as a series of feminine nesting rituals, which allow him to create comfort and reassuring order in a domestic space he totally controls. Like Thoreau at Walden, Hemingway's hero establishes his own self-sufficient, cozy home without the intrusion of any female. This is a different kind of androgyny than that associated with Cather's protagonists and their sturdy Nebraska farmhouses where food and warmth symbolize fertility in harmony with earth's plenty. Hemingway's is male appropriation of women's domestic traditions not to extend or broaden concepts of human possibility or participation in the building of community, but rather to narrow and exclude. He erases most of the world so that Nick Adams can nurture himself.

Nick comes down a logged-off hillside covered with stumps to the meadow beside the river where he will set up his camp. On rising ground overlooking this pastoral scene, he selects a level place between two jack pines. Two of their roots are projecting, however, so Nick chops them out with his axe, rips out inconvenient ferns by their roots, and smooths the uprooted earth. "He did not want anything making lumps under the blankets" (185). All discomforts must be chopped and ripped away. Nick is certainly not an eco-camper concerned about environmental impact. Then he carefully spreads out his bedding, stretches his tent drum-tight, and stows his belongings neatly inside or in the pack he hangs above ground from a nail he has driven into a tree. When Nick crawls inside his tent, Hemingway describes him for the first time as happy.

> Inside the tent the light came through the brown canvas. It smelled pleasantly of canvas. Already there was something mysterious and homelike. Nick was happy as he crawled inside the tent. He had not been unhappy all day. This was different though. Now things were done. There had been this to do. Now it was done. It had been a hard trip. He was very tired. That was done. He had made his camp. He was settled. Nothing could touch him. It was a good place to camp. He was there, in the good place. He was in his home where he had made it. (186–87)

Completion, control, safety . . . home. These create positive happiness and define "the good place." Hemingway wrote elsewhere that "Prose is architecture, not interior decoration" (*Death* 191), thus signaling a masculine distaste for the effeminate arts that shape a living space, yet he spent immense effort in "Big Two-Hearted River" arranging the domestic spaces of Nick's "good place."

The other strong expression of pleasure in part 1 also comes from homey physical comforts—the food Nick cooks himself once his camp is established. Much has been written about Nick's menu of canned pork and beans combined with canned spaghetti and tomato catsup. More important than what he eats, however, is the loving attention devoted to food and the rituals of preparation and eating. As Virginia Woolf remarks in *A Room of One's Own*, food has seldom been an important subject in fiction (12). That is because the body and its functions, as well as domestic experiences, have been treated by masculine culture as the trivial business of women. Woolf herself set out to change those conventions by making food and its preparation central to her own fictional practice, and writers like Willa Cather and Eudora Welty have similarly shown both its literal and figurative importance in their work. When we turn to Welty, we shall see that for her, food is directly linked to the landscape in a semiotic network that celebrates the body and the lives of women as the communal heart of human experience.

Nick Adams sits by his campfire, enjoying the process of opening his cans of food and pouring them into his skillet, watching the mixture bubble, feeling the keen edge of his appetite, restraining his impulse to eat too soon and burn his sensitive tongue. When he tastes his dinner, he utters his only exclamation of joy in the story. "'Chrise,' Nick said, 'Geezus Chrise,' he said happily" (188). This is a prayer of thanksgiving if there ever was one. The wonderfully detailed and satisfying descriptive technique is repeated for his breakfast flapjacks cooked with the same care and smeared with apple butter and for the making of his onion sandwiches.

As long as Nick concentrates on gratifying his body and attending to its sensations, he is whole and happy. But thought is dangerous, even when it is only memory of other happy camping trips. While considering various methods of making coffee, he thinks back to another fishing trip with friends, including a man named Hopkins whose method he decides to use. But memories of arguments, ambitions, business ventures, and disappointments—in short the complexities of involvements with other people—begin to flood into his thoughts. "His mind was starting to work. He knew he could choke it because he was tired enough" (191). He is able to retreat back into childlike physical simplicity by crawling into the little womb of his snug tent, curling up in a fetal position beneath his blankets, and falling immediately asleep.

Part 2 of "Big Two-Hearted River" is a kind of shaky rebirth, involving the careful, somewhat tentative return to the predatory ritual of fishing that had brought such intense joy to Nick's boyhood. His prowess is as sure as ever, and his success is immediate, with a small trout caught first and gently released. But the shock of the cold water rushing past his legs, the shifting gravel underfoot, and the smooth darkness of the deep places behind logjams begin to suggest dangers lurking even in the pastoral landscape. The second trout Nick hooks is too big, in water that is too deep, pulling so hard that it doubles Nick's rod and breaks the leader.

Nick is so emotionally shaken when the line goes slack that he has to get out of the water. "Nick's hand was shaky. He reeled in slowly. The thrill had been too much. He felt, vaguely, a little sick, as though it would be better to sit down" (204). He climbs out of the stream and sits down on a log, careful not "to rush his sensations" and monitoring the way the feeling of disappointment slowly drains away, almost like the water that runs down his trousers and out of his shoes. Considering Theweleit's evidence for the dangerous "feminine" coding of liquids and the way Hemingway indicates the feminine associations of fishing and landscape in "On Writing," it is tempting to think of Nick's fishing as a probing of the symbolic feminine that is almost too overwhelming for him to withstand. Whatever else this episode may mean, Nick's reactions demonstrate that he cannot completely control his encounters with the natural world. The river is not simply an abundant, nurturing, benign "good place" but instead one that has its own threatening depths and necessities. Nick must protect himself from the emotional extremes caused by unsuccessful encounters, even in the apparently superficial physical activity of fishing. Indeed, as most readers seem to agree, fishing carries a powerful allegorical charge that makes it stand for engagement with life itself. Even after Nick recovers his equilibrium and returns to the stream to gracefully bag two fat trout and then stop and concentrate again on the restorative physical pleasures of rest and food, he has to consider the dangers that lurk in the rushing water. Smoking a cigarette after lunch, he looks downstream, as into his next fishing spot.

> Ahead the river narrowed and went into a swamp. The river became smooth and deep and the swamp looked solid with cedar trees, their trunks close together, their branches solid. . . .
> Nick did not want to go in there now. He felt a reaction against deep wading into the water deepening up under his armpits, to hook big trout in places impossible to land them. In the swamp the banks were bare, the big cedars came together overhead, the sun did not come through, except in patches; in the fast deep water, in the half light, the fishing would be tragic. In the swamp fishing was a tragic adventure. Nick did not want it. (211)

Debra Moddelmog sees the darker depths of this swamp as associated with Nick's uncomfortable feelings about marriage (605). Whether or not this is so, the swamp certainly epitomizes the feminine characteristics thoroughly documented by Theweleit. The contrast to this fearful, gloomy, entangling place is provided immediately by the cleanly defined maleness of the two trout Nick has caught and proceeds to gut: "All the insides and the gills and tongue came out in one piece. They were both males; long gray-white strips of milt, smooth and clean. All the insides clean and compact, coming out all together" (212). Now reassured, Nick returns to his camp. The story ends with Nick thinking, "There were plenty of days coming when he could fish the swamp."

There were plenty of stories and novels coming for Hemingway, in which he could continue to explore the streams of his imagination, fish for and grapple with the psychic problems of his wounded heroes against "untamed" landscapes where they test their fishing and hunting skills and thus test and prove their manhood again and again. In "Hemingway's Indian Virtues: An Ecological Reconsideration," Glen Love calls our attention to "an aggressive and isolated individualism" in much of Hemingway's fiction, "which wars against those natural manifestations he claims to love." Ironically, in spite of his admiration for Native American traditions, Hemingway himself was a game hog who slaughtered remarkable numbers of wild animals (Love 203, 212n). In *Green Hills of Africa* he describes the landscape and its animals with love and admiration, yet he reveals the crass competitiveness of his hunting ethos when he describes his triumphal return to town in a jeep stuffed with antelope heads, and then his bitter jealousy of another hunter who got a bigger kudu than he did. Hemingway complains about the other hunter, "Why does he have to beat me so bloody badly?" (292).

Yet he was aware that he was an invader and part of a colonial process that was destroying the landscape.

> A continent ages quickly once we come. The natives live in harmony with it. But the foreigner destroys, cuts down the trees, drains the water, so that the water supply is altered and in a short time the soil, once the sod is turned under, is cropped out and, next, it starts to blow away as it has blown away in every old country and as I had seen it start to blow in Canada. The earth gets tired of being exploited. A country wears out quickly unless man puts back in it all his residue and that of all his beasts. When he quits using beasts and uses machines, the earth defeats him quickly. The machine can't reproduce, nor does it fertilize the soil, and it

eats what he cannot raise. A country was made to be as we found it. We are the intruders and after we are dead we may have ruined it but it will still be there and we don't know what the next changes are. (284–85)

He trusted in the inexhaustible power of the earth to restore itself after human depredations, something we can no longer afford to do. That he may have repented at the end of his life, as his protagonist's attitude toward hunting in *The Garden of Eden* suggests, does not change the fact that in most of his fiction "there is no room to maneuver except at the edge of death, no arresting of the cycle in which one must go forth to kill one's brothers, turning to the natural world as the arena for human greatness, but effecting thereby its greater diminishment" (Love, "Indian Virtues," 207).

Frederick Busch sees much recent criticism of Hemingway by feminists and Marxists and Freudians "as name-calling and not very useful to the understanding by readers of how literature functions" (19). Busch claims that Hemingway "gave the century a way of making literary art that dealt with the remarkable violence of our time. He listened and watched and invented the language—using the power, the terror, of silences—with which we could name ourselves" (1). Aside from the likelihood that the violence of our time is arguably no less horrible than the slaughters of other eras, Busch is wrong to assert that Hemingway's is the language with which we can name ourselves. As I have tried to demonstrate, and as many feminist readers have done earlier, at least half of us are not likely to see ourselves in Hemingway's encoding of subjectivity. Hemingway's male heroes must be seen, beneath all the sentimental celebration of landscape and majestic animals of prey like lions and elephants and even big trout, as adversaries and conquerors. We can see the underlying values of Hemingway's moral code in Busch's perceptive definition of the vision Hemingway offers his readers: "Hemingway made it clear to his readers that a writer who stared into the truths or evasions of the soul and tried to bring back something of what he had seen was a comrade in arms to the warrior or hunter: each was a laborer at his trade who risked his life in the plying of the trade. Hemingway's work demonstrates that the making of art is a matter of life and death, no less" (17). Busch, like Hemingway, uses the "trade" of killing as the metaphor for art, but there are other ways to live on earth and other ways to imagine writing. Even if life is sustained by death and living things eat each other, death is balanced by birth and decay by growth. An exclusively masculine code of values cannot afford to acknowledge this balance or the centrality of all the fecundity that has been traditionally coded as feminine. Hemingway pared away so much of the world from his fiction, retreating into such a narrow and primitive masculinity, that there was nothing left for him but death.

Hemingway's contemporary William Faulkner wrestled with many of the same demons and also explored the possibility of exorcism by primitive rituals of the hunt, chiefly in *Go Down, Moses*, with its central pursuit of the primordial bear in the Delta wilderness. Faulkner's pastorals, however, are much more skeptical and ironic, and in the end he seems to write his way into an acknowledgment of men's devastation of the land and enactment of their own doom.

In explaining *Absalom, Absalom!* to his editor Hal Smith, Faulkner said, "the theme is a man who outraged the land, and the land then turned and destroyed the man's family" (Blotner 327). This seems an odd claim. The actions of Thomas Sutpen that could be called outrages are betrayals of women and children: putting aside his Haitian wife when he discovers she has "Negro blood," refusing to acknowledge his son by that wife, failing to inform his wife Ellen and daughter Judith and son Henry about this previous wife and son, proposing to Rosa Coldfield that she prove her fertility to him as a prerequisite to marriage, and finally rejecting Milly Jones because she bears him a daughter. Only if we realize that Faulkner equates the novel's women with the earth can we understand how his tangled logic posits Milly's father old Wash Jones as the Grim Reaper who enacts the will of the land. The equation of woman and landscape is a premise that lies behind all of his writing about Yoknapatawpha County. He seems to work his way toward a full understanding of its meaning from his earliest novels to its most direct examination in *Go Down, Moses*.

No other part of the United States has been so minutely fixed in literature as the geography of Faulkner's thinly disguised Lafayette County. Scholars have worked for decades to uncover the real Mississippi equivalents of their fictional counterparts and to explain their complex resonances in Faulkner's hands. Even so, until recently Karl Zink's early study, "Faulkner's Garden: Woman and the Immemorial Earth," was the only close examination of the connection between Faulkner's women and the land. Zink calls attention to the sensuous physical texture of all the fiction, humming and buzzing with insects, pulsing with heat, and heavy with the cloying fragrances of flowering plants like lilacs and wisteria and honeysuckle. More particularly he emphasizes the pervasive opposition of liquids, muck, loam, and plump fruits to "masculine" forces of sun and plow and the heroic will of restless men (140). Earth is wet, fecund, teeming—"the supreme primal uterus"—and women are its avatars. In his first novel, *Soldier's Pay*, Faulkner treated this alliance quite directly and positively, little anticipating the more tangled, tortured use of the same setting and motif in the mature *Sound and the Fury*. In the early novel George Farr finds peace and a kind of sexual completion as he sits in the darkness on freshly turned earth outside the window of the woman he desires.

> The turned flower bed filled the darkness with the smell of fresh earth, something friendly and personal in a world of enormous vague formless shapes of greater and lesser darkness. The night, the silence, was complete and profound: a formless region filled with the smell of fresh earth and the measured ticking of the watch in his pocket. After a time he felt soft damp earth through his trousers upon his thighs and he sat in a slow physical content, a oneness with the earth, . . .
>
> Again he became one with the earth, with dark and silence, with his own body . . . with her body, like a little silver water sweetly dividing . . . turned earth and hyacinths along a veranda, swinging soundless bells.
>
> (*SP*, 238; see Zink 149; Faulkner's ellipses in second paragraph)

In *Faulkner's Rhetoric of Loss*, Gail Mortimer uses object relations theory to define the revulsion toward women and blacks that Faulkner expressed later in his career through associations with liquidity, earth, and darkness, especially in *Light in August* (14–42). Minrose Gwin pursues the inquiry further, drawing on the work of European theorists like Luce Irigaray, Julia Kristeva, Hélène Cixous, and Klaus Theweleit to theorize a profound bisexual tension in Faulkner's writing that is often connected with imagery of decaying materiality and engulfing floods. Gwin's view of such figurations is somewhat more generous than mine, casting *The Wild Palms*, for example, as a text in which flooding is the very language of the speaking subject. For her, the novel is a male text speaking itself in a "feminine" linguistic excess that bursts through "those systems of binary representation which make one thing 'masculine' and another 'feminine' " (129–30). It seems to me, however, that Faulkner's rhetoric only rarely allows a positive experience of the feminine for the ordinary reader. His symbolic practice is similar in many respects to the feminized coding of revulsion in German fascist rhetoric after World War I, which Theweleit examines in *Male Fantasies*, so that André Bleikasten seems right in describing horror toward the body's needs and activities, and in particular toward the feminine, which grows increasingly vivid and grotesque as Faulkner's career progresses.

> The revulsion from thick liquidity is first and foremost a revulsion from the female body, which is phantasmically conceived as soft, fluid, formless matter threatening engulfment and as "matter out of place," as *dirt*. Dirt is earth; earth, fecund and foul, is woman. Dirt is filth, and all filth comes down to "womanfilth," as Doc Hines puts it, the "periodical filth" of menstrual blood, which for Christmas as for other Faulkner males is the visible trace of woman's "curse," the unmistakable sign of her fallen and soiled condition. The "thick still black pool" is indeed "more than water": a metaphor of female blood, a metonymy of female flesh. The circuits of the imaginary have led us once more from the material to the bodily and from the physical to the physiological. In Faulkner's *rhétorique profonde* (to borrow Baudelaire's phrase) there is scarcely a figure that does not turn out to be a figure of the body. (290)

My own purpose is to explore how such horrors affect Faulkner's depiction of the historical and ethical relation of humans to the earth and its life. Zink believes "it is quite possible that the male's ambiguous fear and hatred and love of woman [in Faulkner's fiction] must be explained in terms of his fear and hatred and love of the old Earth itself, to which Woman is so disturbingly related" (149). As Bleikasten phrases the situation, Faulkner's male idealists are caught in a phobia of defilement, doomed to a queasy and hopeless lifelong search for purity in which "that which is denied is . . . coextensive with the entire world of experience" (302). Even so, as Gwin demonstrates, disjunctions shift and clash under and along the narrative surfaces of their struggles, erupting at times with forces that deny those male protagonists' construction of their lives, or even the author's apparent purposes in the text.

Such attitudes have persisted from ancient culture to inform much contradictory treatment of landscapes by male writers from as far back as the Sumerian *Epic of Gilgamesh* and Euripides' *Bacchae* down through Emerson and Thoreau to Faulkner's own generation (Shepard; Oelschlaeger; Westling, "Food," 30–33). But Faulkner's participation in these tropes is so extravagantly anguished and ambivalent that it ultimately exposes their moral evasions. He explores their meaning for his male characters with increasing awareness of the cultural stakes involved and the mechanisms of avoidance which his fellows have used to shift blame from masculine action to the "feminine mysteries" imagined as intrinsic to both Nature and Woman. By the time of *Go Down, Moses*, his attention is focused directly and intensely upon the moral problems of white men's behavior in the New World as revealed through the lives of his Mississippi characters. Gwin describes Faulkner's narrative in geographical terms, "like the flooding river" that reverses itself and sweeps us away to an unexpected place. "Faulkner's art," she says, "is located not here or there, not in water or on solid ground, but in the force that moves between" (151–52). While he voices his own feelings of horror and impotence before what he encodes as the primeval feminine at the heart of Nature, he also dramatizes the hysterical extremes of masculine revulsion, the ruthlessness and violence of male aggression against land and women and dark-skinned peoples, the devastation caused by masculine "heroism," and the moral evasions and bankruptcy of individual characters. He exaggerates and ironizes the very attitudes in which he and his protagonists are trapped.

The first Yoknapatawpha novel, *Flags in the Dust,* establishes conventional associations of women with flowers and the southern landscape, which Faulkner absorbed from his region's literary traditions, from classical pastoral conventions, and from the pre-Raphaelite and Decadent poetry in which he had saturated himself as a young writer.[13] Narcissa Benbow's name links her to a delicate flower, and she is regularly described as inhabiting quiet gardens (*Flags* 66, 244). The sexually ripe and knowing Belle Mitchell, on the other hand, is "flowered like a hothouse bloom, brilliant and petulant and perverse" (167). Narcissa's spacial associations are always pure, protected, and fresh by contrast, presented in a riot of mixed metaphors. Her spaces are invaded with hot, crashing violence by Bayard Sartoris's courtship: "His idea was like a trampling of heavy feet in those cool corridors of hers" (134). Or her life is a "grave unshadowed beach" upon which Bayard washes up like a heavy piece of flotsam (136). Yet again, she is a placid pool and Bayard no more than the shadow fleetingly mirrored on its surface and then gone (160).

Faulkner's presentation of Bayard, the wild scion of a crumbling aristocratic family, is clumsy and ambivalent, but intense authorial investment is revealed by the emotive force of passages describing his furious rampages, his mad gallops through the main street of his sleepy hometown, even his drunken escapades through the countryside. Bayard is also ridiculous, however, and enough sympathy is given to Narcissa's perspective to credit her horror at his violence and her determination to save their son from his father's self-destructive heritage. By the end of the novel she has been vindicated:

> All of Narcissa's instincts had been antipathetic to him; his idea was a threat and his presence a violation of the very depths of her nature: in the headlong violence of him she had been like a lily in a gale which rocked it to its roots in a sort of vacuum, without any actual laying-on of hands. And now the gale had gone on; the lily had forgotten it as its fury died away into fading vibrations of old terrors and dreads, and the stalk recovered and the bell itself was untarnished save by the friction of its own petals. The gale is gone, and though the lily is sad a little with vibrations of ancient fears, it is not sorry. (368)

The backdrop for Faulkner's shifts back and forth from sympathy to disgust with Bayard is the fecund, slumbering earth, which seems ultimately impervious to the depredations of men like him. But a note of uneasiness in the portrayal of Bayard's relation to the land anticipates the great split between horrified fascination and grudging awe of the fertile earth's enduring power on the one hand, and unambiguous delight in the idea of retreat into "wilderness" or backwoods on the other. Even though Narcissa has the last word, mistrust and blame accompany Faulkner's description of Bayard's settling into farming on his return from World War I. Behind this resentment lies the heroic soldier code that Bayard and his twin brother John had learned in boyhood from romantic stories of the Confederate Lost Cause. Bayard is furious that his brother had been able to adapt that heroism to modern war and die as an aviator in France, while he has failed and returned home to be trapped in "a smoldering hiatus" after being "so neatly tricked by earth, that ancient Delilah, that he was not aware that his locks were shorn" (194–95). Farming is exactly simultaneous and parallel to Bayard's marriage to Narcissa. In contrast to the domesticated earth that unmans Bayard, the wilderness allows the all-male MacCallum clan to live the frontier life of proud, active, untamed hunters. There Bayard flees just before his death, and in that archaic setting he can bask one last time in the primitive male freedom that defines wholeness in Faulkner's psychic economy.

In his next novel Faulkner catapulted into the fully modernist style and sensibility that define his most accomplished work. This was of course *The Sound and the Fury*, which moved him firmly into the landscape that he would cultivate for the rest of his life. While he often repeated the claim that the image of young Caddy Compson climbing the pear tree in muddy drawers was the original stimulus for the book, the affection he expressed for "his heart's darling" is significantly confused, mingling paternal and maternal tenderness with rueful eroticism in trying to describe his failed effort to tell her story. On one hand he felt he could most passionately capture her through her brothers' eyes (*FU* 1, 31–32, 77, 84). However tender these masculine passions may be, they are clearly erotic. She is the object of abject desire in the cases of Benjy and Quentin, who are utterly dependent on her love, and consuming hatred in the case of Jason. On the other hand, Faulkner also said that the tenderness he felt for the novel was like that of a mother who suffers grief and anguish but "loves the child who became the thief or murderer more than the one who became the priest" (*Lion* 244–46). This "motherly" devotion is also focused on the image of the little girl, but his references to crimes and failure could also apply to the adolescent and adult Caddy, whose sexual independence is construed as dishonor sufficient to doom her to promiscuity and alliance with a Nazi general in an appendix written some seventeen years after the original novel. Yet Faulkner has the elder Jason Compson himself say to Quentin that it is only men who take that kind of attitude toward women's sexuality, men who invented the idea of women's chastity and men who suffer its loss (71).

The whole enterprise of the novel is tangled in an erotic confusion of desire and loathing for an inaccessible and endlessly alluring female object seen in human terms through fleeting glimpses of Caddy, but figured also as Nature, as blossom and rain and trees, comfort and security for her needy brothers, but suffocating honeysuckle and grief when she begins to fulfill her reproductive destiny.[14] Caddy's muddy drawers resulted from the seven-year-old girl's innocent paddling in the stream that ran near her parents' house. Unlike the innocent tone of *Soldier's Pay*'s identification of woman's sexually active body to "a little silver water sweetly dividing," in *The Sound and the Fury* water is separate and equivocal in its associations with Caddy's body. The sensuously positive imagery in *Soldier's Pay* occurs in the mind of her lover who sits in the darkness hearing his watch ticking like an early version of Quentin Compson. But for little Caddy in the later novel, playing in the water and moist earth is already seen as misbehavior by her brothers and prefigures a pollution so profound that it destroys her entire family. She is at home in the flowing materiality of the water and earth and air, but her brothers cannot accept the full expression of this "essential" embodied feminine.

Benjy expresses Caddy's natural vitality most simply and directly. For him, experience is completely embodied, acutely registered by his senses. He is comforted by flowers, water, firelight, and food. But he senses emotional changes through smell, and he can smell death (21, 46). Faulkner said that the idiot child was only an animal who instinctively trusted Caddy's tenderness and love, and he bellowed when he felt the change in her that threatened them (*Lion* 246; *FU* 64). While emotionally true to the text, Faulkner's explanation omits the particular natural imagery of Benjy's thoughts about the comfort of his sister's presence: Caddy smells "like trees in the rain" (12; also 26, 28, 30, 45). While other characters have positive associations with natural smells,[15] Caddy is the crucial one whose smell of trees means freshness and life to him. The threatening change to which Faulkner refers is her ripening sexuality, and every expression of it sends Benjy into howls.

The earliest indication of this problem occurs when she is fourteen and has made herself up to be attractive to boys. Benjy smells the change in the perfume she is wearing, an aphrodisiac that blots out her innocent connection with natural things. When she bathes and thus purifies herself, she smells like trees again (25–26). The refrain, "She smelled like trees" is repeated again and again to indicate Caddy's prelapsarian loveliness as a contrast to the sexual involvement that destroys it.[16] Something is backwards here. Faulkner has taken away Caddy's natural smell for Benjy when she is fulfilling her bodily destiny as a woman, engaging in the sexuality that connects her with all the vitality of nature in its reproductive capacities. Caddy's brothers feel that her body must belong to them in a prelapsarian state that her sexual independence destroys.

Quentin is as physically sensitive and as dependent on Caddy as his simple brother, but because he is intellectually precocious, he understands Caddy's sexuality and its social consequences as Benjy cannot. Thus Quentin correctly associates the smells of "Nature's" reproductive energies with Caddy's sexual blossoming and with his own confused physical yearnings. Caddy's puberty and Quentin's coincide, and they share an awareness of their culture's prudishness. But while Caddy is defiant and actively embraces her "natural" physical destiny, Quentin retreats from his own sexuality in shame. Quentin jealously quarrels with Caddy when she begins consorting with "town squirts" and perhaps partly in retaliation experiments sexually with his sister's playmate Natalie. Significantly, this occurs in the barn with rain falling heavily outside and echoing through "the high sweet emptiness" above them. When Quentin looks up from this "dancing sitting down" to see Caddy standing with her hands on her hips in the doorway, he dismisses Natalie as "Cowface" and signals his shame by jumping into the hogwallow, covering himself with stinking excremental mud, and then rushing out to smear Caddy with the same filth (81–83). Their cooperative purification in the branch is a cleansing ritual repeated a few years later after Caddy's meeting with Dalton Ames. Quentin may be physically aroused at that later time when he offers to kill Caddy and himself with his knife beside the same stream—and Faulkner certainly fills the scene with sexual innuendo and double entendre—but Quentin never again asserts himself sexually in the novel. The same association of sexual coupling and swine that Quentin makes when he smears Caddy with muck recurs in his mind just before he kills himself (107), making it obvious that the very fact of sexual congress remains an earthy horror central to his self-destruction.

Since we see Caddy only through her brothers' eyes, we cannot know her thoughts about these events. But what Faulkner describes as the courage that led her to climb the pear tree at seven and discover the truth of her grandmother's death becomes a fierce sexual independence in adolescence. Her eager embrace of physical love fails only because the boys and men with whom she is involved are unworthy of her. They are cynical exploiters for whom she is only "a bitch" like all other women. Finally, however, the framer of the narrative may be complicit with their view. Faulkner has loaded the dice, however poignant his depiction of Caddy, and however tenderly her brothers Benjy and Quentin may love her.

He saw her from the beginning as doomed, through the image of her muddy drawers up in the pear tree. Five years after he completed the novel he wrote, "I saw that peaceful glinting of that branch was to become the dark harsh flowing of time sweeping her to where she could not return to comfort him, but that just separation, division, would not be enough, not far enough. It must sweep her into dishonor and shame too" ("Intro." 413). Why *must* this be Caddy's fate? It is because Faulkner sees the nature of women as corrupt, allied with decay and death at the heart of earth's teeming fecundity. He said in the same introductory essay that her mudstained drawers were so soiled "that [her] body, flesh, whose shame they symbolized and prophesied," could never be cleansed. Placed beside all the repetitions of images of Caddy in the water, this is the key to what he calls her courage. It is an expression of a "natural" energy immersed in the dizzying flow of the embodied world, just as her body is immersed in the flowing water of the branch, but *not* "the dark, harsh flowing of time" that Faulkner claimed it signified ("Intro." 413–14). It should be no surprise that Quentin's passionate memories of Caddy should so often be visions of her body immersed in the natural liquids that signify both corruption and cleansing, fecundity and decay, and are all part of the teeming physical world that overwhelms him and sends him to his death.

> I was running in the gray darkness it smelled of rain and all flower scents the damp warm air released and crickets sawing away in the grass pacing me with a small travelling island of silence . . . I ran down the hill in that vacuum of crickets like a breath traveling across a mirror she was lying in the water her head on the sand spit the water flowing about her hips there was a little more light in the water her skirt half saturated flopped along her flanks to the waters motion in heavy ripples going nowhere renewed themselves of their own movement I stood on the bank I could smell the honeysuckle on the water gap the air seemed to drizzle with honeysuckle and with the rasping of crickets a substance you could feel on the flesh (91, no punctuation in the original)

This is the night when Caddy goes to meet Dalton Ames after Quentin's frantic efforts to dissuade her. His sexual hysteria rises to a crescendo expressed by the frantic repetition of his sense of drowning in or being smothered by the smell of honeysuckle. Even the water of the branch flows together with the cloying fragrance in a kind of synaesthesia that makes the water the color of honeysuckle. When he throws himself to the ground, his embrace of the earth provides a kind of alternative sexual union that releases him from participation in the riot of reproductive energy all around him (94–95). Perhaps his suicide, lapped in the "caverns and grottoes of the sea tumbling peacefully to the wavering tides" is just a more complete enactment of the same union with the mindless flow of the oppressive cruel, relentless Mother Nature he cannot endure as a sentient man. No Compson man in *The Sound and the Fury* seems able to endure the independent exercise of what Caddy represents: Benjy is grief-stricken even in his simplicity (after all, he is one of Nature's Naturals), Quentin's father drinks himself to death, and Jason is practically paralyzed with vindictive rage. Mr. Compson has instructed his son that the mysteries of women's sexuality boil down to "periodical filth between two moons balanced" (78), and Quentin can never accept the messy fact of bodily cycles that no stream, however limpid, can wash away.

Nature in *The Sound and the Fury* is the same thing as "the dark, harsh flowing of time," the abnegation of heroic possibility. Women are its human representatives and men's destroyers. We have come a long way from Thoreau's cheerful assertion that "Time is but the stream I go a-fishing in" (66). But at the same time we are still close to the Sumerian Gilgamesh's lament when he saw the bodies of the dead floating in the river: "Man, the tallest, cannot reach to heaven, / Man, the widest, cannot cover the earth" (Kramer 177).

The treatment of Joe Christmas's sexuality in *Light in August* provides a far more extreme expression of masculine revulsion at menstruation and women's bodies in general, which Gail Mortimer has called Manichaean (22). His first guilt and his fear of Negro parentage are associated with the body and lovemaking of an orphanage dietician in whose closet he has been engaging in the forbidden act of eating toothpaste. Sweet food and sex and the fragrance of women's clothes are all tangled up together in his mind with the punishment he receives when caught. All his later sexual experience is tainted by the experience: "[h]enceforth womanhood, food, and sexuality will be joined with his racial obsession in a single knot of fear, shame, guilt, and resentment" (Bleikasten 291). Rather than participate in the gang rape of a Negro girl, which would have been his sexual initiation, Joe kills a sheep and paddles his hands in its blood. For him, this is the female body: bestial, bloody, foul, and dead. His later relations with Barbara Allen and Joana Burden develop the sense of pollution and horror to a crescendo that ends in the butchery of the latter. And food is "women's muck," dangerous and degrading (Bleikasten 290–93). Joe is a pathological example of Julia Kristeva's abject subject and Kaja Silverman's feminized male masochist, finally achieving a blissful ejaculation of blood when castrated by the fascist ex-soldier Percy Grimm.[17]

With *Absalom, Absalom!* Faulkner returns to the doomed southern families he had treated in *Flags in the Dust* and *The Sound and the Fury*, to begin a deeper explanation of their historical roots. Once again Quentin Compson serves as the consciousness in which the drama is most trenchantly played out, but this time the principal cause of downfall is a man rather than female sexuality. *Absalom, Absalom!* is a southern creation myth that might remind us faintly of Cather's heroic construction in *O Pioneers!* But Thomas Sutpen is a very different kind of "hero" than Alexandra Bergson. He is at once monstrous and tragic, an elusive figure at the heart of a mystery whose unraveling questions both the concept of the hero and the very meaning of history. The conflicting voices that seek to construct the "real" Thomas Sutpen provide only a shifting ground of evidence for an understanding of his failure, and through him, that of the South. As Eric Sundquist has suggested, some of this confusion may stem from Faulkner's own reluctance or inability to confront the problems represented by his quintessential southern patriarch and the myth of the Lost Cause: "The numerous analogies and metaphors of design and reconstruction that pervade the novel refer at once to Sutpen's and to Faulkner's, each of them the 'sole owner and proprietor' and, more significantly, the 'father' of a vast domain on the edge of collapse. In Faulkner's case, the 'final defeat' represents both the agony of literary composition and the historical trauma with which it is intimately involved" (124). Enough "facts" are nevertheless provided by witnesses of Sutpen's actions—even if some testimony is second- or third-hand—to establish two centrally opposed versions of Thomas Sutpen's life.

Miss Rosa Coldfield's version is an outraged feminine picture of a demon who assaults the land in a satanic parody of creation stories in Hesiod and Genesis.

Out of quiet thunderclap he would abrupt (man-horse-demon) upon a scene peaceful and decorous as a schoolprize water color, faint sulphur-reek still in hair clothes and beard, with grouped behind him his band of wild niggers like beasts half tamed to walk upright like men, in attitudes wild and reposed. . . .

Then in the long unamaze Quentin seemed to watch them overrun suddenly the hundred square miles of tranquil and astonished earth and drag house and formal gardens violently out of the soundless Nothing . . . creating Sutpen's Hundred, the *Be Sutpen's Hundred* like the oldentime *Be Light*. (8–9)

In Rosa Coldfield's words, Sutpen "tore violently a plantation" out of the land in a kind of rape of the wilderness. Quentin is annoyed to be burdened with her notion that "the land of the earth . . . got tired of him at last and turned and destroyed him" (12). She has identified her own abuse by Sutpen with that of the implicitly feminine land, imagining that a power within Nature has avenged this gendered injustice. As we have seen, Faulkner agreed with this interpretation on at least one occasion. Quentin's uneasiness surely grows from his realization that Miss Rosa feminizes him by seeking to make him the receptacle of her vision; as Minrose Gwin suggests, "he simply cannot bring himself to participate in Rosa's killing of the masculine" in her tale of Sutpen's depredations (106). The text of the novel thus offers not Rosa's own words but instead Quentin's masculinized rephrasing of her story, related in annoyance to his father. The result is yet another version of the Euramerican construction of the "empty wilderness" awaiting the shaping hand of patriarchal civilization, but even Quentin's admiring image of Sutpen as creator seems ironic in its hyperbole, colored by Miss Rosa's sense that such a presumption denies the independent being of the land and its teeming life.

The fully sympathetic male view of Sutpen that comes down through Quentin's father and grandfather (apparently the only friend and confidant of the bold pioneer) attributes the collapse of Sutpen's grand design to innocence—a kind of backwoods Horatio Alger naïveté (220). Enough has been written about his moral failure in recapitulating the very system of injustice that had so deeply humiliated him as a fourteen-year-old boy. What interests me more is the pattern revealed by the biographical facts Quentin's grandfather told his father and the kind of story they have formed in Jason Compson's mind. We cannot know how much of this interpretation came from Sutpen himself or how much came from the grandfather who actually knew Sutpen and witnessed some of the events. But certainly Jason's biography results from a collective masculine narrative construction that is sympathetic to Thomas Sutpen's heroic effort to raise himself from poverty.

As Jason Compson describes it, Sutpen's childhood was one of Arcadian innocence on the crudely egalitarian frontier, up in the Appalachian Mountains where "the land belonged to anybody and everybody." As this backwoods paradise is defined, however, access to the land is contested and unequal. White men and boys are the "anybody and everybody" Mr. Compson has in mind, "who hunted or lay before the fire on the floor while the women and older girls stepped back and forth across them to reach the fire to cook" and "the only colored people were Indians and you only looked down at them over your rifle sights" (221). With women to attend to their domestic needs and only Indians to push out of the way (or as "colored" enemies), white men were comfortable and free, hunting for their food and needing only whiskey, a gun, and a simple log cabin. "So he didn't even know there was a country all divided and fixed and neat with a people living on it all divided and fixed and neat *because of what color their skins happened to be and what they happened to own, and where a certain few men not only had the power of life and death and barter and sale over others*," but also the power to force others to serve their simplest needs (221–22, my emphasis).

When Sutpen is rudely awakened from this prelapsarian dream he is about the same crucial age—thirteen or fourteen—as Caddy Compson when her "fall" occurs, but instead of being caused by sexuality, his awakening begins with the death of his mother, which unmoors the family and sends them sliding back down the mountains into the corrupt civilization from which only the mother's energy had freed them (223). The loss of his biological mother, in other words, causes his loss of his "innocent," unconscious unity with Mother Wilderness. The boy's response to the deep social humiliation he encounters when insulted by a plantation slave is regression—escape to a womblike retreat in the woods, a kind of cave into which he crawls and where he leans against symbolically "uptorn roots" (Pikoulis 91) to think out the meaning of his experience. The notion of Sutpen's "innocence" is belied by his decision to avenge himself by beating the Virginia planters at their own game. Such complicity with racial injustice was already present in the backwoods contempt for "colored people" and "Indians" we saw above. To accomplish his design Sutpen recreates himself twice, descending into primal chaos figured in the first instance as Haiti, and after the failure of that attempt, in the Mississippi wilderness. Faulkner describes the landscape of Haiti in terms that make it stand for a social and evolutionary "fact" as well as a geographical one, as if racial differences and the political and ethical problems that Faulkner sees inextricably involved with race were part of the physical reality of the earth and the evolution of life upon it. Haiti is a strange and violent nether world,

> which was the halfway point between what we call the jungle and what we call civilization, halfway between the dark inscrutable continent from which the black blood, the black bones and flesh and thinking and remembering and hopes and desires, was ravished by violence, and the cold known land to which it was doomed, the civilized land and people which had expelled some of its own blood and thinking and desires that had become too crass to be faced and borne longer, and set it homeless and desperate on the lonely ocean—(250–51)

Presumably Faulkner means here to contrast Africa (jungle) with England (civilization) as the extreme landscapes and climates that Haiti mediates. But the island becomes an emblem of the social and political tensions caused by the mingling of African and northern European races, and that in turn is meant to suggest some terrible truth about the earth itself.

As a young overseer on a sugar plantation, Sutpen has begun the process of recreating himself, but he retains an innocent trust in Nature from his wilderness boyhood, which remains a disabling ignorance until almost the end of the novel. He rides over the plantation just before a slave revolt, "not knowing that what he rode upon was a volcano, hearing the air tremble and throb at night with the drums and the chanting and not knowing that it was the heart of the earth itself he heard, who believed (Grandfather said) that earth was kind and gentle and that darkness was merely something you saw, or could not see in" (251). The heart of this Faulknerian darkness is personified by primitive blacks, as it is in Conrad, and it is in fighting them single-handedly that Sutpen proves his mettle and earns his first fortune. He is able to subdue the slave revolt when all seems lost because he goes out alone into the night and confronts primitive darkness with his own body, triumphing perhaps because in him the slaves at last recognized "an indomitable spirit which should have come from the same primary fire which theirs came from" (254). For this reason Sutpen continues to stage trials by combat between himself and his slaves later in Mississippi (28–30, 253), reenacting his victory over savage men and the violent spirit of the land to prove his right to dominate them. Perhaps we should think of him as one of Robert Bly's Wild Men, playing out the male myth of combat and then bonding with a personification of Nature—or Green Man—like Gilgamesh's Enkidu or the Grimms' Iron Hans, who links him with Nature's power but also signals his heroic sovereignty.

In the "tainted" blood of Sutpen's Haitian wife, Faulkner echoes Charlotte Brontë's conflation of African body with femininity, primal violence, and disaster in Edward Rochester's Jamaican wife of *Jane Eyre*. But in Faulkner's story it is the male Thomas Sutpen who *actively* participates in the violence and darkness of the Haitian slave revolt. The daughter of the plantation owner whom he wins to wife by these acts is blamed for the collapse of his ambitions, but her presumed African heritage is only passive. Given the landscape imagery Faulkner has set up for this episode, the debased wife stands for the land and wealth Sutpen earned by his heroism, and both are corrupted by slavery and miscegenation. Involvement in such an environment infects Thomas Sutpen, and the disease smoulders in him only to break out again and destroy him later. When he goes to Mississippi to try again, in the symbolic terms of the myth Jason Compson passes down to Quentin, he goes armed more appropriately than he had been in Haiti. That is, he takes savage allies—the "wild niggers" who represent the bond he made with "primal fire" during his testing there. The Mississippi landscape where he makes his second attempt at rebirth is figured as a tangled jungle where he and the wild men literally immerse themselves, returning to primal slime in order to emerge from it thickly coated with mud and engineer their own evolution into civilization. Over a period of several years he "dragged house and gardens out of the virgin swamp" (40), using the very materials of the wilderness for brick and board. This process is one of separation and control so that Sutpen gains the illusion that he has transcended the land and become its god. Continuing his evolution upward toward "higher" forms of life, he eventually metamorphoses into a white man of property with a "pure white" wife and two unsullied Caucasian children.

But Sutpen's real marriage has been his violent foray into the "virgin" wilderness from which he has torn his plantation. That reshaped landscape is his truest offspring, molded by his own hands from the earth's body. The human drama of miscegenation, incest, and betrayal that is the novel's explicit subject is only an allegory of the deeper dynamic of the landscape's revenge, by which Charles Bon is a product of the seething Haitian earth that his father entered and bonded himself to but later tried to repudiate. Bon's arrival at Sutpen's Hundred is a reassertion of his father's primal bond with violence, night, and volcanic earth, which Faulkner has coded as African flesh throughout *Absalom, Absalom!*

In *Go Down, Moses*, his next effort to confront these historical problems, it seems clear that Thomas Sutpen's "disease" still poisons the American South and by extension the whole nation. Faulkner's connection of miscegenation and doom with the landscape derives, as we saw earlier, from his investment in the archaic analogy between women and earth as reproductive bodies and the notion voiced again and again through his male characters, that women have a special affinity for evil. Philip Fisher has shown in *Hard Facts* how Cooper and other writers of historical fiction used such tricks to create slippages from one logical track to another and thus disguise and evade the responsibility of white men for the displacement of another people on the land and the ravishing of an existing ecosystem for their own gain. Faulkner writes his way toward an understanding of this process in *Go Down, Moses*, and he comes very close to exposing it totally.

Isaac McCaslin's pastoral childhood is more blessed than Thomas Sutpen's, with the Indian Sam Fathers presiding over initiation rituals that unite him with the holy wilderness in the manner of prelapsarian tribal man. R. W. B. Lewis rhapsodizes about "The Bear," calling it a New Testament succeeding the gloomy Old Testament atmosphere of the earlier novels and stories, "Faulkner's first sustained venture towards the more hopeful and liberated world after the Incarnation" (188). But it seems rather a failed venture when taken in the context of the whole of *Go Down, Moses*, as many recent commentators have remarked.[18] Ike McCaslin's old age does not fulfill the promise of his youth, and the Incarnation of which Lewis speaks is only a last visitation of a power that has almost completely faded away by the end of "The Bear." Nevertheless, the novella is a powerful retelling of an archetypal masculine initiation story with particularly resonant American features.[19] Faulkner has complicated and ironized this traditional American story by continuing to tie human moral failure into Nature's energies and "her" fate at men's hands. He has also quite consciously portrayed Ike McCaslin's failure to atone for his grandfather's sins in "Delta Autumn," setting the crucial event in a degraded landscape where there is virtually no more Big Woods and the men who hunt are not worthy of the animals they pursue. The archaic code of manly honor that Sam Fathers had taught Ike will die with him, and even it was insufficient to teach him to behave responsibly.

"The Old People" sets the stage for "The Bear" by describing the hunting society into which Ike is introduced and the primitive heritage he adopts from his Indian teacher and spiritual father. Sam Fathers represents both the landscape and the Chickasaw and African peoples who are closer to its primary essence than any white man could ever be (166–68). Faulkner makes much of the noble blood of chieftains that Sam inherited from both parents but portrays him as "himself his own battleground, the scene of his own vanquishment and the mausoleum of his defeat" (168) because he has been betrayed, as the land has also, by the corrupt influence of Europeans and the bondage they have imposed. What is particularly interesting, however, is the way Faulkner slides the responsibility for this taint onto Sam's slave mother. He has spent several pages detailing the murderous ambition of Sam's father Chief Ikkemotubbe and his casual sale to a Negro slave of the quadroon woman pregnant with his son. Yet it is the mother who Faulkner claims has betrayed the son; Sam Fathers is "not wilfully betrayed by his mother, but betrayed by her all the same, who had bequeathed him not only the blood of slaves but even a little of the very blood which had enslaved it" (168). Once again, men are the agents of sin in Faulkner's universe, but women—trapped though they may be in a masculine network of power and exchange—are to blame. Like women, the inert land is also culpable, as we earlier saw in the life of Bayard Sartoris, and as we shall see Faulkner imply very subtly in "The Bear." He treats Ike's wife as a sort of landscape, and then paints her as a seductress, an Eve who uses sex to make him break his word and lie about his plans to deny his birthright. By such logic the act of love becomes the act of claiming the land.

But at the beginning of "The Bear," Ike seems a fortunate boy who is following in the steps of Cooper's Natty Bumppo, led by a Good Indian into a ritual that returns him to prelapsarian harmony with wild Nature. At ten, he "entered his novitiate to the true wilderness with Sam beside him," and he felt the wild landscape open to admit them and then close around them like an enormous vulva. Commentators as far back as R. W. B. Lewis have pointed to the imagery of return to primal womb here (199), and Faulkner tells us explicitly that Ike remembers feeling as if "he was witnessing his own birth" (195). Then begins an education of some five or six years that prepares him for his vocation. "If Sam Fathers had been his mentor and the backyard rabbits and squirrels his kindergarten, then the wilderness the old bear ran was his college and the old male bear itself, so long unwifed and childless as to have become its own ungendered progenitor, was his *alma mater*" (210, my emphasis).

Here we find the crux of Faulkner's confusion in figuring the landscape: in spite of the bear's supposed maleness or ungendered self-begetting, he also has maternal qualities, as R. W. B. Lewis pointed out long ago (194, 200). *Alma mater* means nourishing mother in Latin, and while it could be considered a dead metaphor used as a synonym for college, there are many other places in the story where the essentially feminine nature of the bear—and the wilderness whose spirit it represents—unmistakably breathes through the masculine qualities Faulkner tries to project upon the landscape. For a start we should remember that Ike is himself the product of the accidental but irrevocably entrapping encounter in the story "Was" between Theophilus McCaslin and a woman whom the narrative humorously conflates with both the landscape and a bear. Sophonsiba Beauchamp's family name means beautiful field (French *beau, champ*), and her brother Hubert explains his hapless friend's responsibility to marry her in terms of a bear hunt: "You came into bear-country of your own free will and accord. . . . You had to crawl into the den and lay down by the bear. And whether you did or didn't know the bear was in it dont make any difference. . . . Yes, sir. She's got you, 'Filus, and you know it" (22–23).

A more sensual bedroom scene is conjured in the forest setting where Ike McCaslin recognizes at age ten the taste of fear in the presence of the bear, "as a boy, a youth, recognizes the existence of love and passion and experience which is his heritage but not yet his patrimony, from entering by chance the presence or perhaps even merely the bedroom of a woman who has loved and been loved by many men" (204). So the bear's wilderness glade is the fearfully exhilarating realm of the erotic feminine, and Ike's masculine heritage is defined as sexual union with the animal who personifies the land.

This idea reaches a kind of fruition in a passage describing Ike's final visit to the woods after the climactic killing of the bear and the accompanying deaths of Sam Fathers and the dog Lion, all signaling the death of the wilderness. This is one last peaceful interlude before Ike leaves adolescence—significantly also just before a lumber company arrives to cut the forest down. Ike wanders musing through its green summer loveliness, thinking that this timeless place is his true mother, and indeed all womanhood for him: "summer, and fall, and snow, and wet and saprife spring in their ordered immortal sequence, the deathless and immemorial phases of the mother who had shaped him if any had toward the man he almost was . . . and he would marry some day . . . but still the woods would be his mistress and his wife" (326).

Such loyalty to Mother Nature touches familiar chords, but it finally represents a retreat from responsibility, as many have observed (Stewart, Claridge, McGee). Faulkner underlines the futility of seeking sanctuary in the embrace of this female wilderness with the irony of its impending destruction by the logging company. David Stewart has sourly remarked that if Ike really cared about the wilderness, he would have joined a conservation organization (216–17), and Faulkner himself admitted the inadequacy of Ike's passive behavior (*FU*, 246).

In the climactic ledger scene when Ike repudiates his inheritance, the text describes him and his cousin McCaslin Edmonds as "juxtaposed and alien now to each other against their ravaged patrimony, the dark and ravaged fatherland still prone and panting from its etherless operation" (298). Presumably the operation was its rape by settlers and planters such as Thomas Sutpen and Ike's grandfather Lucius Quintus Carothers McCaslin, for the narrative goes on to define the cursed landscape as "that whole edifice intricate and complex and founded upon injustice and erected by ruthless rapacity and carried on even yet with at times downright savagery not only to the human beings but the valuable animals too" (298), and as indicated elsewhere, rapacity toward the very earth gouged and eroded by the destruction of the Delta forests and the relentless planting of cotton. All of Faulkner's previous practice has established a context for this passage that denies Ike's reference to the landscape as a "fatherland." It is clearly a motherland whose defilement is also implied in the famous passage from Keats's "Ode on a Grecian Urn" which McCaslin Edmonds uses in trying to link Ike's respect for the bear to his relationship to the farmland he has inherited from his father and grandfather. Faulkner has already eroticized this patrimony and conflated it with the bear hunt, as we saw in the earlier passage about the forest glade and taste of fear. Thus the crucial passage from Keats's description of the painted urn should be read as only one more attempt to reinforce the equation of land/bear/erotic feminine body.

Although, as Sundquist remarks, the whole ledger section describing Ike's repudiation is obscured "in a cloud of loose ends and illogical argument" (137), I think that confusion merely expresses the difficulties through which Faulkner was working his way and which he did finally clarify at the end of "Delta Autumn." The narrative enacts the process of struggling toward an understanding. And Ike is the vehicle for Faulkner's journey through his own psychic Delta of tangled emotions and metaphoric habits. Keats's "Ode" was a poem Faulkner loved and one to which he referred many times in previous fiction (Bleikasten 9, 43, 104, 280). It encapsulates much of the metaphoric tradition he inherited from English literature, quite typically personifying the object of desire and art in feminine terms. As he struggles to articulate Ike's idealism, Faulkner brings the gendered terms and consequences of the tradition into the open, making its problematic nature much more obvious through Ike's questioning of McCaslin Edmonds's paternal authority and the emblematic text.

The opening line of Keats's "Ode on a Grecian Urn" addresses the vase as a "still unravished bride of quietness" in contrast to the arrested scene of rape painted on "her" sides. "What men or gods are these? What maidens loath!" exclaims the poet. "What mad pursuit? What struggle to escape?" The poem seeks to fix the reader's gaze upon an idealized "mad ecstasy" of sexual pursuit captured in the eternal beauty of art (288–89). Faulkner critics have offered useful explanations of the complex symbolic functions served by McCaslin's quotation from the poem but have not really focused on the problem of rape in relation to the wilderness and its denizens.[20] McCaslin Edmonds chooses Keats's image for "beauty and truth" as an analogue to the bear hunt, uncomprehending that Ike's determination not to participate in the injustice and violence of his heritage is the same impulse that kept him from killing Old Ben when he had the chance. "She cannot fade, though thou has not thy bliss," intones McCaslin, "Forever wilt thou love, and she be fair" (GDM 297). He seems not to notice that this "love," aestheticized into a Platonic ideal, is nothing more than lust. Bliss for the poet would derive from sexual assault, though McCaslin adapts it to refer to blood lust. The maiden's (or

bear's) reluctance is not even an issue. Ike fails to see the connection between the girl and the bear, instead drifting off into a reverie in which
the bear endures forever in the wilderness. We know, however, as do both
Ike and McCaslin at the time of this conversation, that the bear is dead
and the wilderness almost gone. If we have been attentive readers, we
must see that in the novel's semiotic terms, an enormous feminine vastness has been devastated, and no amount of romantic poetry can bring it
back. In fact, Faulkner demonstrates, perhaps inadvertently here, that
romantic formulations like Keats's "Ode on a Grecian Urn" function to
aestheticize acts of rapacity that destroy the object of desire.

Remarkable similarities exist between the story's main shape and the
Gilgamesh epic—a wild man mediator between the prince and the forest, male bonding that substitutes for alliances with women, the magical
beast who is the holy forest's guardian and who is associated with feminine powers at the heart of nature, the killing of the beast in a context of
great ambivalence, the resulting destruction of the forest and death of
the wild man guide, a long period of grief and renunciation, and an un-
shakable doom for the protagonist. Faulkner's atavistic yearnings have
drawn him back into patterns of the earliest epic tales of uneasy combat
with the landscape and its life, patterns of masculine thought that are at
least five thousand years old.[21] But Faulkner forced himself to continue
Ike McCaslin's life into adulthood and old age before he completed the
narrative line of *Go Down, Moses*. Isaac McCaslin attempts to enter the
"new country" of marriage and social responsibility, founders on its
shores, and lives out a sterile compromise. Faulkner makes Ike's ultimate
failure very clear in "Delta Autumn," and thus he writes his way into a
twentieth-century renunciation of archaic yearnings.

Marriage for Ike McCaslin means entry into a new landscape of desire
and promise and ultimate betrayal. At first Faulkner defines it in positive
terms: "it was the new country, his heritage too as it was the heritage of
all, out of the earth, beyond the earth yet of the earth because his too was
of the earth's long chronicle, his too because each must share with another
in order to come into it" (311). But Ike is surprised by his new wife's demand that the availability of her body be contingent upon his claiming
the farm that he had tried to repudiate. In the climactic lovemaking scene
that determines Ike's married fate, Faulkner equates the land with his
wife's body in an eternal feminine "composite of all woman-flesh since
man that ever of its own will reclined on its back and opened" (314).

"Promise," she whispers. "The farm." Ike's chorus of "No, . . . No, . . . No, I tell you. I wont. I cant. Never," is punctuated by his interior monologue on the superior wisdom of women, but when he finally capitulates and says "Yes," he thinks, "*She is lost. She was born lost. We were all born lost.*" His acceptance of her demand—that he take his inherited land as he takes her body—is the acceptance of original sin from the temptress Eve, producing a transcendent sexual ecstasy that utterly exhausts him: "it was like nothing he had ever dreamed, let alone heard in mere man-talking until after a no-time he returned and lay spent on the insatiate immemorial beach" (314–15). Isaac McCaslin has violated his pledge of renunciation, but his wife knows he did not mean to do so. Thus no child can come from their union, and she will never again offer herself to him. The rhetorical structure of the story continues the biblical tradition of associating all guilt with the feminine, for the final section of "The Bear," coming immediately after the lovemaking scene, is a flashback to Ike's last visit to the Big Woods on the eve of their destruction by the logging company. A causal connection is suggested by this anachronistic juxtaposition; feminine sexuality seems to lead to destruction of the Delta Eden where Ike has spent his charmed boyhood. The real culprit, Major de Spain—Civil War hero and leader of the yearly hunting ritual—has been replaced by authorial sleight of hand.

In "Delta Autumn," the penultimate story of *Go Down, Moses,* Isaac McCaslin implicates himself in his grandfather's sins and betrays a kinship with Thomas Sutpen, in spite of the weight of an ethical self-consciousness that anticipates environmental values of a much later generation. While "The Bear" might be read as another version of the American myth of pastoral escape through primitive male initiation rituals, with "Delta Autumn" Faulkner has written himself and Isaac McCaslin into the demystified present, where men have to face what they have historically done to the land and its inhabitants. Even in Ike's boyhood hunting years the wilderness is described by the narrative as "doomed," whatever mythic power might also be ascribed to it. And we have seen how the metaphoric network used to connect the disparate thematic materials of "The Old People" and "The Bear" feminizes the landscape and indicates that it has been abused in many respects the way women and African-Americans and Indians have been abused. In "Delta Autumn" Faulkner presents Ike's final dilemma in a form that combines all of these victims into a woman and child who are, in Diane Roberts's words, "the embodied evidence of the crimes of southern history" (87). This is an ambush in the archaic Greek sense—from a *lochos* or hidden wooded place like the one from which Chronos leaped to castrate his father Uranos, metaphorically the place of childbirth (Liddell and Scott 478–79). Suddenly a "castrating woman" appears with the son who will accomplish her revenge. Her baby gives the lie to the pretense of McCaslin honor and, by extension, white male honor. She also gives the lie to the myth of women as castrators, entrappers, and betrayers. She is fertile proof of male sexual potency, she is independent of Roth's and Ike's control, and she is proudly and defiantly true to her agreement with Roth that she will make no claim on his life. Like the Chronos of Hesiod's *Theogony* and all the other Indo-European mythic fathers who fear their offspring (Puhvel 21–32, 45–67), Ike and Roth know that women exercise the untidy fecundity at the heart of life on the land. The "castration" they fear is this continuing cycle of bodily life that forces old Ike and his cowardly cousin to see the consequences of their actions. The McCaslin family continues, the untidy mingling of forms and substances, genders and races, goes on and on. And the McCaslin men are still actively involved in it.

In this story Faulkner has taken pains to visually engrave the archaic icon of the female genitalia upon the Delta landscape by taking the place name literally. He uses the inverted triangle familiar from paleolithic and neolithic fertility religion, calling it "this inverted-apex, this $\bigtriangledown$-shaped section of earth between hills and River . . . arrested in one tremendous density of brooding and inscrutable impenetrability at the ultimate funnelling tip" (343). Of course this landscape has been penetrated, as we read in the earlier sections of *Go Down, Moses*, and the taming process seems to have been necessary to release its fecundity for human use, "as if man had to marry his planting to the wilderness in order to conquer it" ("Delta Autumn" 342). The result is "rich black land, imponderable and vast, fecund up to the very doorsteps of the negroes who worked it and of the white men who owned it"(340). This description carries obvious racial overtones.

When the young woman appears at the all-male hunting camp with her and Roth Edmonds's illegitimate baby, Ike refuses to accept his family responsibility to her. Her skin is light, but she turns out to be his cousin from the mixed-blood Beauchamp side of his family, a descendant of his grandfather's miscegenation and incest. The baby boy is the fusion of the white and African-American branches of the family, since Roth

Edmonds is the sole remaining "white" descendant of the McCaslin patriarch. Ike desperately asserts that racial equality can only come in a thousand or two thousand years and that she should go back "up North" and marry a man of her "own race." This is a ridiculous moral retreat whose prevarications Faulkner has anticipated in a revealing syntactic slippage just previously, during Ike's musings on the old subject of his rejection of his inheritance. He remembers his first blooding by Sam Fathers and the code of humility and reverence for the wild creatures he slew:

> *I slew you; my bearing must not shame your quitting life. My conduct forever onward must become your death*; marking him for that and for more than that: that day and himself and McCaslin juxtaposed not against the wilderness but against the tamed land, the old wrong and shame itself, in repudiation and denial at least of the land and the wrong and shame even if he couldn't cure the wrong and eradicate the shame. (351)

Ike's sense of this ancient code of honor slides into the renunciation scene in which he and his cousin are defined in opposition to ("against") the tamed landscape, which is renamed by an appositive identifying it with the injustice and shame enacted upon it. Then the sentence's syntax slips over further into the abstract language of moral trespass, assuming that the object has become the injustice that can then be repudiated. The point is summarized in the phrase "the land and the wrong and shame" that Ike believed he repudiated at the age of twenty-one. A few lines later Ike's memory returns to the crucial lovemaking scene and juxtaposes his wife and himself against "that same land, that same wrong and shame" (351).

In spite of his acute awareness of the guilt and shame he has designed his life to expiate, he fails the ultimate test when his young female cousin confronts him. He sits defeated and bleary-eyed in a huddle of blankets as "she blazed silently down at him. . . . 'Old man,' she said, 'have you lived so long and forgotten so much that you dont remember anything you ever knew or felt or even heard about love?'" (363). She has the last, withering, word. Ike is left to recognize his and his fellows' failure, which has destroyed the pastoral dream. "No wonder the ruined woods I used to know dont cry for retribution! he thought: The people who have destroyed it will accomplish its revenge" (364).

She knew from him that what people ate in the world was earth, river, wildness and litheness, fire and ashes. People took the fresh death and the hot fire into their mouths and got their own life.
EUDORA WELTY, "At the Landing"

CHAPTER 6

Eudora Welty's Sacramental Vision

Eudora Welty was born only twelve years after William Faulkner and has spent her life in the same Mississippi landscape of hills and wide alluvial bottomland that nourished both their talents. But Welty's fictional evocations of that world have a radically different aura from Faulkner's. While the thick smell of honeysuckle, the heat, the rich Delta soil, the "musing, inattentive, myriad, eternal, green" (*GDM* 322) tangle of woodland are both awesome and horrifying for Faulkner's characters, that environment means pleasure, ease, delight, and intimacy in Welty's fiction. The differences can be seen most clearly in the contrast between "Delta Autumn" and *Delta Wedding*, and it could even be argued that Welty's novel is an answer to the bleak fable of masculine exhaustion defined by Ike McCaslin's apocalyptic vision of social chaos and moral bankruptcy. Both works were written against the backdrop of World War II, in counterpoint to war and the heroic code it justifies. While Faulkner remained deeply invested in that code, even to the point of trying to enlist (Blotner 418, 425), Welty clearly rejected it. Her novel is a celebratory epithalamion meant to serve as an antidote to the horror of military violence that was psychologically devastating a man she loved and endangering the lives of her brothers and male friends. For Isaac McCaslin, Hitler is only "one Austrian paper-hanger" lumped together with other enemies of the South like Roosevelt and Willkie, whom decent men will fight in defense of women and children and their land (338–39).

Defending one's homeland in war is an important activity on a par with hunting in "Delta Autumn." But Welty's plantation world of Shellmound has been deeply scarred by the Civil War and then by World War I in which family hero Denis Fairchild has been killed and his successor and brother George wounded both physically and psychically. These brothers dialogically counter Faulkner's John and Bayard Sartoris of *Flags in the Dust,* who also fought in that war, with the elder killed and the younger crippled by his own failure to achieve martyrdom. Sartoris martial heroism—and indeed the honor of all of Faulkner's protagonists—is a continuation of the ancient masculine code we saw in *Gilgamesh* and Euripides' *Bacchae*, defining itself in violent opposition to the landscape and to "feminine" forces of reproduction that nourish its life. Welty's Delta world by contrast is centered in the consciousness of women whose existence is defined in harmony with those forces. The landscapes of *Delta Wedding* flow right in the open doors and windows of Shellmound Plantation, just as family and community flow in and out into gardens, fields, and bayous in a pulsing continuum. Welty was just as conscious of the ancient erotic connotations of the name and shape of the Delta as Faulkner was, but for her they were a cause for affirmation rather than recoil. She found in the European pastoral tradition and in fertility myths of Greece and Rome and northern European fairy tales the means for shaping affirmations of this physical world.[1] But Eudora Welty did not begin her career with the profound sense of the sensuous interconnectedness of land, plants, creatures, and weathers that we encounter in *Delta Wedding*. She began with a sense of the power of vital forces but also some revulsion and uncertainty, as her first short story collection reveals.

A Curtain of Green is the result of Welty's apprenticeship as a Mississippi writer, including a wide range of early experiments in fictionalizing the native state she felt she only really began to discover in her travels as a WPA Junior Publicity Agent during the 1930s, after finishing her education in Wisconsin and New York. Neither her sheltered childhood in Jackson nor her two years at Mississippi State College for Women in Columbus had given her a sense of "the diversity and all the different regions of the state, or of the great poverty" (*Conversations* 155). Her WPA work provided the primarily human themes she developed through comedy, farce, and documentary realism in her early stories. The only two stories in the collection that begin to suggest her later absorption in the physical world of Mississippi are "A Memory" and the title story "A Curtain of Green."

The first of these is the odd recollection of revulsion experienced by a shy adolescent at a beach, when her infatuated daydreams are rudely interrupted by the grotesque antics of a family of fat swimmers. The story carefully establishes the narrator's sheltered position through a vegetable metaphor describing her parents, "who believed that I saw nothing in the world that was not strictly coaxed into place like a vine on our garden trellis to be presented to my eyes" (*CS* 75). She herself seeks to frame and control her vision by squaring her hands over her eyes, "finger tips touching, looking out by this device to see everything" (75). A warning is suggested in her daydreams about the boy she adores from a distance, through her memory of a nosebleed that once suddenly covered his handkerchief and hand with vermillion in Latin class.

Her reveries are assaulted by the rudely physical family cavorting nearby on the sand, and particularly by her vision of the central fat woman who seems coextensive with the dynamically shifting earth. "Fat hung upon her upper arms like an arrested earthslide on a hill. With the first motion she might make, I was afraid that she would slide down upon herself into a terrifying heap." The description of this unstable earthy substance comes to a focus on breasts like those belonging to the "Venuses" of Paleolithic cave art: "Her breasts hung heavy and widening like pears into her bathing suit" (78). Land, fruit, and female flesh are conflated into an image of horror for the pubescent observer. When the husband of this monstrous creature slowly covers her with sand and then pours it down inside her bathing suit between her breasts, the narrator is stunned to be included in his smiling gaze. She closes her eyes and tries to recapture the disembodied private romance of her daydream, but it is banished by the thudding sounds of fat bodies falling upon one another. When she opens her eyes, she sees the tableau inverted, with the fat woman now bending over the man, pulling down her bathing suit, "turning it outward, so that the lumps of mashed and folded sand came emptying out. I felt a peak of horror, as though her breasts themselves had turned to sand, as though they were of no importance at all and she did not care" (79). Control, gentility, stability, distance—all are banished by this messy, fleshy, earthy, unstable Rabelaisian display. That is Welty's point in writing the story. The reader is left to share the young narrator's feeling of victimization. The adult sexuality that awaits her is a mystery far other than she had imagined; it is linked with sudden flows of blood, loud noises, untidily violent rompings, frightening changes of form, ultimately dissolving into the shifting and mutable earth itself.

"A Curtain of Green" is posterotic, obsessed with the death and senseless violence lurking within the tumbled plant life and weather of the Mississippi landscape. Ostensibly set in the safely genteel domestic realm of middle-class ladies and gardening, the story is actually a meditation upon the uncontrollable and unknowable riot of energy surrounding all life. As the neighborhood women pause in their upstairs windows to await the explosion of summer's daily afternoon thunderstorm, they watch their newly widowed neighbor wander through her garden, "over-vigorous, disreputable, and heedless." Since her husband was killed by a falling chinaberry tree, Mrs. Larkin has retreated into "this slanting, tangled garden, more and more over-abundant and confusing" (CS 107). With tangled hair and wearing her husband's old overalls now turned green like the plants themselves, she seems to be merging into the vital element that caused her husband's death. Venturing further and further into the inchoate fertility of the garden does nothing to ease her desperation, however, and this afternoon in the tension before the storm, she turns with upraised hoe upon the bent back of the Negro boy who helps her.

> Such a head she could strike off, intentionally, so deeply did she
> know, from the effect of a man's danger and death, its cause in
> oblivion; and so helpless was she, too helpless to defy the workings

of accident, of life and death, of unaccountability. . . . Life and death, she thought, gripping the heavy hoe, life and death, which now meant nothing to her but which she was compelled continually to wield with both her hands, ceaselessly asking, Was it not possible to compensate? to punish? to protest? (110–11)

Mercy falls with the rain, whose beginning breaks her mood into gentle resignation; she falls fainting into the flowers as she will fall into bed at night. "It has come, she thought senselessly, her head lifting and her eyes looking without understanding at the sky which had begun to move, to fold nearer in softening, dissolving clouds." The motionless peace she anticipates is the only possible response to the incomprehensible abundance and violence of physical life; "against that which was inexhaustible, there was no defense" (111). As in "A Memory," the central character is finally overwhelmed by the mutability and power of the physical world, but this time she actively moves into and with it rather than attempting to preserve the illusion of detachment or control. Mrs. Larkin's one effort at violent assertion is only tentative, quickly dissolved by the falling rain.[2] The narrative's explicit concern with the plant world and natural forces of earth and sky stands in dramatic contrast to Faulkner's exploration of such settings. While Faulkner's heroes tremble or recoil before the feminine qualities they have projected upon the land, Welty's Mrs. Larkin wades right into the deathly tangle of plants and suffers the thunderstorm to let fall its rain upon her head. She seems a kind of female Lear, attempting to meet and join the forces that have destroyed her happiness.

With these stories Welty was feeling her way into an exploration of the mysteries that weave human lives together with plants and earth, water, weather, and other animals. She wrote to her agent Diarmuid Russell not long before the publication of *A Curtain of Green*:

Every evening when the sun is going down and it is cool enough to water the garden, and it is all quiet except for the locusts in great waves of sound, and I stand still in one place for a long time putting water on the plants, I feel something new—that is all I can say—as if my will went out of me, as if I had a stubbornness and it was melting. I had not meant to shut out any feeling that wanted to enter. —It is a real shock, because I had no idea that there had been in my life any rigidity or refusal of anything so profound, but the sensation is one of letting in for the first time what I believed I had already felt—in fact suffered from—a sensitivity to all that was near or around. But this is different and frightening—no, not really frightening—because for instance when I feel without ceasing every change in the garden itself, the changes of light as the atmosphere grows darker, and the springing up of a wind, and the rhythm of the locusts, and the colors of certain flowers that become very moving—they all seem to be part of some happiness or unhappiness, an unhappiness that something is lost or left unknown or undone perhaps—and no longer simple in their own beautiful but *outward* way. And the identity of the garden itself is lost. (Kreyling 78–79)

This is a prophetic description of the direction in which her fiction would move, but it took several years to clarify and deepen in the stories about the Natchez Trace that she had begun writing near the end of 1940 (Kreyling 44).

The Robber Bridegroom and *The Wide Net* signal her movement into this landscape material. The first book was a playful tour de force she tossed off very quickly (Kreyling 44–45), blending fairy-tale motifs from "The Fisherman and his Wife," "The Little Goose Girl," "Cinderella," "Beauty and the Beast," and "Bearskin" with mythic materials like the story of Cupid and Psyche and historical records of life on the Mississippi frontier along the Natchez Trace. In this novella the wilderness is only an enchanted forest where hero and heroine romp through their harmless adventures. Through this medium Welty was testing out an approach to virility that handles male assault and violence as an unavoidable, ultimately harmless consequence of natural energies. Young Rosamond Musgrove simply accepts whatever the dashing robber Jamie Lockhart does to her. He steals her clothing, eventually kidnaps and rapes her, and then takes her to live hidden in the wilderness in a log cabin with him and his band of rude bandits. She becomes pregnant and is abandoned when she discovers his identity, but all problems are quickly resolved with the lovers united in marriage and a respectable life in New Orleans.

An instructive contrast can be found in the story of a real girl in the Mississippi wilderness, recently told in *Trials of the Earth*, the autobiography of pioneer Mary Hamilton. Hamilton remembers a childhood visit to a neighbor on the frontier in 1874, when a fourteen-year-old niece in the family is snatched away in the night by a drunken "redheaded and red bearded fearce looking giant of a man." About three in the morning, a moaning is heard at the log cabin door, and "there was that poore child crawling up the steps . . . brused and bleading her clothes almost all tore off begging her sisters to kill her and end it all" (254–55). The ravished girl died a week later.

Welty instinctively shrank away from such scenes. She was sharply aware of her own inability to bear pain and afraid that it weakened her writing. As she explained to Russell, "the sight of pain makes me inarticulate and real distortion & monstrosity, of the flesh and the spirit, makes me want to run away. So there you see why I can never be very good. The time comes when I can't bear things on their immediate, ugly, unexplained level but have to look back at them through some vision or reason" (Kreyling 78). This personal orientation helps explain her affection for the pretty, childlike safety of fairy tale and the tendency of her fiction at its weakest to stray toward cuteness or self-indulgent charm. Welty's treatment of sexual assault darkened as her career progressed, moving toward a recognition in her best work of the brutality and pain at the heart of sexuality and indeed all experience, but she never seems fully able to confront it from within the consciousness of a female character who is its victim. She never directly condemns it, but instead almost always seems to sympathize with the need of the man who "takes" a woman.

In the stories of *The Wide Net*, Welty, like Faulkner, assumes erotic powers in the landscape, but for her they are more consciously and systematically developed through the medium of fertility myth. Sir James Frazer provided her introduction to the serious cross-cultural study of myth. From the time just after college when she first encountered Frazer, she kept *The Golden Bough* with her as a kind of bible on a par with Brewer's *Dictionary of Phrase and Fable*.[3] From Frazer she learned the grim reality of human sacrifice at the heart of fertility ritual in cultures as widely different as those of the Mycenaean Greeks and the classical Mayans, whose cousins the Choctaws inhabited Mississippi before European settlement. Welty's use of mythology developed in acknowledgment of this archaic reality, and she came to practice a comic art that includes a tough sense, often obliquely indicated, of the pain and violence at the core of vital forces. As Peter Schmidt has demonstrated, Welty was concerned with grotesque suffering from her earliest stories (3–48), but with *A Wide Net* her gaze hardened to include the kind of violence dramatized in Euripides' *Bacchae*. There, as we saw in chapter 2, animals are torn to pieces and eaten in a sacramental *omophagia* celebrating the "Earth power and Liquid power" of Demeter who gives life-nourishing bread and Bacchus "who found a vital juice in the grape cluster" (Bagg 28). From such a perspective males are necessary vitalizing elements, akin to explosive elements like thunder and lightning that flash through or over the landscape and must be endured.

A Wide Net includes a range of stories focused on Bacchic males that move from the light tone of Don McInnis's goatish antics frightening maiden ladies in "Asphodel" or the cheerful frolics of "A Wide Net," to the spring energies of new life breaking through the paralysis of winter in "Livvie," and finally the darkening sexual initiation of "At the Landing." The title story celebrates the virile energy of young William Wallace and his band of friends dragging the river, splashing in the water, gorging on the fish their net scoops from the depths, and paying homage to an enormous snake that seems both the spirit of the river and an embodiment of their own urges. William Wallace makes this connection, seeming to call forth the vision of the great snake by "leaping all over the place . . . over them and the feast and the bones of the beast, trampling the sand, up and down," doing a crazy dance with a big catfish hooked to his belt buckle. This phallic magic brings on a thunderstorm, itself described as a monster whose "huge tail seemed to lash through the air" and make of the river "a wound of silver" (182–83). Nevertheless it is Wallace's wife whose extravagant threat of suicide had set the whole carnival in motion to punish her young husband for staying out carousing all the previous night.

More typically, Welty repeats the pattern of assault and ravishment seen in *The Robber Bridegroom*, setting the passive heroines of "Asphodel," "Livvie," and "At the Landing" in sheltered spaces away from open landscape and wilderness. Like the metaphoric garden where Narcissa Benbow of Faulkner's *Flags in the Dust* endured the storm of Bayard Sartoris's violent energies, the ordered scenes of these Welty stories are invaded by increasingly frightening Dionysian males.[4] While all three stories share a dreamlike tone and fairy-tale plot elements, "At the Landing," develops toward a rather grim depiction of the necessary interrelationship of vitality and destruction, sexuality, violence, and death. Here, in what seems at first a safe retelling of a classic fairy tale, a wild young man named Billy Floyd frees a maiden from the tomblike ancestral home where her grandfather has kept her immured. Floyd catches huge catfish like the one hanging from William Wallace's belt in the earlier story, but Floyd is as inscrutable and dangerous as Wallace is silly. Jenny Lockhart first sees him from the dead space of the graveyard where her mother is buried. He is across a stream in a sunny, wild-smelling pasture where he leaps upon the back of a red horse and races in a circle three times before disappearing into the surrounding woods. Jenny is clearly not at ease with the disruptive energies he represents: "she knew that he lived apart in delight. That could make a strange glow fall over the field where he was, and the world go black for her, left behind. She felt terrified, as if at a pitiless thing" (CS 245). After Floyd has saved her from the flooding Mississippi, he makes a camp on a dry bluff and rapes her, then cooks wild meat and fish over his campfire, spearing the meat with "the same thoughtlessness of motion" that marked his violation of Jenny's body. Like the action of killing the wild animals he has cooked, "it was all a taking freely of what was free" (251). Jenny Lockhart tries to adapt but will never find her way into the world where he dwells: "She knew from him . . . that what people ate in the world was earth, river, wildness, and litheness, fire and ashes. People took the fresh death and the hot fire into their mouths and got their own life. She ate greedily as long as he ate, and took what he took" (251–52). Floyd does not respond to her efforts to join him, and she vomits up the wild food, recoiling from all it represents.

The story ends with no resolution of the contrarieties it has defined, no clear embrace of the male energy that is linked with natural disasters like Mississippi floods and figured in human terms in Floyd's hunting and fishing, in men and boys practicing their aim by throwing knives at trees, in the casual raping of women. The timid heroine may be freed from imprisonment in her grandfather's static garden, but she finds herself at the mercy of other men who muddy and violate her much as the flood has invaded and soiled her house. Billy Floyd, both billy goat and flood, has moved through her life and disappeared. She wanders to a rivermen's camp in search of him and is reduced to calling out her protests while a succession of strange men impose their bodies upon hers.

Delta Wedding comes right on the heels of this story in Welty's career but submerges sexual violence and its relation to food as embodiment of "earth, river, wildness and litheness, fire and ashes" in a fuller, more realistic comedy of manners owing much to Jane Austen and Virginia Woolf, as I have tried to demonstrate elsewhere (SG and EW). Nevertheless, the raw vision of "At the Landing" is always hovering behind or

just at the edges of the family comedy unfolding at Shellmound Plantation during the week before Dabney Fairchild's wedding. Dabney's older
sister Shelley functions as the sensitive observer who occasionally voices
its meaning within the text, but Welty has controlled the novel's tone so
subtly that most readers fail to notice the deaths, bloody knife fights, and
cruel emotional battles at the heart of the action.[5] Unlike the sterile protected spaces of feminine retreat or imprisonment in *The Wide Net*, the
farmland and houses of *Delta Wedding* are open, full of motion, and bubbling over with life. Attention is centered in the domestic activities of
women who appear to control the novel's action.

As I have suggested elsewhere, I believe Virginia Woolf's *To the Lighthouse* made it possible for Welty to focus on such characters in this novel
and to endow them with an independence of action and mind that she
had not previously been able to portray (*SG* and *EW*). Woolf's novel affirming a domestic world centered on the mother as source of life,
maker of food, and caretaker of house and garden and family was the
example that "opened the door," as Welty explained (*Conversations* 75). I
have discussed the links between Woolf and Welty's rich exploration of
human sexuality in harmony with the Delta landscape at some length in
other places,[6] but here I want to call attention to Woolf's connection of
food to the fertile land, in a way that supported the links that Welty had
already begun exploring in "At the Landing."

Woolf uses traditional metaphors of earth's abundance to define Mrs.
Ramsay's power in *To the Lighthouse*, setting up patterns that Welty
adapted in creating her Mississippi Delta world.[7] Woolf's queenly *mater-
familias* is "this delicious fecundity, this fountain and spray of life" (58); or
she is "a rosy-flowered fruit tree laid with leaves and dancing boughs"
(60); or a presence full of magnetic and comforting sweetness who is
herself both domestic hive and queen bee (80). Males in *To the Lighthouse*
are isolated from such fertile embodiment by codes of heroic striving
against the world and by a dedication to abstract reasoning that Woolf
playfully damns. Mr. Ramsay's distinguished reputation as a philosopher
of "subject and object and the nature of reality" is explained as thinking
"of a kitchen table . . . when you're not there."

The long first section of the novel culminates in Mrs. Ramsay's trium-
phant creation of community out of the disparate and testily jostling
group of her family and guests. Woolf dramatizes this achievement in the
ritual of the formal evening meal, beginning with the warm glow of

light Mrs. Ramsay orders her children to create by lighting the candles, then following Mrs. Ramsay's glance to fix upon a symbolic bowl of fruit in the center of her dining table, and finally climaxing in the arrival of the bubbling casserole of *boeuf en daube* she serves as an offering to her guests. The fruit display is described in terms that clearly mark its cultural associations in the myths we have been examining and that identify the bounteous products of the earth with the landscapes that produce them:

> Now eight candles were stood down the table, and after the first stoop the flames stood upright and drew with them into visibility the long table entire, and in the middle a yellow and purple dish of fruit. What had she done with it, Mrs. Ramsay wondered, for Rose's arrangement of the grapes and pears, of the horny pink-lined shell, of the bananas made her think of a trophy fetched from the bottom of the sea, of Neptune's banquet, of the bunch that hangs with vine leaves over the shoulder of Bacchus (in some picture), among the leopard skins and the torches lolloping red and gold. . . . Thus brought up suddenly into the light it seemed possessed of great size and depth, was like a world in which one could take one's staff and climb hills, she thought, and go down into valleys. (146)

This long passage establishes a matrix of landscape, food, beauty, comfort, celebration, sensuous enjoyment, and human community that is the center of Mrs. Ramsay's—and by extension all women's—fruitful and creative power. It is an ode to the beauty of the earth, with the feminine identified as its heart.

The substance of the world's body is distilled and *fed* by Mrs. Ramsay to her family and guests in the great brown casserole of fragrant beef stew, both sacrament and sacrifice:

> And she peered into the dish, with its shiny walls and its confusion of savoury brown and yellow meats and its bay leaves and its wine, and thought. This will celebrate the occasion [the engagement of Minta Doyle and Paul Rayley]—a curious sense rising in her, at once freakish and tender, of celebrating a festival, as if two emotions were called up in her, one profound—for what could be more serious than the love of man for women, what more commanding, more impressive, bearing in its bosom the seeds of death. (151)

Thus sexuality, celebration, and death are all commingled with the food she serves her guests at this, the novel's last supper. Lily Briscoe thinks of Mrs. Ramsay at this moment as a priestess who leads the young engaged couple as victims to the altar (153).

Eudora Welty understood completely what Woolf was about, and she applied the lessons she learned to her project of expanding a short story, "The Delta Cousins," into a paean to human sexual fulfillment in harmony with the harvest landscape during a Mississippi September. Welty has said that she thinks of food as working almost like a language, a way of talking, in southern life (personal interview), and she explores this understanding in her work. As she wrote in the early story that eventually grew into *Delta Wedding*, cooking is like a secret told to girls by older women, "in confidence, without words, the secret of women's work."[8] Far more than simply reflecting southern traditions of hospitality and delight in feasting, female rituals of food in Welty's novels of family life return to the mystery that our ancient ancestors understood as a sacramental connection between our being and the rest of the world. This is the bodily mystery of eating, requiring that we kill other living things, put them in our mouths, and rend them with our teeth so that we may absorb their strength. By insisting on this untidy physical reality, Welty rejects the philosophical idealism that has dominated self-conscious intellectual culture in the Western world as long as we have had writing, and which Woolf mocked in *To the Lighthouse*. Welty's symbolic language of food identifies physical nourishment with the landscape and the feminine in a poetics of the body as part of a mutable, heterogeneous, and cyclical ecology.

The importance of this accomplishment should be seen in the context of a contemporary debate that she seems to have anticipated, at least partly under Woolf's influence. Recent books like Mark Johnson's *The Body in the Mind*, Morris Berman's *Coming to our Senses*, Maxine Sheets-Johnstone's *The Roots of Thinking*, and Irene Diamond's *Fertile Ground: Women, Earth, and the Limits of Control* emphasize the need to heal the imagined split between mind and body in Western thinking. These efforts at cultural reorientation echo Virginia Woolf's ambitious effort to envision human destiny in ways that include both genders equally and value ordinary bodily experience as part of the natural world. Scenes where food is prepared by women and eaten in communal rituals are particularly useful for this purpose, as we have seen with Mrs. Ramsay's *boeuf en daube* standing for the essence of civilization in *To the Lighthouse*.

The fullest expression of Woolf's vision is her last novel, *Between the Acts*, written under the shadow of the same impending World War that also provided the menacing backdrop for Faulkner's "Delta Autumn" and Welty's *Delta Wedding*. Woolf intended her final novel to counter the heroic and tragic ideology of masculine military power with a comic drama of British history. Mrs. Manresa, one of the novel's most vital characters, defines living in terms of eating and drinking: "Why waste sensation, she seemed to ask, why waste a single drop that can be pressed out of this ripe, this melting, this adorable world?" (56). Within the larger cultural debate about the involvement of body in mind and nature in culture, Woolf's and Welty's practice stands in vivid contrast to Faulkner's Manichaean revulsion from food as nauseating "women's muck." Welty's language of food illuminates these relationships, because eating is literally the action that most intimately involves each of us with physical reality of the world outside the self. The long semiotic history of the imagery of food and sexuality that I have sketched out in chapter 1 should be kept in mind as explanatory background for the cultural power of Welty's accomplishment.

With Faulkner's horror of the body and the feminine as instructive contrast, I want to look directly at how Welty uses food as a medium of exchange between people, connecting them to each other and to the fertility of the landscape. Within the symbolic codes of *Delta Wedding*, food is a language that metonymically enacts these connections: part of nature, it grows out of the land and returns into it, reabsorbed as our bodies eventually are also.

Welty's central organizing principle for *Delta Wedding* is the myth of Demeter and Persephone, which the Delta landscape brought to mind when her friend John Robinson first introduced her to it on a visit to his family's plantation.[9] As goddess of grain and indeed source of all vegetative life in the Homeric Hymn, which is the earliest extended treatment of her nature and character in Greek literature, Demeter is herself the embodied link between food and the living earth. Furthermore, she is associated with Dionysos or Bacchus in this early text, being described rushing forth "as does a Maenad down some thick-wooded mountain," to greet her daughter's return from the underworld (317). We have seen similar associations between Dionysos, Demeter, food, and landscape in Euripides' much later tragedy *The Bacchae*, where the Maenad who worships the god dances over meadow and mountain, kills animals and devours them raw, while "Beneath her the meadow is running with milk / running with wine / running slowly / with the nektar of bees" (Bagg 24). Welty wrote *Delta Wedding* to demonstrate to John Robinson that the horrifying carnage surrounding him during the Allied invasion of Italy in 1944 was only one part of a comprehensible framework of sexuality, birth, death, past and present, the flow of seasons in a farming community, war and peace, misunderstanding and reunion, marriage and domestic discord—all flowing in a cyclical, dialogic pattern for which food is a central symbol.

Welty's sense of the Delta landscape as mysterious and evocative of the Demeter-Kore myth naturally involved her imagination with the complex of images and associations sacred to the Greco-Roman world and reaching back from them to the Neolithic traditions encoded in the Inanna poetry of Sumer. Walter Burkert reminds us in *Greek Religion* that the Athenians "called the dead *Demetreioi* and sowed corn on graves" (161). Many scholars of the Athenian Thesmophoria and the Eleusinian Mysteries sacred to Demeter believe that the goddess's rituals involved the handling of grain or bread during an enactment of death and rebirth (Kerenyi 56–80; Harrison 154–55; Gimbutas 214–15).

The happy events of *Delta Wedding* are celebrated by food but shadowed by death from the beginning, as Laura McRaven sits in the train remembering her dead mother on her journey down into the Delta from the bluffs at Yazoo City. The name of the Yazoo River suggests death and rebirth, the dead hero Denis is constantly brought to mind, the faces of dead Fairchilds stare down on the bustling family from old portraits, and a Kore figure is actually killed by the train just before Dabney's wedding. But these reminders of death are simply the counterparts of physical life. To eat is to feed off death, to be part of the mystery that includes reproduction, growth, ultimate decay, and regeneration.

Welty links food with the landscape in the opening scene of Laura's vision of the Delta from the Yellow Dog, likening the cottony sweep of fields to flour in a barrel. "And then, as if a hand reached along the green ridge and all of a sudden pulled down with a sweep, like a scoop in the bin, the hill and every tree in the world and left cotton fields, the Delta began" (4). Shaken from her awareness of her mother's recent death, Laura begins to eat a banana, burying her face in it as in the cup of a lily. As the sun sets across this glowing, hearthlike landscape, comforting images of womanhood and maternal nourishment linger in the sky: "The sun went down lopsided and wide as a rose on a stem in the west, and the west was a milk-white edge, like the foam of the sea" (5). On her arrival at Shellmound, however, Laura is again reminded of her mother's death in the very form of food, when her Uncle Battle serves her a plate of turkey breast, gizzard, and wing, murmuring, "How Annie Laurie would have loved this very plate!" (12). This is a typical Fairchild joke that simultaneously vents and deprecates grief and tenderness. Significantly, however, the gizzard is stolen from Laura's plate and eaten by Great Aunt Shannon, who belongs to the world of the dead, talking conversationally with all the dead members of the family as if they were at the table with the living.

At a later point in the novel, human bodies are suggestively linked to food and fertile landscape, when the bridegroom Troy Flavin, a Hades figure associated metaphorically with dangerous underground powers of earthquake, proudly opens a womblike sack of his mother's quilts, shaking them out and displaying them to the women of his new family. One is called Hearts and Gizzards, and another is Delectable Mountains. These cover human bodies in sleep, making bumps and hollows of an intimate bedroom landscape, which is called to mind elsewhere by Robbie when she thinks of her sleeping husband as a comforting mountain (148). The quilts' erotic associations are clearly indicated when Troy links Delectable Mountains with his and Dabney's ability to produce children (111–13).

The central power of food imagery in *Delta Wedding* is invested in two complementary cakes that unite opposite forces in the social world of the plantation. The cakes function both metonymically and metaphorically to connect humans to the landscape in complex cycles of fertility and history. One cake is white—a coconut cake made by the "aristocratic" Ellen Fairchild. The other is black—a magical patticake made by the old Negro servant Partheny. Both are aphrodisiacs with complicated symbolic associations, and they work sympathetic magic when eaten by the two pairs of lovers who need to be united in the marriage ritual central to the novel.

Metonymically both Ellen Fairchild's coconut cake and Partheny's patticake stand for the landscape and their human communities. Flour, sugar, egg whites, and all the other ingredients of Ellen's cake are fruits of the land that are physically absorbed when eaten. The completed product suggests in its fluffy sweetness the luxury of the wealthy and leisured class of white planters. The ingredients of Partheny's cake are less refined, frighteningly linked with wild forces of swamp and bayou, for they include dove's blood, dove's heart, and blood of a snake. They suggest a folk tradition of Black Magic associated with blood sacrifice that is complementary to the White Magic of Ellen's cake.

To eat the coconut cake is to participate in a living part of Fairchild family history, the recipe having been passed down from the pioneer ancestress Mashula Hines. Similarly, Partheny's patticake is made according to her community's inheritance from African ritual and folklore. When Troy and Robbie and Pinchy all eat the patticake, they enact cooperating roles in these traditions that connect the African-American and white elements of their rural world. An important social difference is symbolized by the way the two cakes are treated, however. Partheny conjures the patticake as a gift to her white employers. The white community, on the other hand, gives little to the blacks. Ellen does take broth to Partheny when she hears she is ill, but no blacks are invited to eat the coconut cake.

Metaphorically the patticake and the coconut cake are complex analogies to social and ecological networks. They encode differences—black and white, animal and vegetable, bitter and sweet, robust and delicate—but also combine them and are exchanged in rituals that cross boundaries and embrace paradox. Welty does *not* venture here into the more dangerous mixing of bodies in miscegenation, and thus she ignores or evades the guilt that Faulkner explores as a white man. Of course, as a southern woman she has no reason to consider herself implicated in that crime.

The ritual of combining the ingredients for Ellen's cake is linked to a particularly erotic landscape that stands for the sexual union of George and Robbie. Breaking and separating the eggs, Ellen associates this food from nests with "some secret nest" in which her hope for her daughter's marriage lies entangled with George's happiness. "He had married 'beneath' him too," when he married the lower-class schoolteacher and shop clerk Robbie Reid. As Ellen beats the egg whites and creams the sugar and butter, she conjures "up out of the mixture," a memory of Robbie and George giddily playing in a moonlit landscape of flowers beside the river. After chasing his wife into the Yazoo, George had carried her dripping up the bank and flung her into a bed of sweet peas, where the two lay "smiling and worn out, but twined together" in the moonlight while India sprinkled them with pomegranate flowers and handfuls of grass (24–25). Ellen hopes that the success of her delicate white cake will be paralleled by the happy conjunction of man and woman symbolized by this erotic play in the illuminated darkness of the riverbank. However the cake is actually eaten by George and Dabney, Troy and others, in an atmosphere of crisis, its sweetness belied by the estrangement of Robbie from her husband. Even after Robbie's return and reconciliation with George, Welty retains the association of this cake with pain and loss, extending it to the vegetable world in the thoughts of the sensitive observer Shelley Fairchild. Her uncle George offers her a plate loaded with cake, but she pauses in contemplation before she accepts it, and her gesture of acceptance embraces the knowledge of death in the act of eating. Shelley thinks of her sister Dabney's prewedding tears as she watches her cut a lemon for her aunts' tea and wonders "could the lemon feel the knife?" "Perhaps it suffered; not that vague vegetable pain lost in the generality of the pain of the world, but the pain of the very moment. Yet in the room no one said 'Stop.' They all lay back in flowered chairs and ate busily, and with a greedy delight anticipated what was ahead for Dabney" (193). As if accepting this combination of pain, greed, and death involved in eating and celebrating the fertility rituals of the wedding, Shelley takes the piece of cake George offers.

As we have already seen, Partheny's patticake is much more directly connected with death, including the very blood and inner organs of sacrificial animals among its ingredients. Though it has gloomy associations with primitive chthonic rituals and the debased social community of black Brunswick-town, Partheny's cake is as positive in the magic it conjures as Ellen's. Her instructions about how George must perform the ritual of eating it make its benign power clear: "You take dis little patticake to Mr. George Fairchild, was at dis knee at de Grove, and tell him mind he eat it tonight at midnight, by himse'f, and go to bed. . . . Mr. George got to eat his patticake all alone, go to bed by himse'f, and his love won't have no res' till her come back to him" (131). The fact that the ritual is not followed literally does not matter, for the patticake ends up being eaten by those who need it: Troy and Robbie, the outsider members of the two pairs of lovers, and also by the black girl Pinchy who is undergoing an African-American spiritual and sexual initiation—"coming through."[10] Thus male and female partners are symbolically brought together by the patticake, non-Fairchilds prepared to unite with Fairchilds, and a connection of the two races is also suggested. The eating of the black cake occurs in a very bright landscape— the blinding noonday white of the cotton field called The Deadening where Robbie rests in the darkness of a cotton shed and Pinchy hovers in a strip of shade outside the door. Robbie eats a lunch of opposites—

pickles and cakes, sweet and sour—uniting the qualities that suggest her conflicting emotions toward her husband. Then Troy appears and gives her the black patticake whose magic will restore her to George. Pinchy takes the patticake away, presumably to try it herself, and the next thing we know, she has "come through."

When Robbie moves on after eating a piece of the patticake, across the fields to the big house at Shellmound to find her husband, she stumbles into another meal—the midday dinner, scene of the climactic turning point of the novel. Her inability to eat the peach she is offered parallels her inability to break through the wall of Fairchild solidarity she encounters in George's absence. But George's sudden return breaks the mounting tension. Ellen, who has tried to feed Robbie and welcome her, enacts her final effort of reconciliation in charging George with having caused his wife to suffer. She makes the pronouncement and then faints, in the frightening repetition of an act that had caused the death of an unborn child during a previous pregnancy. Her danger draws the family swirling back together to revive her and protect the child she is carrying.

The chaos of family life surrounding this moment is analogous to the exuberant, surprising, sometimes dangerous activity of Maureen. This daughter of the dead family hero Denis is perverse and occasionally even malicious, as when she overturns a woodpile on her cousin Laura or pulls the wings off insects. Maureen has a symbolic value most vividly reflected in the face she makes at Dabney across the dinner table, sticking out her tongue "through her smiling and fruit-filled mouth" (117). This is the real face of the Fairchild family—Dionysiac in celebration but harboring barely controlled destructive forces. And plenty of genuine death and suffering has preceded the events of the novel—Denis's death, George's pain in war, Maureen's mother's derangement, untimely deaths of grandparents and the loss of Aunt Mac's and Aunt Shannon's husbands in the Civil War, and a fatal duel over cotton. Ellen is central in maintaining the women's rituals that keep those forces in check, and feeding is the central ritual among them.

Eating is finally a sacramental enactment of metamorphosis, predicated on death, but part of an endless flow of reshaping and renewal like the cyclical alternations of day and night and repeating seasons, even the geologic heavings of land and sea. We have examined a succession of scenes from the early stories up to *Delta Wedding* in which Welty associates eating with water and eroticism, for instance those connected with immersion and fishing in Mississippi Delta rivers of "The Wide Net" and "At the Landing." The mixing of Ellen Fairchild's coconut cake is a much fuller realization of these connections, whereby the gooey concoction of sugar, butter, eggs, flour, and milk in the mixing bowl are conflated with Robbie and George's giddy but also dangerous playing in the Yazoo River earlier in the summer. That had been "happiness covered with danger," for Robbie had lured George into the water even though a war wound hampered his ability to swim. After he had carried her dripping out of the water and flung her into a bed of sweet peas, the two "lay there smiling and worn out, but twined together—appealing, shining in moonlight, and almost—somehow—threatening," Ellen remembers as she adds nutmeg and grated lemon rind, then milk, egg whites, and flour (24–25).

Robbie and George's flirtation with drowning is recapitulated later in the novel in a more innocent form by the almost-pubescent children Roy and Laura. In this second occurrence of ritual baptism, Roy throws Laura from a rowboat into the river, not realizing that she does not know how to swim. The old Choctaw name means "river of death," but Laura's brief experience of immersion figures the watery grave as a womblike space like the inside of old Aunt Studney's sack, which according to local children's lore is the place babies come from (*DW* 178). Roy pulls Laura out by the hair and thus completes a complex series of ritual events that serve, as I have argued previously, to pollinate the bridal house, prefigure the sexual awakening of Laura and Roy, and wash away the taint of her mother's recent death so that Laura can participate in her cousin Dabney's wedding (*SG* 89–91).

A similar complex of associations is explored in Welty's next book, *The Golden Apples*, in the story "Moon Lake," but this time the drowning comes much closer to realization, while its association with adult sexuality is more explicit and disturbing. Moon Lake is an erotic liquid realm of snakes and phallic cypress knees poking up from beneath the water. It is dangerous to the timid girl campers of the story, who only reluctantly wade into its dark waters every morning for their obligatory swim. Only adults and the boy lifeguard Loch Morrison move comfortably along its surface or explore its depths. Loch's plunging dives are ridiculously overstated assertions of his adolescent masculinity: "He went through the air rocking and jerking like an engine, splashed in, climbed out, spat, climbed up again, dived off" (*CS* 34). When the boldest of the girls at the camp is tricked into a dive by a black boy who is Loch's double, death and sexual initiation are intertwined in a striking mimicry of rape. Loch retrieves Easter's body from the lake and flings her on a picnic table, kneeling over her to administer artificial respiration.

> By now the Boy Scout seemed for ever part of Easter and she part of him, he in motion on the up-and-down and she stretched across. He was dripping, while her skirt dried on the table. . . . [Easter's] face was set now, and ugly with that rainy color of seedling petunias, the kind nobody wants. Her mouth surely by now had been open long enough, as long as any gape, bite, cry, hunger, satisfaction lasts, any one person's grief, or even protest. . . .

> It was a betrayed figure, the betrayal was over, it was a memory. And then as the blows, automatic now, swung down again, the figure itself gasped. (CS 370–71)

Suddenly Easter's body arches, draws itself up, then falls back, kicking Loch off the table; finally she sits up and slowly pulls her ruined dress downward. Like so many other vitalizing masculine figures in Welty's fiction, Loch Morrison is an abrupt but necessary initiator and rescuer. All the male characters in *The Golden Apples* who share these functions are treated comically even though their actions bring suffering to women and even death in one instance. As Patricia Yaeger established some time ago, Welty is in the process of deflating their traditionally heroic associations (444–50). I would argue that she does so in order to insist on the vital energy of women characters who are identified with tremendous powers in the landscape, as in the case of the German music teacher Miss Eckhart of "June Recital," who plays Beethoven with such passion during a thunderstorm that she assumes "the face a mountain could have, or what might be seen behind the veil of a waterfall" (CS 300–301).

A deeper, more complex assertion of the identification of woman with landscape and indeed the whole biota comes in Welty's description of Virgie Rainey's immersion in the Big Black River in "The Wanderers," a scene that echoes Thoreau's pond experience in its evocation of the material presence of nature, in the interrelationship of water and sky as symbolic of the unity of the whole physical world, and in the transcendent mystery of the subject's experience. However, Welty defines a fully embodied participation in the watery material of life, one significantly different from Thoreau's cerebral imagining of his relation to the pond. The evening after Virgie's mother has died and her body has been laid out by old women friends, the daughter walks down to the river for solace.

> She stood on the willow bank. It was bright as mid-afternoon in the openness of the water, quiet and peaceful. She took off her clothes and let herself into the river.
>
> She saw her waist disappear into reflectionless water; it was like walking into sky, some impurity of skies. All was one warmth, air, water, and her own body. All seemed one weight, one matter—until as she put down her head and closed her eyes and the light slipped under her lids, she felt this matter a translucent one, the river, herself, the sky all vessels which the sun filled. She began to swim in the river, forcing it gently, as she would wish for gentleness to her body. Her breasts around which she felt the water curving were as sensitive at that moment as the tips of wings must feel to birds, or antennae to insects. She felt the sand, grains intricate as little cogged wheels, minute shells of old seas, and the many dark ribbons of grass and mud touch her and leave her, like suggestions and withdrawals of some bondage that might have been dear now dismembering and losing itself. She moved but like a cloud in skies, aware but only of the nebulous edges of her feeling and the vanishing opacity of her will, the carelessness for the water of the river through which her body had already passed as well as for what was ahead. The bank was all one, where out of the faded September world the little ripening plums started. Memory dappled her like no more than a paler light, which in slight agitations came through leaves, not darkening her for more than an instant. The iron taste of the old river was sweet to her, though. If she opened her eyes she looked at blue-bottles, the skating water-bugs. If she trembled it was at the smoothness of a fish or snake that crossed her knees. (CS 439–40)

Virgie's skin functions as major organ of perception, and her thoughts move in as full a harmony with the watery environment as her immersed body does. The moment is set in a sky-water unity similar to Thoreau's, but while Thoreau sees himself abstracted from his body and "Nature," while his thoughts wander in celestial spheres, Welty merely erases the bounds of the subject's particular body so that Virgie's thoughts seem to merge into a continuum with the physical world around her. The outer layers of Virgie's body become surfaces of contact rather than separating boundaries as she puts down her head and closes off her sight. Her particular physical definition "disappears" when the specific constraint of gravity is released, and she feels part of "one warmth," "one weight, one matter" in sensuous unity with the medium surrounding her. In this state her self has the same existential value as river and sky, all vessels filled by the life-giving sun.[11]

Virgie moves in the water with a consciousness of her relation to Nature that is opposed to Thoreau's. Where he thinks of his mind as a cleaver or says he comes to know pine trees by chopping them down and shaping them with an axe, Virgie respects the physical integrity of the world outside herself—"forcing [the water] gently, as she would wish for gentleness to her body." Her breasts become the major signifiers of her body, in this watery weightlessness that is only a denser sky, and link her to birds and insects in exquisite sensitivity to her physical environment. The history of the earth as she experiences it through contact with grains of sand and the skeletal remains of ancient generations of tiny creatures becomes analogous to her own biography. They touch her and leave her as do the consoling touches of her women neighbors in the previous scene, and also as the memories of her life with her mother will flow away in the movement of time. Virgie's consciousness seems to merge with passive, nonsentient matter as she feels herself move "like a cloud in skies, aware but only of the nebulous edges of her feeling and the vanishing opacity of her will." Unlike Thoreau, she is always simultaneously contemplative and involved *in* the physical moment, *in her body*, as the last three sentences of the passage make very clear. When she returns to a sense of her individual body's definition at the end of the passage, she knows herself to be harmoniously immersed in the same element as other creatures, rather than seeing herself outside it and superior in the way Thoreau does when he floats in his boat above them on Walden Pond.

Klaus Theweleit insists that "the relationship of human bodies to the larger world of objective reality grows out of one's relationship to one's own body and to other human bodies. The relationship to the larger world in turn determines the way in which these bodies speak of themselves, of objects, and of relationships to objects" (24). Thus by defining one woman's thoughtful physicality, Eudora Welty can explore the traditional associations of women with water and materiality. She revives archaic mythic traditions and follows Virginia Woolf's lead to imagine human consciousness as coextensive with the web of all life on our planet. Under the cover of a dreamy, comic bemusement that owes much to her early passion for fairy tale, Welty quite boldly destabilizes heroic traditions of masculine subjectivity and transcendence, centering the consciousness of her mature fiction in women's insistently embodied experience of a continuum with the intermingling matter and energy through which we move. But after Virgie Rainey has experienced her baptismal ecstasy of union with all life in the Big Black River and freed herself from her old life with her mother, Welty does not seem to know what to do with her. *The Golden Apples* leaves her sitting on a fence in the rain, poised between the realm of the dead in the graveyard and the living world outside it, in the company of an old black woman with a red hen under her arm. Together they listen "to the magical percussion, the world beating in their ears." It is the falling rain, through which they hear "the running of the horse and bear, the stroke of the leopard, the dragon's crusty slither, and the glimmer and the trumpet of the swan" (461). What this is supposed to mean I have never quite understood, unless it is meant to conjure the mysterious energies suggested by the heraldic creatures of myth and fable. If so, the ending of the book seems a regressive evasion of the questions raised by Virgie's career in Morgana and her decision to move on to another place and another life. Fairy-tale monsters cannot lead her into any practical future. Woman, Other, black, voodoo animal, softly falling rain, and a person named Rainey—these elements do conjure the exotic, embodied realm of the nonmasculine, nontranscendent. But they are static, frozen in a tableau that merely reinscribes the coding that has denied them agency in thousands of years of literary figuration.

It is spring. The tiny frogs pull
their strange new bodies out
of the suckholes, the sediment of rust,
and float upward, each in a silver bubble
that breaks on the water's surface,
to one clear unceasing note of need.

Sometimes, when I hear them,
I leave our bed and stumble
among the white shafts of weeds
to the edge of the pond.
I sink to the throat,
and witness the ravenous trill
of the body transformed at last and then consumed
in a rush of music.

Sing to me, sing to me.
I have never been so cold
rising out of sleep.
LOUISE ERDRICH, "The Sacraments"

CHAPTER 7

Brave New World

None of the writers examined so far in this study has succeeded in breaking out of the archaic gendered sense of the human relation to the landscape and its life. Efforts have ranged from Emerson and Thoreau's attempts to define a freshly American understanding of Nature, to Cather's placing of women in positions of heroic accomplishment, to the defensive masculinism of Hemingway's and Faulkner's modernist primitivism, and finally to Welty's revaluation of an embodied feminine identity with the Mississippi landscape. Paul Shepard has recently remarked on the increasingly narcissistic quality of human consciousness, separated from vital integration within the whole Biota and suffering profound psychic disorientation as a result. "Among primal peoples," he claims, "contact with the living nonhuman world is hedged with circumspection, caution, and sometimes ceremonial formality" ("On Animal Friends" 276). Now all we have is a sentimentalized instrumentalism projected out upon the world through monstrous genetic tampering to produce "the mindless drabs of the sheep flock, the udder-dragging, hypertrophied cow, the psychopathic racehorse, and the infantilized dog who will age into a blasé touch-me-bear." We have engineered whole categories of animal slaves "whose heartwarming compliance and therapeutic presence mask the sink of their biological deformity and the urgency of our need for other life" (286–87). We can assume that the landscapes domesticated over the millennia of human agriculture have been similarly degraded and crippled.

Is it possible to retrace our steps and return to some kind of "wild" state? Gary Snyder thinks so: "The nature spirits are never dead, they are alive under our feet, over our heads, all around us, ready to speak when we are silent and centered" (206). Many in the environmental movement, from writers like Snyder to anthropologists and biologists, urge recourse to the remaining tribal peoples who still practice ancient lifeways in gathering and hunting societies such as those of the Amazon forest or the Athabascan lands of far northern America. Anthropologist Richard Nelson is fairly typical in arguing for a recovery of the lost wisdom of "biophilia—a deep, pervasive, ubiquitous, all-embracing affinity with life—[which] lies at the very core of traditional hunting-fishing-gathering societies" like the Koyukon Indians of Alaska among whom he conducted fieldwork (224). Perhaps the only way to escape the embattled gender dualism of European-American culture is to somehow adapt the metaphoric systems of tribal peoples for contemporary figurations of humans in the landscape. That is not to suggest that other cultures lack gender distinctions, taboos, and conflicts, for the ethnographic literature richly documents their existence almost everywhere in human culture. But tribal cultures like the Koyukon do not gender the land and other animals quite the way our tradition does, opposing a feminized "Nature" to masculine transcendent intellect. Theirs is almost always an animate universe where everything shares sentience and community.

Postmodern theorists like Donna Haraway warn of the danger that contemporary writers and thinkers in the technologized world may be merely projecting their own desires upon groups of animals and people they use to construct origin stories that will justify their ideological programs. As Haraway explains in *Primate Visions*, primatology is a field in which women have been placed in the age-old role of mediators between "wild Nature"—primate species like the chimpanzee and the gorilla—and (masculine) civilization (133–85). So the work of Jane Goodall and Diane Fossey, for example, plays out a narrative of the woman servant of a male scientific establishment who links technological civilization with primitive creatures defined as mirrors of our primal past. Haraway demonstrates how qualities valued in our own culture are projected upon observed primate groups, or at least emphasized in their social behavior. Thus, even in the apparent attempt to break out of old assumptions and discover keys to our evolution, traditional hierarchies are reinscribed.

> Woman in these narratives fulfills her communicating, mediating function because of a triple code [gender/science/race], only one part of which is gender. Gender in the western narrative works simply here: Woman is closer to nature than Man and so mediates more readily. . . . Positioned by the symbology, real women are put into the service of culturally reproducing Woman as Man's channel. That modality of gender is required to heal man's expulsion from the garden after the bomb and in the ultimately threatening world that followed. The *National Geographic*'s late twentieth-century story is not about transcendence, but immanence, the possibility of survival on earth. (149–50)

Haraway continues her exposition of the symbolic triad by arguing that the research of Goodall and Fossey was initiated and supervised by a scientific *patriline* chiefly in the person of archaeologist Louis Leakey but also sponsored by giant industrial conglomerates which had an interest in "discovering" tool-making and violent meat-eating behavior among both australopithecine fossils and chimpanzees (151–52).

The third element in Haraway's code, more directly related to the patterns of landscape figuration we have inherited from our ancient European past, is that of race. In this system, white is a marker of civilization and mind. The system is clearly at work in Hemingway's treatment of Indians and in Faulkner's confused identification of Indians, blacks, and animals with the feminine and with "evil" in *Go Down, Moses*. At the same time, as we saw in chapter 5, Faulkner also tried to masculinize the bear and define an all-male wilderness paradise of hunters. For most "white" male writers, dark-skinned people and women are inevitably close to animals, associated with matter, body, and ultimately the degradation of undifferentiated merging with nature. Thus the heroic actions of both Nick Adams in "Big Two-Hearted River" and Thomas Sutpen in *Absalom, Absalom!* involve temporary immersion in the landscape for mastery that allows triumphal emergence *out of it*. As Haraway analyzes the dynamics of such coding,

> Women and animals are set up *as* body with depressing regularity in the mind/body binarism in story fields, including scientific ones. The man/animal binarism is crosscut by two others which structure the narrative possibilities: mind/body and light/dark. White women mediate between "man" and "animal" in power-charged historical fields. Colored women are often so closely held by the category *animal* that they can barely function as mediators in texts produced within white culture. In those cultural fields, colored women densely code sex, animal, dark, dangerous, fecund, pathological. (153–54)

In the last couple of decades women writers from communities defined as "colored" have belied such categorization, moving powerfully into the center of the American literary scene to tell their own stories.[1] Haraway focuses on one such writer, African-American science fiction writer Octavia Butler, as a postmodern storyteller who is able to break down the boundaries between nature and culture and gender and race with a success that has eluded most white feminists. Butler provides an ideal fictional elaboration of the new constructions Haraway defines as necessary to "shift the webs of intertextuality and to facilitate perhaps new possibilities for the meanings of difference, reproduction, and survival" (377). For Haraway, postcolonial politics allow women of color to tell "the main story" (378). A woman speaking from the position associated with the body, with animals, with dangerous powers and substances, and with the land itself, as we have seen, is in a very different place from the white male anthropologist who studies "primal" gathering/hunting peoples and wants to gain access to what he terms their "biophilia."[2] Even though Nelson describes the enmeshment of Koyukon peoples within their physical world, he gives their orientation the European (Greek, Indo-European) name *biophilia* that objectifies Nature or Life as passive object of love. But Haraway's turn to women of color for postmodern figurations of dynamic heteroglossia and destabilizing of categories could be seen as a similar appropriation by a white colonizer, even if she does happen to be a woman. In a 1989 essay Valerie Smith protests the use of black women writers for access to embodiment by Anglo-American feminists (44–45), and more recently Margaret Homans has questioned this tactic. After closely examining the theoretical debates surrounding the problem and especially its discussion by African-American feminist writers, Homans decides that it is legitimate for a white woman to turn to a black writer as an example, *only if* she uses her "as a figure for her own effective and pragmatic ambivalence (perhaps, one might say, her strategic ambivalence), not, as Haraway . . . might, as a figure for a philosophically pure but deconcretized position" (90). However, I would argue that Haraway is simply pointing us to Butler's own fictional experiments, and in a way that avoids essentializing, colonizing reductionism.

In *Playing in the Dark*, Toni Morrison condemns "white" American culture's use of the Africanist presence, "deployed as rawness and savagery" to provide "the staging ground and arena for the elaboration of the quintessential American identity" (44). Morrison's critique could be extended to include the "wilderness" landscape and its indigenous inhabitants as the wider staging ground in this effort. But in the end Morrison suggests that there is an alternative. Her purpose has been "to avert the critical gaze from the racial object to the racial subject; from the described and imagined to the describers and imaginers; from the serving to the served" (90). Therefore, to read the fiction of African-American (or Native American or indeed *any*) writers appropriately is to accept their imagined worlds and learn to serve their visions. Barbara Christian has said that these writers are engaged in the play of language for survival; if we accept and absorb their "pithy language that unmask[s] the power relations of their world" (68), then we are not coercively importing their work to subordinate it to the traditional system of power relations. Rather, we are destabilizing and changing that system. In fact, that is how all culture works—by mingling and synthesizing and shifting. The question is where value and power come to rest.

Native Americans have an especially direct access to the ancient tribal ways of understanding that Richard Nelson admires in the Koyukon society where he briefly lived, and in the past twenty years Indian poets and novelists have moved into the literary mainstream to claim their cultural authority. I would like to turn to the work of Louise Erdrich for suggestions about the kind of ecological thinking that might be possible from perspectives not limited to European-American traditions. As Americans writing in English, of course, Native Americans work both inside and outside those traditions.

Louise Erdrich's tetralogy of novels about a large and mixed Chippewa clan in North Dakota over five or six generations is a history of one Native American community. At the same time it is a rewriting of the American literary story of Manifest Destiny as Philip Fisher describes it. We have seen the imperialist nostalgia of the European-American pastoral vision inscribed by such "classic" authors as Thoreau, Cather, Hemingway, and Faulkner. Erdrich is deeply engaged with this tradition at the same time that she is the inheritor of Anishinabe, Ojibwa, or Chippewa worldviews from her mother's family on the Turtle Mountain Reservation in North Dakota. She was a member of the first class at Dartmouth College that included women, and she was also an Indian scholarship student. Made to feel doubly marginal in that bastion of white male privilege, she nevertheless gained access to an elite education there, in the company of a small cadre of other Native American students supported by a Native American Studies Program. She gained formative childhood experience from her Chippewa family on the reservation, but Erdrich has said that she also had to recover some elements of her tribal past from library materials that include ethnographic reports of European-American anthropologists. She has always been candid in book dedications and interviews, as well as in the fabric of her novels and short stories, about the complicated cultural mix of her upbringing and thus of the world she depicts.[3] Erdrich's work and her public comments about it clearly admit the tentative, constructed nature of her fictional histories. So much the better. She cannot be accused of essentializing her people, and as we shall see, she is under no illusions about anyone's access to the past.

What is striking for my purposes about her first published novel—the closely related stories that make up *Love Medicine*—is the absence of the gendered landscape of traditional European-American fiction. Land and air and weather simply compose the vital element in which her characters live, shifting and moving especially through the imagery of water that flows through the stories. Men and women feel it equally, acknowledging their lives as immersed in it. Unlike Hemingway's *In Our Time* or Faulkner's *Go Down, Moses, Love Medicine* has no single, authoritative narrative voice. Instead many voices and perspectives shape a communal relation to the reservation land parceled out by the U.S. government to grandparents and great-grandparents, and then denuded by logging companies and eroded much as the tribal community has been.

The opening story begins in the third person, describing the suicide of June Kashpaw in 1981, but it quickly shifts to the first-person voice of her niece Albertine Johnson. The second story moves back to 1934 and is the first-person account of Marie Lazarre's "sanctification" in a broken-down convent at the hands of a pathological nun who we learn in a later book is actually her mother. And on the stories go, moving up into the 1940s and 1950s, 1960s, 1970s, and 1980s, with different members of closely linked and often feuding families, to end with a story set in 1984 that reconciles some of their most embattled members. The question of narrative gaze and subjectivity is far too complex to anatomize here, but it is shared by women and men of various ages and generations. Most of them are Chippewa, but most are also mixed-blood people, struggling with the confusion of identity that besets so many Native Americans after the concerted efforts of the U.S. government to destroy their cultures and languages.

On the shifting ground of personal and cultural identity, the characters of *Love Medicine* work out lives as twentieth-century Americans, but flowing through them like a deep river is the current of their Anishinabe cultural past, dimly remembered or sensed by the older members of the families, and used as a metaphoric scaffolding by Erdrich. As many commentators have already pointed out, elements in this metaphoric frame include the trickster figure Nanabozo, the fear of going *windigo* in winter (falling prey to the cannibal ice-monster), awe for the power of lakes, and fear of drowning.[4] But the land is sustaining, and pervasive water imagery suggests that the manitous of the lakes are still potent for the Nanapushes and Kashpaws, Pillagers, Morriseys, Lamartines, and Lazarres of the stories. Nector Kashpaw in "The Plunge of the Brave" defies a white artist's idea of the Indian's "tragic" drowning in a painting for which he poses as Noble Savage. The rich white woman who insists that he pose nude, or as Nector puts it, stand "stock still in a diaper"(124), participates in the same anticipatory nostalgia for the "end" of the Indian presence in North

America that Philip Fisher finds so characteristic of nineteenth-century historical fiction. But Erdrich shapes a Native American gaze that turns the trope inside out. Nector understands the game: "There I was [in the painting], jumping off a cliff, naked of course, down into a rocky river. Certain death. Remember Custer's saying? The only good Indian is a dead Indian? Well, from my dealings with whites I would add to that quote: 'The only interesting Indian is dead, or dying by falling backwards off a horse'" (124).

Nector Kashpaw is far from dead or willing to further enact the roles the majority culture wants him to play. In a wryly comic identification with both Ishmael and Queequeg of *Moby Dick*, he sees his life buoyed up in a swiftly flowing river. "I knew that Nector Kashpaw would fool the pitiful rich woman that painted him and survive the raging water. I'd hold my breath when I hit and let the current pull me toward the surface, around jagged rocks. I wouldn't fight it, and in that way I'd get to shore" (124). At one crisis point he walks naked into Lake Matchimanito and considers drowning himself, only to be popped back up to the surface by unseen forces. When he finally dies in "Love Medicine," he returns metaphorically to the depths of the lake where his life has had its source, and his wife Marie's grief nearly pulls her in with him. Their symbolic relation to this central lake on the reservation has been established in earlier stories with imagery likening both Marie and Nector to stones worn smooth at the bottom of the lake by the action of water that is like the flow of events in their lives (95–96, 127). The one character in *Love Medicine* who drowns is Henry Lamartine, Jr., of "The Red Convertible," a man so psychically damaged by service in the Vietnam War that he cannot recover his place in his family or community.

Erdrich has focused the book's water imagery by writing a new story, "The Island," for the revised and enlarged 1993 edition of *Love Medicine*. The island in Lake Matchimanito seems to be a place out of ordinary time, serving as a refuge for Moses Pillager, the last of his clan, a hermit who wears his clothes backwards and walks backwards. Moses lives a kind of death-in-life in a womblike cave full of cats in order to escape the diseases and devastation of white culture. Young Lulu Nanapush goes to Moses for her sexual initiation, drawn by intuitive need for reconnection to the land and world of her people's tribal past. Gaining what she needs, she also brings Moses back to life.

Touch by touch, I took down his gravehouse. With my kisses, I placed food for living people between his lips. He told me his real name. I whispered it, once. Not the name that fooled the dead, but the word that harbored his life.

Did spirits hear us?

Then he was *Small Mouth. Close Lightning.* He was *Stick Across. Beaver.* He was *Facing Sky. Ending Hawk.* Or perhaps he was *Dressed in Clay. All Hill. Steps Over Track. Hard Sky. Reflection of the Sun.* He was *With Horns.* Call him *Long Moose Limp* or *Swampy Woman Man.* His name was *Small.* It was *Hind Quarters.* It was *Face Appearing.* It was none of these. (82)

Such names suggest the multiplicity and protean dynamism of relations to land, weather, plants, and other animals. Together Moses and Lulu hibernate in the womblike center of the landscape's old power, and from their union a child is born who will grow up to be an Indian activist modeled after Leonard Peltier, an elusive trickster leading successful protests against the U.S. government in the 1970s.

Lake Matchimanito represents for Erdrich the element of life washing around all the characters in the book, and its power is personified in the water manitou Misshepeshu, variously described in Erdrich's later novels as a lion or horned creature who can be lover or killer or sustainer, depending on whose story we are reading, whose vision we share. For those who are attuned to the vitality of the land, Misshepeshu embodies its mystery. A contrasting vision of Misshepeshu is offered in *Tracks*, the third novel in Erdrich's tetralogy, by the sadistic and jealous assimilationist Pauline Puyat, who genders Misshepeshu as a man. Pauline projects her own twisted lust into her vision of the horned and clawed and finned lover with green eyes and copper skin who is ultimately "a thing of death by drowning, the death a Chippewa cannot survive" (11). Pauline uses this concept to fuel the resentful gossip of the community against her rival Fleur Pillager, Moses's cousin who, like him, remains powerfully embedded in the old way of life. Though Pauline claims that Fleur sleeps with the water monster under the lake and works evil powers that she gains from him, we never see corroboration in the text but know only that Fleur is drawn to the water, wears green, is said to metamorphose into a bear, and is generally allied with the powers of the land. In Erdrich's recent fourth novel, *The Bingo Palace*, Fleur's grandson Lipsha has a vision recalling his near-drowning as a very young child, when his mother June wrapped him in a burlap sack and threw him in a slough. He was saved by Misshepeshu:

> Darkened and drenched, coming toward me from the other side of drowning—it presses its mouth on mine and holds me with its fins and horns and rocks me with its long and shining plant arms. Its face is lion-jawed, a thing of beach foam, resembling the jack of clubs. Its face has the shock of the unburied goodness, the saving tones. Its face is the cloud fate that will some day surround me when I am ready to die. What it is I don't know, I can't tell. I never will. But I do know I am rocked and saved and cradled. (218)

This time the Chippewa water manitou is a benign and lifesaving being, who may be a dream-vision to help Lipsha understand the sustaining elements in his environment, or who can be taken literally as a traditional superhuman presence still occasionally experienced. Yet earlier in the story Lipsha's Aunt Zelda has shocked him by confiding her own memory of the event, in which she herself had been his savior, wading into the mud and then into water over her head to dive under and search for the gunnysack weighted with rocks (49–51). In this personal account, Zelda acts as an avatar of Misshepeshu.

The point about all these encounters with Misshepeshu is their indication that the landscape is full of active forces, equally associated with males and females, that animate the lives of Erdrich's Chippewa characters. As Richard Erdoes and Alfonso Ortiz explain, such an attitude is characteristic of Indian traditions all over North America. "Mysterious but real power dwells in nature—in mountains, rivers, rocks, even pebbles. White people may consider them inanimate objects, but to the Indian, they are enmeshed in the web of the universe, pulsating with life and potent with medicine" (xi). Erdrich's location of particular vitalizing powers underwater can be traced back to the Earth-Diver creation stories of the Algonquin peoples among whom the Anishinabe or Ojibwa or Chippewa peoples are numbered. All life in these stories emerges from the primal waters and rests on the back of a great turtle. The land is created by various water animals who dive down and bring up soil (Johnston 11–15, 50–51; Turner 36–37).

Throughout *Love Medicine*, both men and women characters are associated with powerful forces in the landscape. June walks "home" through the snowstorm as a Christ figure on Easter, reunited with the whole natural world from which her tormented life had estranged her, though literally dying (7). At the end of the novel, in "Crossing the Water," her son Lipsha is restored to his home on the reservation, saved from potentially disastrous service in the Army by a reunion with the father who links him with the powerful medicine of the Pillager past descended from his grandfather Moses who never surrendered to the white world and whose power Lipsha has inherited as "the touch." It is, however, quite a tentative and ironic power that must be treated with reverence. When he tries to fake a traditional love potion in the story "Love Medicine" by using frozen turkey hearts from the supermarket instead of the hearts of a pair of wild geese, he inadvertently kills his grandfather and loses his "touch." Lipsha regains "the touch" from the land itself, by probing the earth for dandelion roots after this disaster: "With every root I prized up there was return, as if I was kin to its secret lesson" (257–58). The hope of the community lies with this confused young man who does not know who he really is, drifts from playing pinball machines to scoring brilliantly on the A.C.T. exam and then dropping out of school to work in a sugar beet factory.

Lipsha's dilemma is given a historical context by *Tracks*, the novel Erdrich published after *Love Medicine* and *The Beet Queen*. Here she reshaped four hundred pages of material written early in her career into a postmodern origin story (Peterson 982) that self-consciously constructs an answer to mainstream histories of frontier settlement and the figurations of imperialist nostalgia employed by such writers as Cooper, Hemingway, and Faulkner. In *Tracks* two conflicting versions of events interweave to question and destabilize each other but also to construct a field of possibilities for the reader's engagement.[5] The more reliable of the two narrators is Nanapush, a turn-of-the century embodiment of the archetypal Chippewa trickster Nanabozo; he opens the novel with a litany of emblematic claims that situate him as the final authentic witness of the tribal past. Because he is telling his story to his "grandaughter" Lulu in an attempt to restore her Indian identity and connection with her family after disorienting years in government schools, he functions as a link with the pre-European past, the time before disease and American government betrayals destroyed tribal population, cultural unity, autonomy on the land (cf. Peterson 985).

My girl, I saw the passing of times you will never know.

I guided the last buffalo hunt. I saw the last bear shot. I trapped the last beaver with a pelt of more than two years' growth. I spoke aloud the words of the government treaty, and refused to sign the settlement papers that would take away our woods and lake. I axed the last birch that was older than I, and I saved the last Pillager.

Fleur, the one you will not call mother. (2)

With this self-consciously ritualized claim of authority, Erdrich replaces the figure of Faulkner's Sam Fathers, the native guide for the white boy in "The Bear" who almost wordlessly passes on his ancient traditional knowledge to the scion of his people's oppressors. Unlike Faulkner's Indian, Erdrich's last witness lives with his own people and tells a whole tribal and family saga of the land to a girl who will carry it on. As readers, our access to the history of the American landscape is now achieved through the playful language of the old trickster, and we are in the position of the girl who needs to be reconnected to the land in the old relationship of respect and humility.

Nanapush is a healer and elder guide for Lulu as he has also been for her mother and putative father. He saved Lulu's mother Fleur from the pestilential Pillager cabin by Lake Matchimanito where all her family lay dead around her, and together he and Fleur patched up a new family to continue living according to the traditional ways of sacramental involvement with the land. Nanapush became a father figure and teacher for young Eli Kashpaw as well, initiating him to the hunting secrets that depend on kinship with animals. As Nanapush explains it to Lulu, "I think like animals, have perfect understanding for where they hide, and in my time I have tracked a deer back through time and brush and cleared field, to the place it was born. You smile! There was only one thing wrong with teaching these important things, however. I showed Eli how to hunt and trap from such an early age that I think he lived too much in the company of trees and wind" (40). Yet these very traits made him the appropriate mate for Fleur, who also lived "in the company of trees and wind." Once she recovered from her near death with Nanapush's help, went away to live in the white town of Argus for a time and then returned as a young woman, she retreated to the Pillager cabin by the lake and took up a solitary existence according to traditional ways. Eli was led to her while hunting a doe he had wounded; their courtship began in contestation over the carcass of the doe, and in conflation with the act of tracking and killing. Here Erdrich inscribes a traditional Chippewa identification of hunting with human sexuality, which she had earlier expressed in the title poem of her first book, *Jacklight*. The epigraph that precedes the poem quotes scholar R. W. Dunning: "The same Chippewa word is used both for flirting and hunting game, while another Chippewa word connotes both using force in intercourse and also killing a bear with one's bare hands" (3). Fleur and Eli's relationship developed in the context of the intimate network of hunting and killing animals for food, with an understanding of the sacred relation of food to death and love.

During a time of estragement when Fleur refused to cook for him, Eli won her back with the renewed help of Nanapush, who not only counseled psychological strategies for softening Fleur's heart but also guided him in the hunt for desperately needed meat to keep the family alive. Nanapush sang Eli along the track of a moose through the snow, almost in a parallel with the songlines that indigenous people of Australia use to map their landscape. Nanapush blackened his face with charcoal, placed his otter bag on his chest with his rattle nearby, and began his ritual song in sympathy with Eli's movements in the forest: "I began to sing slowly, calling on my helpers, until the words came from my mouth but were not mine, until the rattle started, the song sang itself, and there, in the deep bright drifts, I saw the tracks of Eli's snowshoes clearly" (101). In his vision Nanapush directed the hunt to its successful conclusion. When the moose was killed, Eli strapped the meat over his own body in order to carry it out of the woods, thus providing a dynamic physical symbol of the way another animal's flesh shapes and restores the body through eating. "He secured jagged ovals of haunch meat to his thighs, then fitted smaller rectangles down his legs, below the knees. He pressed to himself a new body, red and steaming, swung a roast to his back and knotted its ligaments around his chest. He bound a rack of ribs across his hat, jutting over his face, and tied them on beneath his chin. Last of all, he wrapped new muscles, wide and thick, around each forearm and past his elbows" (103). The offering of this food was the beginning of Eli's return to Fleur's good graces; food and love exist as two parts of a whole.

Pauline Puyat, the second narrator of *Tracks*, sees the world in a way antithethical to Nanapush's vision of sacred wholeness. She is a mixed-blood obsessed with denying her Indian lineage and allying herself with the symbolic economy of her people's oppressors by entering a convent and trading her blood relationships for allegiance to the white Christ. Her narrative is continuously suspect. Defining herself as a savior of her pagan community, Pauline sees herself as Fleur's rival, struggling to win the souls of the Indian community away from the powers of the landscape personified in the figure of Misshepeshu, whom she identifies as Satan.

> Between the people and the gold-eyed creature in the lake, the spirit which they said was neither good nor bad but simply had an appetite, Fleur was the hinge. It was like that with Him, too, Our Lord, who had obviously made the whites more shrewd, as they grew in number, all around, . . . while the Indians receded and coughed to death and drank. It was clear that the Indians were not protected by the thing in the lake or by the other Manitous who lived in trees, the bush, or spirits of animals that were hunted so scarce they became discouraged and did not mate. There would have to come a turning, a gathering, another door. And it would be Pauline who opened it. (139)

By demonizing her own people, she recapitulates the old process Christianity has used for many centuries to colonize and overwhelm competing religious beliefs. As usual the "pagan" religions are identified with animals, the body, the land, and the feminine.[6] But by personifying the construction of these attitudes in a resentful, pathological hypocrite like Pauline, Erdrich starkly exposes the destructive psychological effects of internalized racism caused by the standard "white" view of Indian life. Pauline allies herself with death, punishes her body, and interferes in the relationship of Eli and Fleur. When Fleur begs her help to stop a premature birth, Pauline manages to flounder and delay, spill bags of medicinal herbs, and ultimately destroy the baby's chance for life. In retaliation for her own pregnancy and motherhood, Pauline abuses her body by wearing her shoes on the wrong feet, refusing to bathe, and trying to stop regular bodily processes. She convinces herself that Napoleon Morrisey, her baby's father, is Misshepeshu when he swims out into the lake and pulls in the leaking boat in which she has kept a suicide vigil and hoped to drown. She grapples with the exhausted man, throws him to the ground, and strangles him. At dawn, when she recognizes his human features, she tells herself, "There was no guilt in this matter, no fault. How could I have known what body the devil would assume?" (203). Pauline's attacks on her Indian community and her mortification of her body parallel attacks on both Indians and landscape by the white culture with which she identifies.

In the interweaving of Pauline's and Nanapush's narratives, *Tracks* makes a path back into the history of the American frontier and the formation of a national literary culture. Erdrich starts the story again, revising the white man's master narrative of imperialist nostalgia. In particular, she rewrites Hemingway's portraits of the Chippewa and Faulkner's version of the defeat of the Indians and end of the forest wilderness, as well as the long lineage of other descendants from Cooper's historical romances. We have seen in chapter 5 some of the ways Hemingway feminized and animalized the Chippewa he had known in Upper Michigan as a boy. The key story of *In Our Time* for Erdrich's revision is "Indian Camp," with the white doctor and his brother and his son rowing across a lake by Indians to the scene of bloody birth and suicide in a squalid cabin. In Erdrich's rewriting, the narrative belongs to the Chippewa elder Nanapush, and the power of resolving the crisis lies with the Indians and their allied spirits in the landscape. As in Hemingway's story, the agony of his wife's labor drives the husband to inflict violence upon himself with a knife, but in Erdrich's version, Eli Kashpaw merely slashes his arm and runs into the woods. Nanapush describes the gathering of animal spirits as the crisis draws to a focus on the second day, when "it was as if the Manitous all through the woods spoke through Fleur, loose, arguing. I recognized them. Turtle's quavering scratch, the Eagle's high shriek, Loon's crazy bitterness, Otter, the howl of Wolf, Bear's low rasp" (59). A she-bear drunk on the Trader's wine shambles into the birth house and confronts Fleur in her labor, so astounding and energizing her that Fleur raises herself up and gives birth. Thus Erdrich has snatched the power of birth away from Hemingway's white male representative of science who glories in his superiority to the abject, animalized Chippewas. Erdrich's Indian people are an intelligent, wily, humorous, complex part of a world that posits no chasm between humans and other animals but rather suggests a potentially enormous reservoir of mutual energy.

In contrast to Faulkner's bear, Erdrich's bear is Fleur's mirror image, her totem animal and one of the most potent of all in the Chippewa symbolic system (Barnouw 7, 10; Landes 27–28; Grim 78–79). She is symbolic of the life of the forest, appearing as a comic drunk on one level but also serving to help Fleur give birth before she turns and stumbles away into the woods to disappear forever. Throughout Erdrich's tetralogy Fleur is associated with bear—Pauline says her tracks turn into bear tracks, and the bear's cough is said to be heard in her presence in both *Tracks* and *The Bingo Palace*—but Fleur is a healer and shaman all her long life.

When the forest falls at the end of *Tracks*, it is white men's doing, though Fleur allies herself with the forest in orchestrating a final scene of temporary vengeance. The Turcot Lumber Company has seized allotment after allotment of Indian land around the lake and clear-cut the timber. Nanapush later describes the carnage almost as the battering of his own body. "From where we now sit, granddaughter, I heard the groan and crack, felt the ground tremble as each tree slammed earth. I weakened into an old man as one oak went down, another and another was lost, as a gap formed here, a clearing there, and plain daylight entered" (9).

After Fleur's dogged efforts to save the Pillager allotment have been thwarted by the betrayal of her lover Eli Kashpaw's family, she waits beside her cabin for the final insult, the arrival of the white loggers with their teams of horses and equipment. Nanapush understands the sinister tension in the air as Fleur stands with her hands on her hips, glances up at the sky, and then closes her eyes. The wind rises, the waves slap lightly on the shore of the lake, and Nanapush hears the low murmur of Indian spirits in the woods. First one tree crashes down in the distance, then another closer by, as the white men bite their lips and glance over at Fleur, who flashes her fierce Pillager smile. Nanapush remembers:

> Around me, a forest was suspended, lightly held. The fingered lobes of leaves floated on nothing. The powerful throats, the columns of trunks and splayed twigs, all substance was illusion. Nothing was solid. Each green crown was held in the air by no more than splinters of bark.
>
> Each tree was sawed through at the base.
>
> One man laughed and leaned against a box elder. Down it fell, crushed a wagon. The wind shrieked and broke, tore into the brush, swept full force upon us. Fleur held to me and gripped my shirt. With one thunderstroke the trees surrounding Fleur's cabin cracked off and fell away from us in a circle, pinning beneath their branches the roaring men, the horses. The limbs snapped steel saws and rammed through wagon boxes. Twigs formed webs of wood, canopies laced over groans and struggles. Then the wind settled,

curled back into the clouds, moved on, and we were left standing together in a landscape level to the lake and to the road. (223)

This is a Pyrrhic victory. The forest is gone, Fleur moves off down the road pulling a small cart made of the green wood of Matchimanito oaks, and the remaining Indian community is left as refugees in a demystified modern world.[7] The historical evasions of Thoreau, Cather, Hemingway, and Faulkner have been blasted away by Erdrich's story of the frontier's close. Colonization, genocide, legal chicanery, and corporate pillage are all experienced in miniature from within Nanapush's family, but seen with a clear and bemused gaze almost innocent of hatred for the agents of all these disasters.

Fleur eventually returns to Lake Matchimanito and regains her family land, as we learn in Erdrich's most recent novel, *The Bingo Palace*, whose title refers to the fate of that land on Fleur's death at the age of more than one hundred years. A contemporary world of taverns and pickup trucks, senior citizens' retirement centers, double-wide trailers, and gambling halls has grown up all around the lake to make her old cabin in the wild brush a complete anachronism. Her great-grandson Lipsha comes to her desperate for guidance, but the identity confusions that beset him through the stories of *Love Medicine* continue. Any search for answers from the tribal past is doomed to be partial for him and all his people in the 1990s, even though he gains some insight from encounters with elders, in sweat lodges, or on vision quests.

From his uncle Lyman Lamartine, Lipsha hears the story of a vision "of an ungrazed hill where the grass was moving, going, rushing, as if a great hand was pushing it from underneath" which his dead Uncle Henry Jr. saw as "the earth breathing, coming at me, almost like it's playing with me." Lyman remembers the experience of seeing that hill with his brother and feeling they were in the grip of modest but unrelenting power: "Wind, earth, water—all of it flowed together as the lick of green flames, as the grass" (162–63). Lyman calls Lipsha "Little Brother" and says that he sees in him the same ability as Henry Jr.'s to understand the powers of the land and the spirit world.

Fleur herself, the most frightening and powerful elder in Lipsha's community, is waiting for her great-grandson to accept his role as her successor, "someone to carry on her knowledge," and even the gossipers in town call him "that medicine boy," though they use the term with some irony (7). He avoids this calling throughout the novel but has a powerful experience with the old lady when he begs her to help him with love medicine to win Shawnee Ray Toose. Though Fleur is over one hundred years old, Lipsha can hardly keep up with her when he walks several miles home with her from town and grows frightened in the woods around her cabin. "This is a one-way woods. She has me. She is drawing me forward on a magic string coughed up from her insides" (134). Yet he survives his fear and ends up for the evening in her cabin, experiencing a mystery he cannot fully report, when she turns to respond to his request for love medicine and looks so steadily into his eyes that he blinks. "When I open my eyes again, she broadens, blurs beyond my reach, beyond belief. Her face spreads out on the bones and goes on darkening and darkening. Her nose tilts up into a black snout and her eyes sink. I struggle to move from my place, but my legs are numb, my arms, my face, and then the lamp goes out. Blackness. I sit there motionless and my head fills with the hot rasp of her voice" (136–37).

Some months later, after the love medicine has worked, but only temporarily, Lipsha goes out to the lake with his Uncle Lyman to fast for three days in an attempt to learn his fate in the traditional Chippewa ritual of vision quest. But he cannot imagine "What is so great, what is so wonderful, what is so outrageously fantastic about the woods." Most of his visions are of hot dogs smeared with mustard, nachos, frozen Dairy Queen slush and ice cream. His reward for the vigil is to be sprayed by a skunk whose crabby voice tells him that the sacred land of Lake Matchimanito "ain't real estate" (198–99). This is belated and hopeless advice, because his cousin Lyman Lamartine has already begun the planning for a gambling center to be planted exactly where Fleur's cabin stands.

Such uncertain magic as the profits from gambling casinos seems to be the only hope for tribal people in late-twentieth-century America; Erdrich is describing a reality that has sprung up on reservations all over the United States. Gambling was a traditional Native activity, but it is uncertain whether the modern mechanized version can support the restoration of land and people that many tribes anticipate. Certainly reservation life has made a radical break from everything Fleur Pillager and the old way of life have represented in Erdrich's fiction. Knowing that her land is foreclosed and that she is to be removed from her cabin, Fleur walks away to her death, pulling a toboggan over the winter ice to join Moses and all the other old ones in the island cave, leaving the daylight landscape to her confused and mercenary descendants. But sometimes they feel her return.

> She doesn't tap our panes of glass or leave her claw marks on eaves and doors. She only coughs, low, to make her presence known. You have heard the bear laugh—that is the chuffing noise we hear and it is unmistakable. Yet no matter how we strain to decipher the sound it never quite makes sense, never relieves our certainty or our suspicion that there is more to be told, more than we know, more than can be caught in the sieve of our thinking. For [the day of her death] we heard the voices, the trills and resounding cries that greeted the old woman when she arrived on that pine-dark island, and all night our lesser hearts beat to the sound of the spirit's drum, through those anxious hours when we call our lives to question. (274)

Under one cultural guise or another, most of humanity shares to some degree in this sense of the presence of the animistic past. Yet Erdrich questions the possibility of its recovery through her portrait of Lipsha Morrisey's comic failures, even while she acknowledges the continued presence of enormous powers in the landscape and Lipsha's connection to them. Polish philosopher Leszek Kolakowski defines an essential alienation for humans resulting from the development of self-consciousness.

> It is not the fact that we are feeling and sensitive *subjects* that distinguishes us among living creatures, but the fact that we can be *objects* for ourselves, that is, be capable of splitting our consciousness so that it becomes its own observer. . . . Contact with nature is not per se comprehensible, because even though we understand that contact we are unable to identify permanently our own observing consciousness with our own consciousness as an element of nature under observation. Our life in culture is incapable of being non-reflectingly accepted as a continuation of a natural ecological situation, as it contains the unceasing memory of the observer doubling himself in a projection towards himself as a object. (115)

Reintegration under these circumstances is unattainable, except through the creative activity of fiction: "Mythology is an attempt to overcome the amnesia of Being" (118).

Such fictions cannot be supplied by explorations of the past but instead must be suggested by projections into the future. Environmental philosophers, ecofeminists, ecocritics, New Biologists, poets, and science fiction writers are all working busily to create such narratives or mythopoeic forms.[8] Max Oelschlaeger himself participates in this effort, but an alarming thing happens at the end of *The Idea of Wilderness* that is predictable in light of his reliance on the notion of the Magna Mater as the benign ground of archaic philosophies.

> We, the spoiled children of the Great Mother, we who refuse to see, to hear and heed Her message, Her laws. Is salvation possible? Or have we so fouled this earth, so covered the green world beneath our second world, that no light can penetrate the world's midnight? Is there hope for the plant and animal people? Is there hope for us all? These are questions that must be answered by the postmodern mind, for only through that exercise of consciousness can our modern dilemma be transcended. (353)

It seems to me that the "postmodern mind" cannot afford to fall back into the destructive gender oppositions that we have seen to be central to American literature and to the long European/Mediterranean/Mesopotamian cultural tradition from which it descends, as Patrick Murphy and Paul Shepard have recently warned.[9] Concerted efforts must be made to shape new metaphors for the land that are neuter and non-anthropomorphic. Anthropologists have documented many cultures that have existed without feminizing the landscape or positing the extreme separation that is the European heritage;[10] thus we know that such conceptual reorganizations must be possible.

James Lovelock's Gaia Hypothesis, asserting that "the biosphere is a self-regulating entity with the capacity to keep our planet healthy by controlling the chemical and physical environment" (*Gaia* xii), has suffered from both scientific skepticism and attacks by ecotheorists like Murphy and Shepard who emphasize the gender implications in the theory's name. But Lovelock's basic scientific argument is a neuter concept of an organic cybernetic system. It offers one possible metaphor for a landscape where we might both be conscious and working within a much wider living system than we can understand or pretend to control. Octavia Butler's conception of the living ship that is a symbiotic host for its sentient Oankali inhabitants in her *Xenogenesis Trilogy* offers another. The alien creatures who attempt to repopulate postapocalypse Earth in this work are interplanetary gene traders whose ship is a metaphoric landscape meant to reinterpret that of our own Earth. It is entirely animate, a large and complex body in symbiotic relationship with the panoply of creatures it houses. Oankali "houses" are actually compartments inside treelike organisms whose walls open to the touch of Oankali "hands." These "trees" produce vegetable foods that the Oankali have trained to make them tasty and similar to foods humans eat. Also, fabrics used for clothing are produced by the living hosts. Animals living in the ship have been genetically manipulated to serve as transportation. Wastes are buried in the living soil of the ship and are metabolized. Carnivorous plants have been genetically changed into healing sleeping-chambers. The difference between the Oankali ship and the earth is that it is a mobile biota governed by wise, restrained beings who act for the good of the entire living community. But of course such extensive genetic manipulation as the Oankali practice raises troubling ethical questions and depends in any case on an almost godlike restraint and wisdom in their behavior. Butler makes it clear that humans are far too selfish, violent, and destructive to be capable of Oankali cooperation and disinterestedness.

Donna Haraway discusses the complex mix of benign and dangerous communication and interdependence of life among these beings, calling attention to the fact that "Catastrophe, survival, and metamorphosis are Butler's constant themes" (378). Butler's main character in the first novel of the trilogy is an African-American woman named Lilith who ends the novel having been forced into reproductive interaction with the aliens so that, as Haraway summarizes the situation, she is "pregnant with the child of five progenitors who come from two species, at least three genders, two sexes, and an indeterminate number of races" (378). Butler seems to insist on a radical interrelation among living creatures that involves constant metamorphosis and adaptation. The Oankali understand this and have evolved values that support balance and reciprocity within an extensive larger Self that is a world. If we were to imagine consciousness in some of the smaller elements of an individual human body, say lymphocytes or white blood cells, we might more easily understand the necessary relation between the "ship" or mobile whole and the individuals who make it up—like the earth and the individual animals who make up its biota. Octavia Butler seems to have done something of the sort in developing the idea of the Oankali ship and the gene trading needed for the community's life. James Lovelock implies an analogy similar to Butler's at the end of *The Ages of Gaia: A Biography of Our Liv-*

ing Earth, when he attacks the exploitative model of contemporary technological thought.

> It all depends on you and me. If we see the world as a living organism of which we are a part—not the owner, nor the tenant; not even a passenger—we could have a long time ahead of us and our species might survive for its "allotted span." It is up to us to act personally in a way that is constructive. The present frenzy of agriculture and forestry is a global ecocide as foolish as it would be to act on the notion that our brains are supreme and the cells of other organs expendable. Would we drill wells through our skins to take the blood for its nutrients? (237)

This is not just an American problem, as the long history I have tried to sketch in chapter 1 should indicate. There were once great pine and cedar forests in Mesopotamia and Lebanon, which Sumerians and Semites plundered for their great public buildings; Crete was deforested by the Minoans 3,500 years ago; first Greece and then Rome ravaged the whole northern coast of the Mediterranean for their naval fleets and building projects. To this day, the bleaching bones of the Greek mountains testify to the severity of landscape degradation accomplished by the supposed originary paragons of Western civilization. In the Western hemisphere, there is archaeological evidence that the Mayans destroyed the landscapes on which their city-states depended. Whatever the ideology or mythic shape all these peoples gave their actions, the result was devastation for the land, changes in weather and rainfall, and widespread extinction of wildlife.

I have attempted to trace the ancient symbolic background for a peculiarly self-conscious chapter in the human exploitation of the ecosystem—the European appropriation of North America—and then to look closely at the gendered semiotic practices that have been used to mask and excuse destructive behavior. This kind of special pleading lies at the very heart of the humanistic traditions we have inherited from our European ancestors, in particular, as I have tried to show, the heroic masculine codes at the heart of the American pastoral for the past two hundred years. The "melodramas of beset manhood" which predominate in the official version of American literary culture require a feminized landscape where solitary heroes can escape the demeaning responsibilities of communal life. Women writers have challenged these versions of human self-definition and morality, and women from non-European ethnic backgrounds have revised standard male histories or substituted new stories that suggest other ways of living in the land. It is time for us to use these new figurations to rethink our place on earth, as one of the grand decimal periods in our European calendar draws to a close amidst the environmental fears and increasing eca-tastrophes that beset us.

However, we must entertain the possibility that the environmental movement is itself a kind of imperialist nostalgia. Can it be an accident that ecological consciousness has appeared in the industrialized world of Euro-America? Jean Baudrillard calls it a "maleficent ecology" by which the whole concept of nature has been reconceived.

> The modern discovery of nature consists in its liberation as energy and in a mechanical transformation of the world. After having first been matter, and then energy, nature is today becoming an inter-active subject. It is ceasing to be an object, but this is bringing it all the more surely into the circuit of subjection. A dramatic paradox, and one which also affects human beings: we are much more com-promised when we cease to be objects and become subjects. This is a trick that was pulled on us long ago, in the name of absolute lib-eration. Let's not pull the same one on nature. For the ultimate danger is that, in an interactivity built up into a total system of communication, there is no *other*, there are only subjects—and very soon, only subjects without objects. (80)

Baudrillard believes we have stepped out of history and "passed a point beyond which *nothing is either human or inhuman any longer* and what is at stake . . . is the tottering of the species into the void" (82–83).

Increasingly all over the globe, and with the political stimulation and encouragement of American and European environmental organizations, indigenous peoples of India, South America, Indonesia, and Africa are working to save their remaining forests and preserve traditional ways of subsistence living on the land. But this may be only a last flicker be-fore extinction. Our species may only be engaged in creating a series of zoological parks to entomb relics of the earth's past, while the powerful of our kind work frenetically to create a technological virtual reality under glass or underground like the one described in E. M. Forster's eerily prophetic story of 1909, "The Machine Stops." Baudrillard claims that Walt Disney was the true prophet of our human future, an "inspired precursor of a universe where all past or present forms meet in a playful promiscuity" (118).

Octavia Butler comes closest to anticipating in a realistic way how our future might look, though her warily utopian vision of Oankali/construct plantations on Earth assumes that humans first destroyed most life on their planet in apocalyptic warfare. For her, the playfulness of Baudrillard's promiscuous future can never hold sway because of political injustice and the biological consequences of human technology. Butler's most recent novel, *Parable of the Sower*, moves back closer to the present and forgoes the science fiction fabrications of an alien deus ex machina, to imagine the collapse of American cities, technologies, and political structures in class warfare only twenty or thirty years away, with streams of ragged refugees flowing up and down Interstate 5 and Highway 101 in California as cities burn and survivors turn to savagery and cannibalism. We must hope that the more positive vision of the *Xenogenesis Trilogy* can be a possible guide and that the scientific reorientation suggested by Lovelock's Gaia Hypothesis in its recently revised forms and by the Biophilia Hypothesis implied in Kellert and Wilson's anthology are the beginnings of new landscape myths for humankind.

NOTES

CHAPTER 1: Lost Innocence

1. See her discussion of this final passage of Fitzgerald's novel, 138–39.

2. Lawrence 67–92; and Fiedler 168–200. Fiedler seems clearly to have begun his analysis where Lawrence left off, exploring the way Cooper uses the dark-haired Cora as repository of passion and connection with unbridled forces in the indigenous culture and landscape. See also Klaus Theweleit on the psychic drama of imperialism, 323–25.

3. Annette Kolodny briefly refers to this ancient tradition of gendering the landscape (8–9), but the fullest recent exploration of the archaeological evidence for its origins is found in Marija Gimbutas's *Goddesses and Gods of Old Europe* and *The Language of the Goddess*. Maxine Sheets-Johnstone calls the origin for such analogical traditions "a biological disposition to use one's body as a semantic template" (308).

4. See G. R. Levy 29–53; Christopher Vecsey 52; Black Elk, through Joseph Epes Brown, in Tedlock and Tedlock 22–26; Oelschlaeger 12–17; McLuhan 5, 6, 22, 56. Marija Gimbutas finds surviving elements of this worldview among European peoples of isolated areas such as the Basque region of Spain, Ireland, Brittany, and Lithuania; see, for example, pp. xvii–xviii, 219, 249, 275, and 290 of *Language*.

5. Joseph Campbell l–lvii.

6. Continuing the emphasis of Bachofen and his followers are Jungian archetypal works like Eric Neumann's *The Great Mother* and C. Kerenyi's *Eleusis*; and Gimbutas's *Goddesses and Gods* and *The Language of the Goddess*; and feminist historians of religion like Rosemary Radford Reuther and Merlin Stone. Herbert Schniedau uses James Mellaart's excavations at Catal Huyuk as evidence for matriarchal cultural origins in *Sacred Discontent* 234–38. Working counter to these efforts has been the main body of archaeologists and mythographers—for example, Walter Burkert, whose *Greek Religion* seems at least in part to be a revision of Harrison's *Prolegomena*, which deemphasizes feminine forces in Greek religious practice; and Jaan Puhvel, who pays very little attention to female divinities in his *Comparative Mythology*.

7. One of the most ambitious and intriguing works in this area is Alexander Marshack's *The Roots of Civilization*; see also Paul Shepard, *Man in the Landscape*; Henri Delporte, *L'image de la femme dans l'art préhistorique*, and Gimbutas, *Language*.

8. "Deep history" is a term used by Paul Shepard at least as early as *Nature and Madness* ix.

9. See also Cixous and Clément; Irigaray; and Ortner.

10. See *Goddesses and Gods* 18, 145–50, 196–200, 236–38, and *Language* xvi–xxi. Colin Renfrew has led recent challenges to Gimbutas's migration theory, especially in *Archaeology and Language*, but most Indo-Europeanists still assume that migrations were central to the spread of Indo-European culture.

11. In his classic article on "The Historic Roots of Our Ecological Crisis" Lynn White, Jr., makes a distinction between the relatively gentle ancient Middle Eastern technique of scratch-plowing and the later Northern European system of deep plowing that attacked the land with great violence and a friction requiring eight oxen to pull the plow (345–46).

12. Shepard devotes a chapter of *Man in the Landscape* to "Varieties of Nature Hating," 214–37, but does not directly consider the part that gender plays in the attitude.

13. The field of neuroanatomy is very active at the present time, with sophisticated neurological imaging techniques allowing close observation of blood flow and electrical activity deep within the brain as well as on its surface while activities such as speaking and reading are occurring. Churchland's *Neurophysiology* is a sophisticated introduction to the field. For an ambitious recent attempt to relate literary criticism to neuroscience, see Karl Kroeber, *Ecological Literary Criticism: Romantic Imagining and the Biology of Mind*.

14. See Susan Star for an analysis of the historical development of the debate on localization theory.

15. Teresa De Lauretis comments on similar processes operating in Greek tragedy, specifically Sophocles' *Oedipus the King*, but she assumes—with Vladimir Propp—a much later era for the enactment of the conflicted shift from a matrifocal power center to a patrifocal one. Landscapes such as forests are assumed to be identified with feminine powers, in a gradual evolution of narrative structures that posit the male hero as active agent and the feminine as space, obstacle, matrix, and matter. See her discussion in *Alice Doesn't* 113–19.

16. For comparative purposes, see Thorkild Jacobsen's translation of these passages in *The Harps That Once* 3–23, 91–94.

17. Kramer believes that the history of ancient Mesopotamia is characterized from its beginnings by the interplay and competition between sedentary agricultural peoples of the Tigris and Euphrates valleys and nomadic Semitic pastoralists from the West (234–41), but he also suggests (95) that the mother-goddess Ki was originally the primary Sumerian deity and was displaced by later male gods. See Lerner's hypothesis delineating the historical displacement of goddess religions by male-dominated pantheons of deities in the ancient world (141–60). This process occurs in the narrative structure of Hesiod's *Theogony*,

leading to the displacement of the earth-mother Gaia (Gey, Gaia—echo of Sumerian Ki by a pantheon of predominantly male gods, ll. 115–22, pp. 86–87).

18. See also Maureen G. Kovacs, *The Epic of Gilgamesh*, xxi.

19. For a discussion of the various textual sources and levels of the epic, see Kramer, 181–98, and Jeffrey Tigay.

20. Inanna is her Sumerian name, Ishtar her Babylonian name.

21. Marshack 335–40; Gimbutas, *GG*, 196–200; Burkert, *GR*, 42, 124, 149, 154; and *HN*, 115–16; and Puhvel 136.

22. H. W. F. Saggs sees this passage as reflecting historical changes in Mesopotamian religious concepts (19).

CHAPTER 2: European Tradition and Figuration of a New World

1. The relatively late tradition of Jewish wisdom literature, represented by the books of Ecclesiasticus, Baruch, and Wisdom in the Roman Catholic Bible, stand as a significant exception. In *The Feminine Dimension of the Divine*, Joan Chamberlain Engelsman describes the historical repression of the female divine figure of Sophia in the early Church and replacement of the feminine Greek word for wisdom, *sophia*, with the masculine word *logos*, word, cited in Susan Cady, Marian Ronan, and Hal Taussig, *Sophia, The Future of Feminist Spirituality*, 11–38.

2. See Oelschlaeger on differences between the ancient J and E sources of the biblical text as we have it, 375–76, n. 55.

3. See Merlin Stone's discussion of this implicit attack on female reproductive power, and indeed on the chthonic religious traditions of the ancient Near East (198–223); also Paul Shepard, *Nature and Madness*, 47–74; and Oelschlaeger 46–53.

4. Kramer describes specific Sumerian backgrounds for the biblical story and explains in particular the painless childbirth of Sumerian goddesses as contrast to the painful labor decreed as punishment for the biblical Eve, in *History Begins*, 141–47.

5. My interpretation of the play differs markedly from Robert Pogue Harrison's idea that the subject is the collapse of civic order into the forest, "the abyss of precivic darkness from which civilization is merely a deviation, and a precarious one at that" (38). Harrison reads the play as a consistent aesthetic whole, whereas I see it as an archaic core sandwiched between a rationalized beginning and ending. For me, Euripides' attempt to blame Agave for the tragedy does not articulate with the meanings established in the body of the play. It seems to me that Nietzsche comes much closer to a workable explanation, even though he ignores the play of gender at the heart of the dramatic conflict between Pentheus and Dionysos.

6. And the god himself can be seen as another version of the goddess's annually dying lover like Dumuzi/Tammuz and Osiris, as William Anderson and Clive Hicks explain in *Green Man* 37, 39–40.

7. See Shepard's discussion of the complex evolution of hostility toward the natural world, from the Hebrews down to Greek and Christian thought, *Man in the Landscape* 219–21.

8. Leo Marx traces this idea back to the work of Friedrich Schiller, whose *Letters upon the Aesthetical Education of Man* (1795) was introduced to England by Carlyle (169–84). Marx's chapter "The Machine" is a thoughtful examination of the European origins of the metaphor and its application in the United States early in the nation's history.

9. See Keller also, 43–65. She follows Merchant in connecting the birth of science with the persecution of witches but stresses the battle of the new scientists against an alchemical tradition steeped in erotic imagery, as part of a complex set of economic, social, and political changes in European life that gradually transformed the ideology of gender.

10. See Roderick Nash 44–47; and Oelschlaeger's chapter on romanticism: "Wild Nature: Critical Responses to Modernism," 97–132.

11. In *The History of the Seneca Indians* Arthur C. Parker describes how Huron chiefs drew French colonial authorities into previously existing conflicts between themselves and the Iroquois. The Iroquois then courted the English and Dutch as allies for their defense, and thus indigenous tribal hostilities became a European war as well (24–26).

12. Johansen describes the effect on Hobbes and Locke, Marx and Engels, as well as Rousseau, 119–26.

13. P. 16. See also Tichi's discussion of Bradford's and Mather's rhetoric of condemnation of the land, 22–27.

CHAPTER 3: Pastoral Ambivalence in Emerson and Thoreau

1. Cheyfitz goes so far as to claim that Emerson grew up in "a mob of hermaphroditic figures," with his father dying when the boy was eight and the widowed household run by a grimly frugal mother and the paternal aunt whom he called "Father Mum" and "my heroine" (160–63). Ellison (7) tells us that Emerson associated his Aunt Mary with the sublime, but Barish balances the picture with a fuller biographical study crediting Mary Moody Emerson's warmly supportive role in her nephew's development while also tempering Cheyfitz's overemphasis upon Emerson's one epistolary use of the term "Father Mum" (36–53).

2. This same contradictory dynamic can be seen more clearly in the movement back and forth between sentimental homage and condescension in Emer-

son's 1855 address on "Woman," reluctantly presented to a women's rights convention (*Complete Works* 6: 335–55).

3. See Ellison 75–77. F. O. Mattheissen's attempts to find organic unity in both Emerson and Thoreau have been followed by more recent efforts like Jehlen's argument that Emerson was attempting to define a transcendent unity behind his apparently oppositional dualisms (83–84). Cheyfitz, Ellison, and Barish are more interested in the forces causing such instabilities and in his courage in facing them. Ellison sees Emerson as a typical romantic, writing the "heterogeneous, self-critical prose" that characterized his era and prepared for our own century (232–37).

4. See, for instance, James McIntosh 21, and Michaels 140–46.

5. Sattelmeyer explains that Thoreau read Lyell's *Principles of Geology* (1830–33) in 1840 and continued through the rest of his life reading widely in the controversial new work in natural history by writers including Louis Agassiz and Charles Darwin (*Thoreau's Reading* 81, 78–110). Rossi discusses in detail the influence of Lyell's work on the Journals and *Walden* in "Thoreau and Nineteenth-Century Science."

6. Leo Marx, for example, calls attention to the traditional pastoral unreality of the setting, the temporary quality of Thoreau's sojourn, and the many ways he emphasizes the middle ground he occupies between the industrial modern world of Concord and the untamed landscape of precolonized New England (242–65). Philip Fisher calls Walden Pond "the already pacified and cleared annex of a society" (81), while Joan Burbick takes a more positive position and concentrates on Thoreau's reconciliation of nature and civilization at Walden Pond (59–82).

7. Michael West claims, "No English writer since Milton and Pope has more assiduously sought to adapt the Greco-Roman ideal of nobility to modern culture" (1053). But West sets Thoreau apart from other nineteenth-century "Heroic Vitalists" such as Carlyle and Nietzsche in offering a democratic, egalitarian version of the ideal.

CHAPTER 4: Willa Cather's Prairie Epics

1. Slote discusses Cather's debt to Emerson (34, 36, 40, 42, 211n, 222), to the effect that his prose fixed itself firmly in the young writer's imagination as early as her college years as a journalist. Also, O'Brien describes how the adolescent "William Cather, M.D." listed Emerson as her favorite prose writer, alongside Napoleon as her favorite character in history in an album book (82, 100).

2. Lee argues, "Cather's work gets its energy from contraries. She is pulled between the natural and the artificial, the native and the European. She is a democrat and an elitist. She relishes troll-like energy and primitivism as much as

delicacy and culture. . . . Her fictions are of split selves and doublings" (16). Lee sees Cather's androgyny as another example of these contrarieties.

3. See Smith-Rosenberg's illustrations for photographic examples and Kate Chopin's story "Charlie" for a fictional treatment.

4. See Smith-Rosenberg's discussion of the extreme form of this figure as emblem of explosive, destructive, manic, masturbatory male energy in popular Davy Crockett tales (90–108).

5. See Lee's discussion of the overwhelming power of the land in an earlier Cather story, "The Bohemian Girl," which was later expanded into the love story of Emil and Marie in *O Pioneers!* (103).

6. Fetterley generalizes this dynamic to explain the very source of Cather's genius as "a woman's voice making love to a feminine landscape" (161). Unless otherwise indicated, all quotations from Cather's novels will be taken from the Library of America edition.

7. Josephine Donovan sees the Demeter-Persephone myth beneath the surface of *O Pioneers!* For her, Alexandra "seems to integrate the Artemisian daughter with Demeter the mother," and Marie functions as another avatar of the Kore who will be swallowed by the earth. This confusing scheme translates the "Corn God" into a Corn Mother who is identified with Alexandra's Demeter qualities but who must try to carry away the daughter self (107–8). See also O'Brien's complex but oddly inconclusive psychoanalytic reading of this figure (437–38).

8. See Moers's pioneering discussion of symbolic female landscapes in Cather 257–63; Rosowski's analysis of female sexual symbolism in the Colorado landscape around Moonstone as well as Panther Canyon (70–72); O'Brien's discussion of the canyon as Bachelard's "intimate space" (410); and Lee's insistence that we recognize the androgyny of the passage (126–29).

9. Lee elucidates the complex circularity and sense of renewable time created by the way the Introduction's train trip recapitulates Jim's original arrival in Black Hawk by train (133–34). See also Rosowski 76–88 for a more extensive study of the novel's circularities and connections to similar patterns in romantic poetry.

10. Lee (140) likens this negative space to "the chaos before the Word" of the Old Testament creation story, but it could just as easily be linked to Chaos before the emergence of Gaia in Hesiod's *Theogony*. The idea that Nature is formless "outside man's jurisdiction" is a favorite concept of Willa Cather's that reappears ten years later in *Death Comes to the Archbishop* to describe a similarly "wild" landscape in the Southwest (109).

11. Cather's attention to immigrant families might seem a populist move, made at a time of national xenophobia when public sentiment had turned against the waves of foreigners pouring into the country. In "The Vanishing American" Michaels details the series of laws enacted to prevent both foreign immigrants

and Indians from becoming American citizens. He also discusses the virulent nativist opinions expressed in newspapers and public speeches by political figures of the era during and after World War I (222–29). While it is true that her fiction does celebrate the energy and endurance of the immigrant farmers, Fischer and Michaels (40–41) show how Cather's work is tainted by condescension and racism, and Kaye reminds us that Cather keeps the immigrants in the position of peasants (25). The plight of the invisible Indians of the Plains is closely intertwined historically with that of the central European peasantry that Cather depicts as the earthy and rude mechanicals of her pastoral retreat. And *My Ántonia* plays out a strange dynamic that allies them with the landscape as raw materials for the higher cultural life of American wealth and masculine power.

12. Noel Polk suggests a biblical echo, the notion of beating swords into plowshares, and contrasts the greedy and destructive Spanish search for gold with the natural golden imagery of the setting sun (personal correspondence, September 1992).

CHAPTER 5: Pastoral Regression in Hemingway and Faulkner

1. In *Green Hills of Africa* he mentions Poe and Melville, Emerson, Hawthorne, Whittier, Thoreau (claiming improbably not to be able to read him), James, Crane, and Twain (20–22); Kipling, Flaubert (27); Tolstoi (69–70); Thomas Wolfe, Dostoevsky, Stendhal, and Joyce (71); Turgenev and Mann (108). Though he does allude to Gertrude Stein in *Green Hills of Africa* (65–66) and gives her a large place in *A Moveable Feast* (9–31, 117–19), he is anything but generous. See Reynolds 16–23.

2. Blotner mentions Freud, Frazer, and T. S. Eliot, as well as the indirect influence of Stein and Joyce through Sherwood Anderson. Blotner 396, 399, 417, 457–58. See also Minter 26–27.

3. Blotner 17–19, 36, 246, 631; and Minter 6–7, 10–12. Richard King defines the problem in Freudian terms, seeing Faulkner as defined by a Family Romance also played out in the larger psychosocial context of the devastated post-Reconstruction South with its bankrupt ideal of the heroic Lost Cause.

4. Hemingway's war experience is well known, though often supplemented by his early stories about the war. In fact, he was seriously wounded in the legs by shrapnel while handing out chocolate to combat troops on the line (Lynn, *Hemingway*, 79). Faulkner's exploits are understandably less known. He was only an air cadet training in Canada when the war ended, and it is doubtful that he ever flew a plane in that capacity. Still, he returned home limping, with a cane and a custom-made uniform, telling wild stories about having flown a trainer upside-down through a hangar, crashed, and had a steel plate implanted in his head (Blotner 64–66).

5. See, for instance, Anne Ross for a discussion of such sites in Britain, *Pagan Celtic Britain: Studies in Iconography and Tradition* 19–33. Cerne Abbey is an especially well-known example, and sacred wells are found all over Ireland and very frequently by Breton churches.

6. See, for example, David Stewart's "Ike McCaslin, Cop-Out," and Glen Love's "Hemingway's Indian Virtues: An Ecological Reconsideration."

7. See Young 7. More recently Debra A. Moddelmog has discussed these rejected materials in "The Unifying Consciousness of a Divided Conscience: Nick Adams as Author of *In Our Time.*" Moddelmog accepts the fictional premise of the pages Hemingway excised from the final form of "Big Two-Hearted River" but comments on the negative attitudes toward women and marriage that form a context for the published story.

8. A representative of the Acquisitions Librarian at the Chicago Art Institute said in a 1994 telephone conversation that Hemingway could not have seen Cézanne's work at the Chicago Art Institute, which only acquired its first Cézanne in 1926, five years after Hemingway left Chicago.

9. He says in *The Green Hills of Africa* that "I have not yet been able to read [*Walden*]" (15). Critics have fallen naturally into comparing Hemingway to Thoreau; see, for example, Glen Love's assertion in "Hemingway's Indian Virtues" that in broad terms "Hemingway's primitivism may be seen as a return to earth, Thoreau-like, to front the essential facts of life, and to reduce it to its most elemental terms" (202). Early drafts of the story that became "The Snows of Kilimanjaro" featured a hero named Henry Walden (Busch 3).

10. He speaks of war as a great advantage for a writer, one of the major subjects, and measures many of the writers he most admires by their experience of it (*Green Hills* 47–48). Its centrality to his most successful books needs no emphasis.

11. Posthumously published fragments written around the same time and featuring Nick Adams involve him in lovemaking with a girl who is part of his crowd of summer friends at a lake resort, but he calls the woman "Slut" after he is finished with her, and he goes home to his own bed, leaving her in the woods (*NAS* 228). Complicating the treatment of women in the Nick Adams stories is the unfinished autobiographical narrative "The Last Good Country," describing adolescent Nick's escape from game wardens, with the aid of a favorite sister who accompanies him to an idyllic forest campsite far from town. Nick's fond relation to his tomboy sister and tolerance for her cropping her hair and trying to turn into a boy reappears decades later in the posthumously published *The Garden of Eden*. In its later form, this material is developed into a much fuller exploration of sexual experimentation and androgyny, though the *The Garden of Eden* does not fully indicate the willingness to accept sexual ambiguity of the unpublished original manuscript (as discussed by Debra Moddelmog and Robert Scholes at the Hemingway/Fitzgerald International Conference in

Paris, July 7, 1994). Even in the published version of the manuscript, the language of David and Catherine's discussion of Catherine's "surprise" for her husband (44–47) is very close to the dialogue between Nick and his sister about her excitement in surprising him by cropping her hair:

> "I don't want to trade you for a brother."
>
> "You have to now, Nickie, don't you see? It was something we had to do so I did it for a surprise."
>
> "I like it," Nick said. "The hell with everything. I like it very much." (113)

12. See Jackson Benson's comment on the grotesque suffering and death associated with women and childbearing in Hemingway's fiction (287–88). Jeffrey Meyers suggests in "Hemingway's Primitivism and 'Indian Camp'" that Hemingway understood the husband's suicide in the story as a reaction to the doctor's violation of couvade taboo (308).

13. See Ellen Glasgow's treatment of her heroine as a flower in *Virginia* and Anne Jones's discussion of this tactic in *Tomorrow Is Another Day* 245–46; also Westling, *Sacred Groves and Ravaged Gardens* 10–12, 27–30; and Blotner on Faulkner's early pastoralism 70–72, 78–81, 93–98.

14. See Bleikasten 50–55 for the fullest recent treatment of this imagery.

15. On the night of Damuddy's death, Benjy associates Mr. Compson and Quentin with the rain he hears on the roof. They have both been outdoors and smell like rain, but he seems to register the smell because they are kind to him (40–41). Two black males are also associated with comforting smells: Versh smells like rain and like a dog (42), and T. P. has a smell that Benjy recognizes and likes when he sleeps in his bed (18).

16. At a later time, when Caddy is necking on the porch with a boy named Charlie, Benjy begins to cry and tries to pull her away from him. Only after Caddy has sent Charlie away and washed her mouth out with soap does she smell like trees again (29–30). At her wedding, she wears flowers in her hair and a veil like shining wind, but Benjy smells through this illusion to her sexual fall: "Caddy put her arms around me, and her shining veil, and I couldn't smell trees anymore and I began to cry" (24–25). See Diane Roberts's psychoanalytic perspective on this image and its associations (116–18).

17. See Sundquist's chapter on "The Strange Career of Joe Christmas" for a richly intertextual placement of the novel in a cultural context that supports such associations of racial hysteria, sexuality, violence, and menstrual blood (63–95).

18. See for example Minter 189–91; Sundquist 133 and 158–59; Laura Claridge, "Isaac McCaslin's Failed Bid for Adulthood"; and Patrick McGee, "Gender and Generation in Faulkner's 'The Bear.'"

19. Archetypal studies of the 1950s and 1960s, such as John Lydenberg's "Nature and Myth in Faulkner's *The Bear*" and Francis Lee Utley's "Pride and

Humility: The Cultural Roots of Ike McCaslin" see this ancient material providing access to "essential mysteries" of human life.

20. Sundquist calls attention to the multiple paradoxes of Faulkner's adaptation of the poem and the fact of rape behind Keats's and Faulkner's romantic rhetoric, but he is chiefly interested in its relevance for the problems of miscegenation and incest that Ike's repudiation is meant to expiate (137–38). McGee 51–52 seems to miss the point of McCaslin's quotation and discusses other aspects of the painting on the urn than those McCaslin mentions.

21. See Sandars's "Introduction" to her text of *The Epic of Gilgamesh*, 17–20.

CHAPTER 6: Eudora Welty's Sacramental Vision

1. Eudora Welty herself often speaks of her debt to fairy tale and myth in the interviews collected by Peggy Prenshaw in *Conversations with Eudora Welty*. Some of the major critical discussions of her use of these materials have been provided by John Edward Hardy in "*Delta Wedding* as Region and Symbol"; Peggy Prenshaw in "Women's World, Man's Place"; Carol Manning in *With Ears Opening Like Morning Glories* 89–121; Louise Westling in *Eudora Welty* 26, 43–49, 85–126; and Rebecca Mark in *The Dragon's Blood*.

2. In *Eudora Welty's Achievement of Order* Michael Kreyling offers the most satisfying direct interpretation of the story as Mrs. Larkin's attempt to accept the workings of Nature (16–17). I have previously discussed the story as an exploration of the interrelation of fertility and death in *Eudora Welty* 67–68. Other readings see it as a parable of women's repressed anger (Schmidt 23–27) and as an allegorical rendering of the artist's dilemma (Burgess 136–38).

3. In conversations at her home in Jackson during the summer of 1987, Miss Welty spoke with me about her early enthusiasm for Frazer and her continued reliance on *The Golden Bough*, as well as her long interest in the archaeology of Neolithic England and Ireland, Minoan Crete, and the remains of the Mississippi Mound Culture in her native state.

4. Robert Penn Warren recognized Welty's use of fertility motifs early in her career, referring to the "saturnalian revel" of the fish fry in "The Wide Net" and the "field god" heroes of "Livvie" and "At the Landing" (253–55). Ruth Vande Kieft developed these themes further, and Prenshaw richly defined the affirming feminine consciousness that they are used to dramatize. For fuller development of my arguments, see *Eudora Welty* 74–84. See also Peter Schmidt's emphasis on gender conflict in these stories (123–44).

5. In the *New York Post*, April 18, 1946, Sterling North said that he felt as if he had just eaten a barrel of molasses when he finished reading *Delta Wedding*. Similarly, Isaac Rosenfeld in the *New Republic* and an anonymous reviewer in the

Providence Journal of that same month complained about what seemed a flowery preciousness of the novel's prose. These responses result at least in part from gendered expectations and prejudices that continue to influence some readers. I once had a male student who called the novel's style "pink," and another who said, "Let's face it: a bear hunt is much more interesting than a wedding." The student's reference to Faulkner brings to mind Leslie Fiedler's revealing comment in *Love and Death* that only "the grossness, the sheer dirtiness, the farce and howling burlesque" keep Faulkner from seeming precious (482).

6. A number of critics have commented on Eudora Welty's kinship with Virginia Woolf, beginning with John Crowe Ransom's remarking on similarities in style in the *Kenyon Review* 8 (1946): 505. See Michael Kreyling; my discussion in *Sacred Groves* 65–75 and *Eudora Welty* 85–98; and Albert Devlin, "Modernity and the Literary Plantation."

7. Welty echoes Woolf in writing of a mother of eight children, setting her story under a September harvest moon, focusing on courtship, associating a lost brooch with sexual initiation, emphasing the centrality of food in social ritual and family life, and so on. For fuller elaboration of these parallels, see *Sacred Groves* 65–75.

8. "The Delta Cousins," The Welty Collection, Mississippi State Department of Archives and History, Series 4, C1.a, p. 31.

9. Welty described this experience to me during a conversation at her home, June 16, 1987. She went on to say that the Delta landscape stimulated a rich flow of mysterious associations. She visited Robinson's family a number of times while he was serving in the Army Air Corps in Italy during World War II. This was the same period during which she was writing the novel and sending it in pieces to him. She told me that she wrote the novel and sent the installments to him to cheer him up and remind him of home. For further information see Kreyling 111–12. The connection to Demeter and Persephone has previously been discussed by Peggy Prenshaw 70–72; and Allen 40–41. See also my earlier treatment in *Sacred Groves* 77–83 and *Eudora Welty* 98–106; and Sprengnether. Albert Devlin provides the fullest available description of the circumstances that stimulated the writing of the novel, in "Meeting the World in *Delta Wedding*" 94 and 98.

10. Rossa Cooley describes the religious practice among South Carolina Gullah people as a form of "seeking" in which "the young candidates must 'come through' the praise house [church]" and must see "visions and dreams," which are then interpreted by a spiritual father or spiritual mother "who is chosen after having been seen in a dream" (151). Welty has emphasized a more secular kind of initiation in the treatment of Pinchy.

11. This passage recalls the Panther Canyon episode in Willa Cather's *The Song of the Lark*, in which Thea Kronberg finds a pottery shard in the river and

thinks of this artifact made by long-dead Indian women for holding water in the same way that her own throat holds the musical sounds of her operatic art. See Ellen Moers's discussion of this passage, 257–59.

CHAPTER 7: Brave New World

1. But their entry into the literary mainstream ironically coincides with the advent of postmodern theory in the academy. Barbara Christian protests in "The Race for Theory" that much of the recent theoretical debate has seemed authoritarian, dogmatic, and exclusive to writers of color like herself. This is particularly true of elements of deconstruction, reader-response theory, and Freudian/Lacanian language theory that deny the existence of the author and cede all linguistic agency to males. Arguing that the language of critical theory is as hegemonic as the world it attacks, Christian notes that it "surfaced, interestingly enough, just when the literature of people of color . . . began to move to 'the center'" (71). If Christian is correct in implying that much critical theory exists to do the cultural work of suppressing these disruptive forces in Western symbolic traditions, then the writing of women of color is exactly the place we should be looking for the possibility of breaking out of the trap in which we have found the writers of my study entangled.

2. See also Vera Norwood's assertion at the end of *Made from This Earth* that ecofeminists need to pay closer attention to the "diverse symbolism in women's animality" explored by writers like Toni Morrison and Leslie Silko (284).

3. See interviews collected in *Conversations with Louise Erdrich and Michael Dorris*, especially pp. 65, 77, 81–82, 96–97. The accusations of some that she is not a "real" Native American or that she has not properly politicized her writing should be dismissed as regrettable squabbling that attests to the internalized racism besetting many "minority" groups. See the unfortunate review of *The Beet Queen* by Leslie Silko and Susan Perez Castillo's commentary about the ensuing controversy. In *The Bingo Palace* Lyman Lamartine tells his nephew Lipsha a joke that testifies to this problem: "There's these three fishermen. An Irishman, a Frenchman, and an Indian. They're picking crayfish from a streambed one day, and they each have a bucket. They're all picking at the same rate, the same number of these crayfish. The Irishman fills his, but he turns his back and the crayfish all get out. The Frenchman fills his, but he turns his back and his crayfish get out too. But when the Indian turns around, though, his bucket's still full. The others can't believe it, they ask how come. The Indian says it's simple. He picked out all Indian crayfish—the minute one of them tries to climb out the others pull him back" (102). Sidner Larson provides a useful anatomy of contemporary Indian identity politics and problems of self-defininition in "The Outsider in James Welch's *The Indian Lawyer*." For an indica-

tion of the complex cultural heritage of the Turtle Mountain Chippewa, see Julie Maristuen-Rodakowsi, "The Turtle Mountain Reservation in North Dakota: Its History as Depicted in Louise Erdrich's *Love Medicine* and *Beet Queen*."

4. Translations of the Great Rabbit trickster's name are various, for instance, Wenebojo or Manabozho (Barnouw 3), Nehnehbush (Landes 22), and Manabozho (Erdoes and Ortiz 511). The most useful recent introduction to Anishinabe (or Chippewa or Ojibwa) oral traditions and religious practices is Basil Johnston's *Ojibway Heritage*. See also Gerald Vizenor's *The People Named the Chippewa: Narrative Histories*.

5. For a fuller analysis of such narrative strategies in Erdrich's novels, see Catherine Rainwater's "Reading between Worlds: Narrativity in the Fiction of Louise Erdrich."

6. Lee Schweninger calls Pauline a "patriarchal female," seeing the problem from an ecofeminist perspective (49). Readers familiar with the stories in *Love Medicine* know that Pauline's daughter Marie reverses her mother's betrayal and identifies herself with tribal community.

7. Schweninger argues that Fleur's "power has become perverted by the patriarchy's omnipotence and omnipresence" (49), but I do not think Fleur's behavior in *The Beet Queen* and *The Bingo Palace* supports such a conclusion.

8. See, for example, James Lovelock's *Gaia: A New Look at Life on Earth*, the essays in Stephen R. Kellert and Edward O. Wilson's *Biophilia Hypothesis*, Gary Snyder's *The Practice of the Wild*, Mary Oliver's *American Primitive*, Ursula LeGuin's *Always Coming Home*, and Octavia Butler's *Xenogenesis Trilogy*.

9. See Patrick Murphy's "Sex-Typing the Planet" and "My Mother's Name Is Evelyn, Not Gaia," as well as Paul Shepard's "Gaia Doubts."

10. I am indebted to my seminar student Laura Girardeau's unpublished essay, "The World Tree: Reexamining Gendered Constructions of Nature," for evidence of this variety of landscape figuration.

WORKS CITED

Allen, Gay Wilson. *Waldo Emerson: A Biography*. New York: Viking, 1981.

Allen, John A. "The Other Way to Live: Demigods in Eudora Welty's Fiction." *Eudora Welty: Critical Essays*. Ed. Peggy W. Prenshaw. Jackson: UP of Mississippi, 1979. 26–55.

Anderson, William, and Clive Hicks. *Green Man: The Archetype of Our Oneness with the Earth*. London: Harper Collins, 1990.

Appleton, Jay. *The Symbolism of Habitat: An Interpretation of Landscape in the Arts*. Seattle: U of Washington P, 1990.

Axtell, James. *The European and the Indian*. New York: Oxford, 1981.

Bachofen, Johan Jacob. *Myth, Religion, and Mother Right: Selected Writings of J. J. Bachofen*. Trans. Ralph Manheim. Intro. Joseph Campbell. Princeton: Princeton UP, 1967.

Bagg, Robert, trans. *The Bakkhai by Euripides*. Amherst: U of Massachusetts P, 1978.

Bakhtin, M. M. *The Dialogic Imagination*. Austin: U of Texas P, 1981.

Barish, Evelyn. *Emerson and the Roots of Prophecy*. Princeton: Princeton UP, 1989.

Barnouw, Victor. *Wisconsin Chippewa Myths and Tales and Their Relation to Chippewa Life*. Madison: U of Wisconsin P, 1977.

Baudrillard, Jean. *The Illusion of the End*. First pub. in France as *L'illusion de la fin* 1992. Stanford: Stanford UP, 1994.

Baym, Nina. "Melodramas of Beset Manhood: How Theories of American Fiction Exclude Women Authors." *American Quarterly* 33 (Summer 1981): 123–39.

Benoit, Raymond. "Again with Fair Creation: Holy Places in American Literature." *Prospects: An Annual of American Cultural Studies* 5 (1980): 315–30.

Benson, Jackson. "Ernest Hemingway as Short Story Writer." *The Short Stories of Ernest Hemingway: Critical Essays*. Ed. Jackson Benson. Durham: Duke UP, 1975. 272–310.

Berman, Morris. *Coming to Our Senses*. New York: Simon and Schuster, 1989.

Bleikasten, André. *The Ink of Melancholy: Faulkner's Novels from* The Sound and the Fury *to* Light in August. Bloomington: Indiana UP, 1990.

Blotner, Joseph. *Faulkner: A Biography*. Rev. ed. New York: Random, 1984.

Bly, Robert. *Iron John*. Reading, Mass.: Addison-Wesley, 1990.

Browne, Sir Thomas. *Religio Medici*. Ed. W. A. Greenhill. London: Macmillan, 1960.

Bruccoli, Matthew J. *Some Sort of Epic Grandeur: The Life of F. Scott Fitzgerald*. New York: Harcourt, 1981.

Buell, Lawrence. "Pastoral Ideology Reappraised." *American Literary History* 1 (1989): 463–79.

Burbick, Joan. *Thoreau's Alternative History.* Philadelphia: U of Pennsylvania P, 1987.

Burgess, Cheryll. "From Metaphor to Manifestation: The Artist in Eudora Welty's *A Curtain of Green." Eudora Welty: Eye of the Storyteller.* Ed. Dawn Trouard. Kent, Ohio: Kent State UP, 1989. 133–41.

Burkert, Walter. *Greek Religion.* Trans. John Raffan. Cambridge, Mass.: Harvard UP, 1985.

―――. *Homo Necans: The Anthropology of Ancient Greek Sacrificial Ritual and Myth.* Trans. Peter Bing. Berkeley and Los Angeles: U of California P, 1983.

Busch, Frederick. "Reading Hemingway Without Guilt." *New York Times Book Review.* 12 Jan. 1992: 3, 17–19.

Butler, Octavia. *Parable of the Sower.* New York: Four Walls Eight Windows, 1993.

―――. *Xenogenesis.* New York: Warner, 1989.

Bynum, Carolyn Walker. *Holy Feast and Holy Fast: The Religious Significance of Food to Medieval Women.* Berkeley and Los Angeles: U of California P, 1987.

Cady, Susan, Marian Ronan, and Hal Taussig. *Sophia: The Future of Feminist Spirituality.* San Francisco: Harper, 1986.

Campbell, Joseph. Introduction. *Myth, Religion, and Mother Right: Selected Writings of J. J. Bachofen.* Trans. Ralph Manheim. Princeton: Princeton UP, 1967. i–lvii.

Castillo, Susan Pérez. "Postmodernism, Native American Literature, and the Real: The Silko-Erdrich Controversy." *Massachusetts Review* 32 (1991): 285–94.

Cather, Willa. *Death Comes to the Archbishop.* New York: Knopf, 1927.

―――. *Early Novels and Stories:* The Troll Garden, O Pioneers!, The Song of the Lark, My Ántonia, One of Ours. New York: Library of America, 1987.

―――. *A Lost Lady.* Boston: Houghton, 1923.

―――. *My Ántonia.* Boston: Houghton, 1926.

Chadwick, John. *Linear B and Related Scripts.* Berkeley and Los Angeles: U of California P, 1987.

Chavkin, Allan, and Nancy F. Chavkin, eds. *Conversations with Louise Erdrich and Michael Dorris.* Jackson: UP of Mississippi, 1994.

Cheyfitz, Eric. *The Trans-Parent: Sexual Politics in the Language of Emerson.* Baltimore: Johns Hopkins UP, 1981.

Christian, Barbara. "The Race for Theory." *Feminist Studies* 14 (1988): 67–79.

Churchland, Patricia. *The Computational Brain.* Cambridge, Mass.: MIT P, 1992.

Cixous, Hélène, and Catherine Clément. *The Newly Born Woman.* Trans. Betsy Wing. Minneapolis: U of Minnesota P, 1986.

Claridge, Laura. "Isaac McCaslin's Failed Bid for Adulthood." *American Literature* 55 (1983): 241–51.

Collingwood, Robin G. *The Idea of Nature.* 1945. New York: Oxford, 1981.

Cooley, Rossa. *School Acres: An Adventure in Rural Education.* New Haven: Yale UP, 1930.

Cowley, Malcolm, ed. *The Viking Portable Hemingway.* New York: Viking, 1944.

Creigh, Dorothy Weyer. *Nebraska: A Bicentennial.* New York: Norton, 1977.

Cronon, William. *Changes in the Land: Indians, Colonists, and the Ecology of New England.* New York: Hill and Wang, 1983.

Darville, Timothy. *Prehistoric Britain.* London: Batsford, 1987.

De Lauretis, Teresa. *Alice Doesn't: Feminism, Semiotics, Cinema.* Bloomington: Indiana UP, 1984.

Delporte, Henri. *L'image de la femme dans l'art préhistorique.* Paris: Picard, 1979.

Devlin, Albert. "Meeting the World in *Delta Wedding.*" *Critical Essays on Eudora Welty.* Ed. W. Craig Turner and Lee Emling Harding. Boston: G. K. Hall, 1989. 90–107.

———. "Modernity and the Literary Plantation: Eudora Welty's *Delta Wedding.*" *Mississippi Quarterly* 43 (1990): 163–72.

Diamond, Irene. *Fertile Ground: Women, Earth, and the Limits of Control.* Boston: Beacon, 1994.

Dodds, E. R., ed. *Euripides' Bacchae.* 1944. Oxford: Clarendon, 1960.

Donne, John. *The Complete Poetry of John Donne.* Intro. and Notes by John T. Shawcross. Garden City, N.Y.: Anchor, 1967.

Donovan, Josephine. *After the Fall: The Demeter-Persephone Myth in Wharton, Cather, and Glasgow.* University Park: Pennsylvania State UP, 1989.

Douglas, Ann. *The Feminization of American Culture.* New York: Knopf, 1977.

DuBois, Page. *Sowing the Body: Psychoanalysis and Ancient Representations of Women.* Chicago: U of Chicago P, 1988.

Ellison, Julie K. *Emerson's Romantic Style.* Princeton: Princeton UP, 1984.

Emerson, Ralph Waldo. *Ralph Waldo Emerson.* Ed. Richard Poirier. Oxford Authors Series. New York: Oxford UP, 1990.

———. "Woman." Vol. 6 of *The Complete Works of Ralph Waldo Emerson.* Ed. Edward Waldo Emerson. 12 vols. Boston: Houghton Mifflin, 1903–4. 335–55.

Englesman, Joan Chamberlain. *The Feminine Dimension of the Divine.* Philadelphia: Westminster P, 1979.

The Epic of Gilgamesh. Intro. N. K. Sandars. New York: Penguin, 1972.

Erdoes, Richard, and Alfonso Ortiz, eds. *American Indian Myths and Legends.* New York: Pantheon, 1984.

Erdrich, Louise. *Baptism of Desire.* New York: Harper, 1989.

———. *The Beet Queen.* New York: Holt, 1986.

———. *The Bingo Palace.* New York: HarperCollins, 1994.

———. *Jacklight.* New York: Holt, 1984.

———. *Love Medicine.* 1984. New York: Holt, 1993.

———. *Tracks.* New York: Holt, 1988.

Faulkner, William. *Absalom, Absalom!* New York: Random, 1936.

————. *Collected Stories.* New York: Random, 1934.

————. *Faulkner in the University: Class Conferences at the University of Virginia 1957–1958.* Ed. Frederick L. Gwinn and Joseph Blotner. New York: Vintage, 1965.

————. *Flags in the Dust.* Ed. Douglas Day. New York: Random, 1973.

————. *Go Down, Moses.* New York: Modern Library, 1942.

————. *The Hamlet.* New York: Random, 1954.

————. "An Introduction to *The Sound and the Fury.*" *Mississippi Quarterly* 26 (1972–73): 410–15.

————. *Light in August.* New York: Modern Library, 1950.

————. *Lion in the Garden: Interviews with William Faulkner, 1926–1962.* Ed. James B. Meriwether and Michael Millgate. New York: Random, 1968.

————. *Soldier's Pay.* New York: Boni & Liveright, 1926.

————. *The Sound and the Fury.* New York: Modern Library, 1966.

Fetterley, Judith. "*My Ántonia,* Jim Burden, and the Dilemma of the Lesbian Writer." *Lesbian Texts and Contexts.* Ed. Karla Jay and Joanne Glasgow. New York: New York UP, 1990. 145–63.

————. *The Resisting Reader: A Feminist Approach to American Fiction.* Bloomington: Indiana UP, 1978.

Fiedler, Leslie. *Love and Death in the American Novel.* 1960. New York: Dell, 1969.

Fischer, Mike. "Pastoralism and Its Discontents: Willa Cather and the Burden of Imperialism." *Mosaic* 23 (Winter 1990): 31–44.

Fisher, Philip. *Hard Facts: Setting and Form in the American Novel.* New York: Oxford UP, 1985.

Fitzgerald, F. Scott. *The Great Gatsby.* New York: Scribner's, 1925.

Forster, E. M. "The Machine Stops." *Oxford and Cambridge Review* 8 (Michaelmas term, 1909): 83–122.

Frazer, James George. *The Golden Bough: A Study in Magic and Religion.* Abridged ed. in 1 vol. New York: Macmillan, 1960.

Fryer, Judith. *Felicitous Space: The Imaginative Structures of Edith Wharton and Willa Cather.* Chapel Hill: U of North Carolina P, 1986.

Gelfant, Blanche H. Introduction. *O Pioneers!* By Willa Cather. 1913. New York: Penguin, 1989.

Gilbert, Sandra, and Susan Gubar. *No Man's Land: The Place of the Woman Writer in the Twentieth Century.* Vol. 1, *The War of the Words* and vol. 2, *Sexchanges.* New Haven: Yale UP, 1987 and 1989.

Gimbutas, Marija. *The Goddesses and Gods of Old Europe: Myths and Cult Images.* Berkeley and Los Angeles: U of California P, 1982.

————. *The Language of the Goddess.* San Francisco: Harper, 1989.

Glasgow, Ellen. *Virginia.* Garden City, N.Y.: Doubleday, 1913.

Glees, Paul. *The Human Brain*. Cambridge, England: Cambridge UP, 1988.

Grim, John A. *The Shaman: Patterns of Siberian and Ojibway Healing*. Norman: U of Oklahoma P, 1983.

Gwin, Minrose. *The Feminine and Faulkner: Reading (Beyond) Sexual Difference*. Knoxville: U of Tennessee P, 1990.

Hamilton, Mary. *Trials of the Earth*. Ed. Helen Dick Davis. Jackson: UP of Mississippi, 1992.

Haraway, Donna. *Primate Visions*. New York: Routledge, 1989.

Hardy, John Edward. "*Delta Wedding* as Region and Symbol." *Sewanee Review* 60 (1962): 397–417.

Harrison, Jane Ellen. *Prolegomena to the Study of Greek Religion*. 1907. London: Merlin, 1962.

Harrison, Robert Pogue. *Forests: The Shadow of Civilization*. Chicago: U of Chicago P, 1992.

Hayes, Peter. *The Limping Hero: Grotesques in Literature*. New York: New York UP, 1971.

Heilbrun, Carolyn. *Reinventing Womanhood*. New York: Norton, 1979.

———. *Writing a Woman's Life*. New York: Ballantine, 1988.

Hemingway, Ernest. *Death in the Afternoon*. New York: Scribner's, 1932.

———. *The Garden of Eden*. New York: Scribner's, 1986.

———. *Green Hills of Africa*. New York: Scribner's, 1935.

———. *In Our Time*. New York: Scribner's, 1925.

———. *A Moveable Feast*. New York: Scribner's, 1964.

———. *The Nick Adams Stories*. Ed. Philip Young. New York: Scribner's, 1972.

Hesiod, the Homeric Hymns and Homerica. Trans. H. G. Evelyn-White. Cambridge, Mass.: Harvard UP, 1977.

The Holy Bible. King James Version. Cleveland: World, n.d.

Homans, Margaret. "Women of Color: Writers of Feminist Theory." *New Literary History* 25 (Winter 1994): 73–94.

Hyde, George E. *Pawnee Indians*. Denver: U of Denver P, 1951.

Irigaray, Luce. *Speculum of the Other Woman*. Trans. Gillian C. Gill. Ithaca, N.Y.: Cornell UP, 1985.

Isaacson, Robert. *The Limbic System*. New York: Plenum Press, 1982.

Jacobsen, Thorkild. *The Harps That Once: Sumerian Poetry in Translation*. New Haven: Yale UP, 1987.

Jehlen, Myra. *American Incarnation: The Individual, the Nation, and the Continent*. Cambridge, Mass.: Harvard UP, 1986.

Johansen, Bruce. *Forgotten Founders: Benjamin Franklin, the Iroquois, and the Rationale for the American Revolution*. Ipswich, Mass.: Gambit, 1982.

Johnson, Mark. *The Body in the Mind: The Bodily Basis of Meaning, Imagination, and Reason*. Chicago: U of Chicago P, 1987.

Johnston, Basil. *Ojibway Heritage*. Lincoln: U of Nebraska P, 1976.

Jones, Anne Goodwin. *Tomorrow Is Another Day: Southern Women Writers 1859–1936*. Baton Rouge: Louisiana State UP, 1981.

Kaye, Frances W. *Masquerade and Isolation: Willa Cather's Women*. New York: Peter Lang, 1993.

Keats, John. *John Keats*. Ed. Elizabeth Cook. Oxford: Oxford UP, 1990.

Keller, Evelyn Fox. *Reflections on Gender and Science*. New Haven: Yale, 1985.

Kellert, Stephen R., and Edward O. Wilson. *The Biophilia Hypothesis*. Washington, D.C.: Island P, 1993.

Kerényi, C. *Eleusis: Archetypal Image of Mother and Daughter*. Trans. Ralph Manheim. New York: Schocken, 1977.

King, Richard. *A Southern Renaissance: The Cultural Awakening of the American South, 1930–1955*. New York: Oxford, 1980.

Kolakowski, Leszek. *The Presence of Myth*. Trans. Adam Czerniawski. Chicago: U of Chicago P, 1989.

Kolodny, Annette. *The Lay of the Land: Metaphor as Experience and History in American Life and Letters*. Chapel Hill: U of North Carolina P, 1975.

Kovacs, Maureen G. *The Epic of Gilgamesh*. Stanford: Stanford UP, 1985.

Kramer, Samuel Noah. *History Begins at Sumer*. 3rd rev. ed. Philadelphia: U of Pennsylvania P, 1981.

Kreyling, Michael. *Eudora Welty's Achievement of Order*. Baton Rouge: Louisiana State UP, 1980.

Kristeva, Julia. *Powers of Horror: An Essay on Abjection*. New York: Columbia UP, 1982.

Kroeber, Karl. *Ecological Literary Criticism: Romantic Imagining and the Biology of Mind*. New York: Columbia UP, 1994.

Landes, Ruth. *Ojibwa Religion and the Midéwiwin*. Madison: U of Wisconsin P, 1968.

Larson, Sidner J. "The Outsider in James Welch's *The Indian Lawyer*." *American Indian Quarterly* 18 (Fall 1994): 1–12.

Lawrence, D. H. *Studies in Classic American Literature*. New York: Seltzer, 1923.

Lee, Hermione. *Willa Cather: Double Lives*. 1989. New York: Vintage, 1991.

LeGuin, Ursula. *Always Coming Home*. New York: Harper, 1985.

Lerner, Gerda. *The Creation of Patriarchy*. New York: Oxford, 1986.

Leroi-Gourhan, André. *Treasures of Prehistoric Art*. New York: Abrams, [1967?].

Leverenz, David. *Manhood and the American Renaissance*. Ithaca: Cornell UP, 1989.

Levy, G. R. *The Gate of Horn: A Study of the Religious Conceptions of the Stone Age and Their Influence upon European Thought*. London: Faber, 1948.

Lewis, R. W. B. *The American Adam: Innocence, Tragedy, and Tradition in the Nineteenth Century*. Chicago: U of Chicago P, 1955.

———. "The Hero in the New World: Faulkner's *The Bear*." *Bear, Man, and God: Eight Approaches to William Faulkner's "The Bear."* Ed. Francis Lee Utley, Lynn Z. Bloom, and Arthur F. Kinney. New York: Random, 1971. 188–201.

Lewis, Robert W. "'Long Time Ago Good, Now No Good': Hemingway's Indian Stories." *New Critical Approaches to the Short Stories of Ernest Hemingway.* Ed. Jackson Benson. Durham: Duke UP, 1990. 200–212.

Liddell, H. G., and Robert Scott. *An Intermediate Greek-English Lexicon, Founded upon the Seventh Edition of Liddell and Scott's Greek-English Lexicon.* Oxford: Oxford UP, 1987.

Lord, Albert B. *The Singer of Tales.* 1960. New York: Atheneum, 1968.

Lorenz, Konrad. Introduction. *The Comedy of Survival: Studies in Literary Ecology.* By Joseph Meeker. New York: Scribner's, 1974.

Love, Glen. "Hemingway's Indian Virtues: An Ecological Reconsideration." *Western American Literature* 22 (1987): 201–13.

———. "*The Professor's House*: Cather, Hemingway, and the Chastening of American Prose Style." *Western American Literature* 24 (1990): 295–311.

Lovelock, James. *The Ages of Gaia: A Biography of Our Living Earth.* New York: Norton, 1988.

———. *Gaia: A New Look at Life on Earth.* New York: Oxford, 1979.

Lydenberg, John. "Nature Myth in Faulkner's *The Bear.*" *American Literature* 24 (1952): 62–72.

Lynn, Kenneth S. *Hemingway.* New York: Simon & Schuster, 1987.

———. "The Troubled Fisherman." *New Critical Approaches to the Short Stories of Ernest Hemingway.* Ed. Jackson Benson. Durham: Duke UP, 1990. 149–55.

MacLeod, William Christie. "Celt and Indian: Britain's Old World Frontier in Relation to the New." *Beyond the Frontier: Social Process and Cultural Change.* Ed. Paul Bohannon and Fred Plog. New York: Natural History Press, 1967.

Manning, Carol. *With Ears Opening Like Morning Glories: Eudora Welty and the Love of Storytelling.* Westport, Conn.: Greenwood, 1985.

Maristuen-Rodakowski, Julie. "The Turtle Mountain Reservation in North Dakota: Its History as Depicted in Louise Erdrich's *Love Medicine* and *Beet Queen.*" *American Indian Culture and Research Journal* 12.3 (1988): 33–48.

Mark, Rebecca. *The Dragon's Blood: Feminist Intertextuality in Eudora Welty's* The Golden Apples. Jackson: UP of Mississippi, 1994.

Marshack, Alexander. *The Roots of Civilization.* New York: McGraw, 1972.

Marx, Leo. *The Machine in the Garden: Technology and the Pastoral Ideal in America.* New York: Oxford, 1964.

Mather, Cotton. *The Wonders of the Invisible World.* Vol. 1 of *The Witchcraft Delusion in New England: Its Rise, Progress, and Termination.* Ed. Samuel G. Drake. 3 vols. Roxbury, Mass.: Woodward, 1866.

McGee, Patrick. "Gender and Generation in Faulkner's 'The Bear.'" *Faulkner Journal* 1 (1985): 46–54.

McIntosh, James. *Thoreau as Romantic Naturalist.* Ithaca: Cornell UP, 1974.

McLuhan, T. C., comp. *Touch the Earth: A Self-Portrait of Indian Existence*. New York: Promontory, 1971.

McWilliams, John. *The American Epic*. New York: Cambridge, 1989.

Meeker, Joseph. *The Comedy of Survival: Studies in Literary Ecology*. New York: Scribner's, 1974.

Menchú, Rigoberta. *I, Rigoberta Menchú: An Indian Woman in Guatemala*. Trans. Ann Wright. Ed. Elisabeth Burgos-Debray. New York: Verso, 1984.

Merchant, Carolyn. *The Death of Nature: Women, Ecology, and the Scientific Revolution*. New York: Harper, 1990.

————. *Ecological Revolutions: Nature, Gender, and Science in New England*. Chapel Hill: U of North Carolina P, 1989.

Meyers, Jeffrey. "Hemingway's Primitivism and 'Indian Camp.'" *New Critical Approaches to the Short Stories of Ernest Hemingway*. Ed. Jackson Benson. Durham: Duke UP, 1990. 300–308.

Michaels, Walter Benn. "The Vanishing American." *American Literary History* 2 (Summer 1990): 220–41.

————. "*Walden*'s False Bottoms." *Glyph* 1 (1977): 132–49.

Minter, David. *William Faulkner, His Life and Work*. Baltimore: Johns Hopkins UP, 1980.

Moddelmog, Debra A. "The Unifying Consciousness of a Divided Conscience: Nick Adams as Author of *In Our Time*." *American Literature* 60 (Dec. 1988): 591–610.

Moers, Ellen. *Literary Women*. New York: Doubleday, 1976.

Morrison, Toni. *Playing in the Dark*. New York: Random, 1992.

Mortimer, Gail. *Faulkner's Rhetoric of Loss*. Austin: U of Texas P, 1983.

Murphy, Patrick D. "My Mother's Name Is Evelyn, Not Gaia." *Nature Writing Newsletter* 6 (Spring 1994): 12–13.

————. "Sex-Typing the Planet: Gaia Imagery and the Problem of Subverting Patriarchy." *Environmental Ethics* 10 (1988): 155–68.

Nash, Roderick. *Wilderness and the American Mind*. 1967. Rev. ed. New Haven: Yale UP, 1973.

Neumann, Erich. *The Great Mother: An Analysis of the Archetype*. Trans. Ralph Manheim. Princeton: Princeton UP, 1955.

Nietzsche, Friedrich. *The Birth of Tragedy and the Case of Wagner*. Trans. Walter Kaufmann. New York: Vintage, 1967.

Nilsson, Martin. *The Minoan-Mycenaean Religion and Its Survival in Greek Religion*. Lund: Gleerup, 1927.

Norwood, Vera. *Made from This Earth: American Women and Nature*. Chapel Hill: U of North Carolina P, 1993.

O'Brien, Sharon. *Willa Cather: The Emerging Voice*. New York: Oxford, 1987.

Oelschlaeger, Max. *The Idea of Wilderness: From Prehistory to the Age of Ecology.* New Haven: Yale UP, 1991.

Oliver, Mary. *American Primitive.* Boston: Little, Brown, 1983.

Olson, Paul A. "The Epic and Great Plains Literature: Rolvaag, Cather, and Neihardt." *Prairie Schooner* 55 (1981): 263–85.

Ortner, Sherry B. "Is Female to Male as Nature Is to Culture?" *Woman, Culture and Society.* Ed. Michelle Zimbalist Rosaldo and Louise Lamphere. Stanford: Stanford UP, 1974. 67–87.

Parker, Arthur C. *The History of the Seneca Indians.* Port Washington, N.Y.: Friedman, 1967.

Perluck, Herbert A. "*The Bear:* An Unromantic Reading." *Religious Perspectives in Faulkner's Fiction.* Ed. J. Robert Barth, S.J. Notre Dame: Notre Dame UP, 1972. 173–98.

Peterson, Nancy J. "History, Postmodernism, and Louise Erdrich's *Tracks.*" *PMLA* 109 (1944): 982–94.

Pikoulis, John. *The Art of William Faulkner.* Totowa, N.J.: Barnes and Noble, 1982.

Prenshaw, Peggy W. "Woman's World, Man's Place: The Fiction of Eudora Welty." *Eudora Welty: A Form of Thanks.* Ed. Louis Dollarhide and Ann J. Abadie. Jackson: UP of Mississippi, 1979.

Puhvel, Jaan. *Comparative Religion.* Baltimore: Johns Hopkins UP, 1987.

Rainwater, Catherine. "Reading between Worlds: Narrativity in the Fiction of Louise Erdrich." *American Literature* 62 (1990): 405–22.

Randall, John H., III. "Willa Cather and the Pastoral Tradition." *Five Essays on Willa Cather: The Merrimack Symposium.* Ed. John J. Murphy. North Andover, Mass.: Merrimack College, 1974. 75–96.

Ransom, John Crowe. "Delta Fiction." *Kenyon Review* 8 (Summer 1946): 503–7.

Renfrew, Colin. *Archaeology and Language: The Puzzle of Indo-European Origins.* New York: Cambridge UP, 1988.

Reynolds, Michael S. *Hemingway's Reading, 1910–1940: An Inventory.* Princeton: Princeton UP, 1981.

Roberts, Diane. *Faulkner and Southern Womanhood.* Athens: U of Georgia P, 1994.

Romines, Ann. *The Home Plot: Women, Writing, and Domestic Ritual.* Amherst: U of Massachusetts P, 1992.

Rosaldo, Renato. *Culture and Truth: The Remaking of Social Analysis.* Boston: Beacon, 1989.

Rosowski, Susan J. *The Voyage Perilous: Willa Cather's Romanticism.* Lincoln: U of Nebraska P, 1986.

Ross, Anne. *Pagan Celtic Britain: Studies in Iconography and Tradition.* London: Routledge, 1967.

Rossi, William. "The Limits of an Afternoon Walk: Coleridgean Polarity in Thoreau's 'Walking.'" *ESQ* 33 (1987): 94–109.

———. "Thoreau and Nineteenth-Century Science: The Geological Principles of *A Week on the Concord and Merrimack Rivers*." Oregon Humanities Center, Eugene, Oregon. 8 May 1992.

———. "Thoreau, Lyell, and the Geological Principles of *A Week*." *American Literature* 66 (1994): 275–300.

Ruether, Rosemary Radford. *Sexism and God-Talk: Toward a Feminist Theology*. Boston: Beacon, 1983.

Sagan, Carl. *The Dragons of Eden: Speculations on the Origins of Human Intelligence*. New York: Random, 1977.

Saggs, H. W. F. *The Encounter with the Divine in Mesopotamia and Israel*. London: Athlone, 1978.

Sandars, N. K., ed. *The Epic of Gilgamesh*. 1960. New York: Penguin, 1972.

Sattelmeyer, Robert. "The Remaking of *Walden*." *Writing the American Classics*. Ed. James Barbour and Tom Quirk. Chapel Hill: U of North Carolina P, 1990.

———. *Thoreau's Reading: A Study in Intellectual History*. Princeton: Princeton UP, 1988.

Schneidau, Herbert N. *The Sacred Discontent: The Bible and Western Tradition*. Baton Rouge: Louisiana State UP, 1976.

Schweninger, Lee. "A Skin of Lakeweed: An Ecofeminist Approach to Erdrich and Silko." *Multicultural Literatures through Feminist/Poststructuralist Lenses*. Ed. Barbard Frey Waxman. Knoxville: U of Tennessee P, 1993. 37–56.

Segal, Charles. *Interpreting Greek Tragedy*. Ithaca: Cornell UP, 1986.

———. "The Menace of Dionysus: Sex Roles and Reversals in Euripides' Bacchae." *Women in the Ancient World: The Arethusa Papers*. Ed. John Peradotto and J. P. Sullivan. Albany: State U of New York P, 1984. 195–212.

Sensibar, Judith. *The Origins of Faulkner's Art*. Austin: U of Texas P, 1984.

Sheets-Johnstone, Maxine. *The Roots of Thinking*. Philadelphia: Temple UP, 1990.

Sheldrake, Rupert. *The Rebirth of Nature: The Greening of Science and God*. New York: Bantam, 1991.

Shepard, Paul. "Gaia Doubts." *The Nature Writing Newsletter* 6 (Spring 1994): 11.

———. *Man in the Landscape*. New York: Knopf, 1967.

———. *Nature and Madness*. San Francisco: Sierra Club Books, 1982.

———. "On Animal Friends." *The Biophilia Hypothesis*. Ed. Stephen R. Kellert and Edward O. Wilson. Washington, D.C.: Island Press, 1993.

Silko, Leslie Marmon. *Almanac of the Dead*. New York: Simon & Schuster, 1991.

———. "Here's an Odd Artifact for the Fairy-Tale Shelf." Rev. of *The Beet Queen*, by Louise Erdrich. *Studies in American Literature* 10 (1986): 177–84.

Silverman, Kaja. "Masochism and Male Subjectivity." *Camera Obscura* 17 (1988): 30–67.

Slote, Bernice. *The Kingdom of Art: Willa Cather's First Principles and Critical Statements*. Lincoln: U of Nebraska P, 1967.

Slotkin, Richard. *Regeneration through Violence: The Mythology of the American Frontier, 1600–1860*. Middletown, Conn.: Wesleyan UP, 1973.

Smith, Valerie. "Black Feminist Theory and the Representation of the 'Other.'" *Changing Our Own Words: Essays on Criticism, Theory, and Writing by Black Women*. Ed. Cheryl A. Wall. New Brunswick, N.J.: Rutgers UP, 1989. 38–57.

Smith-Rosenberg, Caroll. *Disorderly Conduct: Visions of Gender in Victorian America*. 1985. New York: Oxford, 1986.

Snyder, Gary. "Good, Wild, Sacred." *Meeting the Expectations of the Land: Essays in Sustainable Agriculture and Stewardship*. Ed. Wes Jackson, Wendell Berry, and Bruce Colman. San Francisco: North Point, 1984.

———. *The Practice of the Wild*. San Francisco: North Point, 1990.

Sprengnether, Madelon. "*Delta Wedding* and the Kore Complex." *Southern Quarterly* 25 (1987): 120–30.

Star, Susan Leigh. *Regions of the Mind: Brain Research and the Quest for Scientific Certainty*. Stanford: Stanford UP, 1989.

Stein, Gertrude. *The Autobiography of Alice B. Toklas*. New York: Harcourt, 1933.

Stewart, David. "Ike McCaslin, Cop-Out." *Bear, Man, and God: Eight Approaches to William Faulkner's "The Bear."* Ed. Francis Lee Utley, Lynn Z. Bloom, and Arthur F. Kinney. New York: Random, 1971. 212–20.

Stone, Merlin. *When God Was a Woman*. New York: Harcourt, 1976.

Sundquist, Eric. *Faulkner: The House Divided*. Baltimore: Johns Hopkins UP, 1983.

Tanner, Nancy. "Matrifocality in Indonesia and Africa and Among Black Americans." *Woman, Culture, and Society*. Ed. Michelle Zimbalist Rosaldo and Louise Lamphere. Stanford: Stanford UP, 1974. 129–56.

Tedlock, Dennis, and Barbara Tedlock, eds. *Teachings from the American Earth*. New York: Liveright, 1975.

Teubal, Savina J. *Hagar the Egyptian: The Lost Tradition of the Matriarchs*. San Francisco: Harper, 1990.

Theweleit, Klaus. *Male Fantasies*. Trans. Stephan Conway, et al. Vol. 1. Minneapolis: U of Minnesota P, 1987. 2 vols.

Thoreau, Henry David. *Journal*. Ed. Robert Sattelmeyer. Vol. 2. Princeton: Princeton UP, 1984. 6 vols. to date.

———. *Walden*. Ed. J. Lyndon Shanley. Princeton: Princeton UP, 1971.

———. *Walden and Resistance to Civil Government*. Ed. William Rossi. New York: Norton, 1991.

Tichi, Cecelia. *New World, New Earth*. New Haven: Yale UP, 1979.

Tigay, Jeffrey H. *The Evolution of the Gilgamesh Epic*. Philadelphia: U Pennsylvania P, 1982.

Todorov, Tzvetan. *The Conquest of America: The Question of the Other.* Trans. Richard Howard. New York: Harper, 1982.

Trehub, Arnold. *The Cognitive Brain.* Cambridge, Mass.: MIT P, 1991.

Turner, Frederick W., III. *The Portable North American Reader.* New York: Penguin, 1977.

Utley, Francis Lee. "Pride and Humility: The Cultural Roots of Ike McCaslin." *Bear, Man, and God: Eight Approaches to William Faulkner's "The Bear."* Ed. Francis Lee Utley, Lynn Z. Bloom, and Arthur F. Kinney. New York: Random, 1971. 167–87.

Utley, Francis Lee, Lynn Z. Bloom, and Arthur F. Kinney, eds. *Bear, Man, and God: Eight Approaches to William Faulkner's "The Bear."* Rev. ed. New York: Random, 1971.

Vande Kieft, Ruth. *Eudora Welty.* 1962. New York: Twayne, 1987.

Vecsey, Christopher. *Imagine Ourselves Richly: Mythic Narratives of North American Indians.* New York: Crossroads, 1988.

Vizenor, Gerald. *The People Named the Chippewa: Narrative Histories.* Minneapolis: U of Minnesota P, 1984.

Warner, Marina. *Alone of All Her Sex: The Myth and the Cult of the Virgin Mary.* 1976. New York: Vintage, 1983.

Welty, Eudora. *The Collected Stories.* New York: Harcourt, 1980.

———. *Conversations with Eudora Welty.* Ed. Peggy Whitman Prenshaw. Jackson: UP of Mississippi, 1984.

———. "The Delta Cousins." Unpublished manuscript. The Welty Collection, Mississippi Department of Archives and History, Series 4, Cl.a, p. 31.

———. *Delta Wedding.* New York: Harcourt, Brace, and World, 1946.

———. Personal interview. 16 June 1987.

West, Michael. "Scatology and Eschatology: The Heroic Dimensions of Thoreau's Wordplay." *PMLA* 89 (1974): 1043–64.

Westling, Louise. *Eudora Welty.* Houndmills, Basingstoke: Macmillan, 1989.

———. "Food, Landscape, and the Feminine in Delta Wedding." *Southern Quarterly* 30 (1992): 29–40.

———. *Sacred Groves and Ravaged Gardens: The Fiction of Eudora Welty, Carson McCullers, and Flannery O'Connor.* Athens: U of Georgia P, 1985.

White, Lynn, Jr. "The Historical Roots of Our Ecologic Crisis." *Science* 10 Mar. 1967: 1203–7. Rpt. in *The Subversive Science: Essays Toward an Ecology of Man.* Ed. Paul Shepard and Daniel McKinley. Boston: Houghton, 1969. 341–51.

Wittenberg, Judith Bryant. "Faulkner and Women Writers." *Faulkner and Women: Faulkner and Yoknapatawpha, 1985.* Jackson: UP of Mississippi, 1986. 270–94.

Wolkstein, Diane, and Samuel Noah Kramer. *Inanna, Queen of Heaven and Earth: Her Stories and Hymns from Sumer.* New York: Harper, 1983.

Wollstonecraft, Mary. *A Vindication of the Rights of Woman.* Ed. Carol H. Poston. 1975. New York: Norton, 1988.

Woodress, James. *Willa Cather: A Literary Life.* Lincoln: U of Nebraska P, 1987.

Woolf, Virginia. *Between the Acts.* New York: Harcourt, 1941.

————. *A Room of One's Own.* 1929. New York: Harcourt, 1981.

————. *To the Lighthouse.* New York: Harcourt, 1927.

Yaeger, Patricia. "The Case of the Dangling Signifier: Phallic Imagery in 'Moon Lake.'" *Twentieth Century Literature* 28 (Winter 1982): 431–52.

Young, Philip. Preface. *The Nick Adams Stories.* By Ernest Hemingway. Ed. Philip Young. New York: Scribner's, 1972.

Zink, Karl E. "Faulkner's Garden: Woman and the Immemorial Earth." *Modern Fiction Studies* 2 (1956): 139–49.

INDEX

Abbey, Edward, 52
Absalom, Absalom! (Faulkner), 10, 111–16,
  151
Aesthetic judgment, 15
Africa, 114
African–American science fiction, 151
African–American writers, 151–52, 167–71
African body, conflated with femininity,
  primal violence, and disaster, 115
Africanist presence, 152
Ages of Gaia, The (Lovelock), 168–69
Aggressive male will, 22
Agricultural discipline of landscape, 78
Agricultural societies, 11
Alexander the Great, 59
Alexandra Bergson, 59, 60, 65–70, 72
Algonquin peoples, 157
Allen, John A., 58
Alma mater, 118
Amazon heroines, 60, 63–64
American Adam, The (Lewis), 39, 83, 92
American colonization, 5
American pastoral, 52–53, 59–81, 122, 169
Anatolia, 7
Androgyny, 81, 95
Animistic past, 166
Anishinabe, 153–67
Annie Pavelka, 71
Ántonia Shimerda, 63, 71–79; as
  embodiment of landscape, 71, 74–79;
  and androgynous role as farm worker,
  75; feminization of, in town, 75; deflated
  in old age, 78; transferred into mythic
  figure by Jim Burden, 78–79; as catalyst
  for creation of male world, 79
Appalachian Mountains, 113
Appleton, Jay, 15
Arapaho, 58
Arcadian innocence, 113
Archaeology, ix, 7, 9, 18

Aristotle, 29
Artemis, 21
"Asphodel" (Welty), 132
Athena, 27
"At the Landing" (Welty), 132–34, 143
Austen, Jane, 133
Australian aborigines, 6, 160
Australian songlines, 160
Autobiography of Alice B. Toklas, The (Stein), 91
Axtell, James, 34

Bacchae (Euripides), x, 7, 28–29, 49, 87,
  104, 126, 131, 137
Bacchus, 28, 132, 135, 137
Bachofen, Johann Jacob, 7, 10
Backlash against feminism and suffrage
  movement, 71, 83
Bacon, Francis, 32, 36, 47
Bagg, Robert, 28–29, 132, 138
Bakhtin, Mikhail, 18
Barish, Evelyn, 40–41
Barnouw, Victor, 162
"Battler, The" (Hemingway), 95
Baudrillard, Jean, 170–71
Baym, Nina, 83–84, 92–93, 95, 169
Bear, as avatar of wilderness, 118, 121
"Bear, The" (Faulkner), 3, 116–22; and the
  Gilgamesh epic, 121
"Bearskin" (Welty), 130
"Beauty and the Beast" (Welty), 130
Beet Queen, The (Erdrich), 158
Benoit, Raymond, 83–84
Berman, Morris, 136
Between the Acts (Woolf), 137
Bible, 12, 15, 23–25, 85; Old Testament,
  24–25; New Testament, 116
Big Black River, 144–47
"Big Two–Hearted River" (Hemingway),
  83, 90–91, 93–97, 144–47, 151
Big Woods, 117, 122

French Realist painters, 79
Freudian theories, 6
Fringe environment, grassland or steppe, 10–11
Frontier, x, 33–38, 57–58, 64–65, 113, 158–64
Fryer, Judith, 64, 79
Fuller, Margaret, 41

Gaia, 26
Gaia Hypothesis, 167, 171
Gaming, on Indian reservations, 164–66
Gate of Horn, The (Levy), 8
Gelfant, Blanche, 69
Gender and race, 150–51
Gender balance, 136–37, 153–71
Gender conflict, 18, 84
Gendering the landscape as female, 5–6
Genesis, 7, 23, 111; antagonism to the landscape in, 24; and primacy of male creation, 24
Genetic manipulation, 167–68
Gentlemen Prefer Blondes (Loos), 85
Georgics, The (Virgil), 5, 72, 82
German fascist rhetoric, 103
German philosophic idealism, 40
Gilbert, Sandra, 45, 61, 83, 87, 93
Gilgamesh, 19–23, 51, 126; and opposition to nature and land, 19; ritual marriage of, to Ishtar, 20; heroism of, defined by ecological tragedy, 21; and rejection of Ishtar, 21
Gimbutas, Marija, 10, 17, 138
Glasgow, Ellen, 82, 84
God: nonmaterial, 24; curse of, upon the earth, 25
Goddess–centered cultures, 10
Go Down, Moses (Faulkner), 101, 104, 116–24, 150, 154
Golden Apples, The (Welty), 143–47, 154
Golden Bough, The (Frazer), 8, 131
"Golden Land" (Faulkner), 84
Goodall, Jane, 150
Great Gatsby, The (Fitzgerald), 3, 4
Greece, 7, 11, 169; Greek people, 7, 17, 25; Greek literature, 25–30

Greek Religion (Burkert), 138
Green Hills of Africa (Hemingway), 84, 99
Green Man, 115
Green world of hunter-gatherers, 8
Grim, John A., 162
Grim Reaper, 101
Guatemala, 6
Gubar, Susan, 45, 61, 83, 87, 93
Gwin, Minrose, 102–4

Haiti: as emblem of racial and cultural mingling, 114; landscape of, as primal chaos, 114–15
Hamilton, Mary, 130
Haraway, Donna, 51–52, 149–51, 168–71
Hard Facts (Fisher), 5, 38–45, 116, 153, 155
Harrison, Jane Ellen, 8, 138
Harrison, Robert, ix
Hawthorne, Nathaniel, 36
Heilbrun, Carolyn, 61
Hemingway, Ernest, x, 4, 81, 83–101, 148, 153–54, 158, 164; contempt of, for women writers, 84; acquaintance of, with Cather's fiction, 84, 92; and resentment of strong mother figure, 85–86; and goal of depicting landscape in fiction, 90–91; grim heroism of, 92–93; and Indians, 94–95, 99–101, 150, 162; and androgyny, 95–96; individualism of, 99; "Hemingway's Indian Virtues," 99–100; and narrow version of masculinity, 101; and portraits of the Chippewa, 162
Heroic individuality, American myth of, 83–84
Heroic tradition, 17–18, 51, 62, 81, 92, 105, 134
Hesiod, 26–27, 111
Hittites, 25
Holy forest, 24
"Holy Places in American Literature" (Benoit), 83–84
Homans, Margaret, 152
Homer, 12, 25, 29
Homeric Hymn to Demeter, 26, 77, 137
Honeysuckle and sexuality, 109–10
Huckleberry Finn (Twain), 80–83